The
POSIX.1
Standard

A Programmer's Guide

The
POSIX.1
Standard
A Programmer's Guide

Fred Zlotnick

Mindcraft, Inc.

Palo Alto, California

The Benjamin/Cummings Publishing Company, Inc.

Redwood City, California • Menlo Park, California • Reading, Massachusetts
New York • Don Mills, Ontario • Wokingham, U.K. • Amsterdam
Bonn • Sydney • Singapore • Tokyo • Madrid • San Juan

Sponsoring Editor: John Thompson

Production Supervisor: Laura Kenney

Freelance Project Management: Gary Palmatier

Copy Editor: Anna Huff

Composition and Illustration: Ideas to Images

Cover illustration: *Rainbow Kite* © 1991 Mr. Screens

Library of Congress Cataloging-in-Publication Data

Zlotnick, Fred.
    The POSIX.1 standard : a programmer's guide / Fred Zlotnick.
        p.   cm.
    Includes index.
    ISBN 0-8053-9605-5

    1. UNIX (Computer file)   2. Operating systems (Computers)—
Standards—United States.   I. Title.   II. Title: POSIX dot one standard.
III. Title: POSIX point one standard.
QA76.76.063Z57   1991
005.4'3—dc20   91-9770
                                                                CIP

2 3 4 5 6 7 8 9 10 –DO– 95 94 93 92 91

The Benjamin/Cummings Publishing Company, Inc.
390 Bridge Parkway
Redwood City, Califomia 94065

Preface

About POSIX

The UNIX® system was 10 years ahead of its time, but it is now more than 20 years old. This is not to say that UNIX is now out of date. On the contrary, it has become the dominant operating system for much of the computing industry. It is a de facto standard.

The fact that UNIX systems run on so many different types of hardware has made it possible for application programmers to write portable programs that are not limited to a single manufacturer's platform. However, the widespread acceptance of UNIX has been accompanied by a number of problems, chief among them a proliferation of different, incompatible versions. In fact, the UNIX system does not represent one standard but several, all mutually incompatible. The POSIX standardization effort began as an attempt to deal with this problem by establishing an official standard that, as far as possible, is compatible—*from the program's point of view*—with the core of most historical UNIX implementations. The purpose is to make portable programs possible.

This book deals with the POSIX 1003.1-1990 standard. That standard—commonly referred to as POSIX.1 (pronounced "pah-zix dot 1") or more informally as "dot 1"—describes an operating system interface for C language programs. It is based on a number of documents; the *1984 /usr/group Standard* is its most direct ancestor. Most of the interface descriptions in POSIX can, with slight variations, be found in one of two documents that describe implementations of UNIX systems: the *System V Interface Description (SVID)* published by AT&T and the *4.3 Berkeley Software Distribution (4.3BSD) Manuals*. In general, the philosophy of the 1003.1 committee was to adhere to existing UNIX system interfaces unless there was a good reason to do otherwise.

The official name of the POSIX.1 standard is ISO/IEC IS 9945-1:1990. The International Standards Organization (ISO) and International Electrotechnical Commission (IEC) jointly oversee international computer standards. In the United States, the American National Standards Institute (ANSI) and the Institute of Electrical and Electronics Engineers (IEEE) are responsible for computer standards, and ANSI/IEEE Std. 1003.1-1990 is another official name for the POSIX.1 standard. We simply use the informal name POSIX.1 or (even more simply) just POSIX when no confusion can arise.

The "-1" in 9945-1:1990 and the ".1" in POSIX.1 both refer to the fact that other operating system interface standards are being developed to cover areas not in the purview of the current standard. These standards are under development by IEEE committees with numbers like 1003.2 (developing POSIX.2). The name *POSIX* is almost an acronym for Portable Operating System Interface. The "IX" suffix is traditional. The name *POSIX* was suggested by Richard Stallman.

All major vendors of the UNIX system either are delivering POSIX.1 conforming systems now or are committed to doing so. Such systems include or will include OSF/1, System V, and BSD. Vendors of some other major operating systems that are not based on the UNIX system, including VMS and OS/2, have also committed to POSIX.1 conformance. Thus, the POSIX effort has moved well beyond the world of UNIX systems in which it originated. Each POSIX.1 implementation will also contain vendor-specific extensions to POSIX, either for compatibility with historical versions or as "value-added" features. If an application programmer is to avoid implementation dependence, he or she must make careful use of the standard's features and avoid nonportable vendor-supplied features.

Goals

The POSIX.1 standard makes it possible to write application programs that are portable across a wide variety of systems and architectures. The goal of the book is to show you how to take advantage of that possibility. Our specific goals are to:

- Explain the syntax and semantics of the 203 C functions and macros supported by the POSIX.1 standard and the data structures that support them.

- Give an understanding of the concepts that you need to use these interfaces and data structures effectively.

- Show how other standards and specifications interact with POSIX.1.

- Show how you can use the POSIX.1 standard to package a portable application, including source code and supporting files.

- Explain the limits of the POSIX.1 standard.

The principal goal of the book is to teach programmers how to write programs that will run under any implementation of POSIX.1—Strictly Conforming POSIX.1 Applications, in the language of the standard. Note that POSIX.1

explicitly addresses application programs only. Interfaces needed for system administration or system programming are not supported.

Audience

This book is written for computer professionals and for students of operating systems.

- Software engineers can only hope to write portable application programs by adhering to the POSIX.1 standard.

- Software engineers who are implementing systems must take POSIX.1 as a partial specification.

- Software engineering managers need to know the possibilities and limits of portable programming using POSIX.1 to understand what degree of portability their programming teams can reasonably be expected to achieve.

- Managers in charge of hardware procurements must understand what vendors do and do not guarantee when they claim to be "POSIX conforming."

- Students should know the features guaranteed by an international operating system interface standard.

Features

This book includes the following features: prototypes for all functions; sample code; appendices for reference; exercises; and a glossary.

Prototypes for All Functions

In the chapters and appendices of this book, C functions are described using the prototype format of the ANSI C standard. Even if you are not familiar with the prototype format, you should be able to understand the code. Here is an example: the C library function *strcpy()* would be described like this in "old style":

```
char *strcpy(s1, s2)
char *s1, *s2;
```

A prototype for this function is written with the argument list, including type information, inside the parentheses:

```
char *strcpy(char *s1, const char *s2);
```

The names of the parameters are optional. Thus, an equivalent way to write this prototype is:

```
char *strcpy(char *, const char *);
```

The reserved word const in front of the second argument is an addition to the language by the ANSI C committee. (It is borrowed from the C++ language.) It indicates that the object pointed to by the second argument cannot be modified by a call to the *strcpy()* function. The absence of this qualifier in front of the first argument indicates that the object pointed to by the first argument can be modified by the function.

As a special case, if a function has no arguments, its ANSI C prototype is written with a parameter list consisting of the single reserved word void. For example:

```
char *getlogin(void);
```

There is a special notation for prototypes of functions that take a variable number of arguments. The fixed arguments, if any, are declared as in other prototypes. In place of the variable arguments, you put an ellipsis (. . .). For example, a prototype for *fprintf()* is:

```
int fprintf(FILE *stream, char *format, ...);
```

The identifiers stream and format also can be omitted:

```
int fprintf(FILE *, char *, ...);
```

Every POSIX.1 function is associated with a header. (The terms *header file* and *include file* are obsolete; see Chapter 1, Section 1.2.) When a prototype for a function is presented, the header in which its prototype appears on C standard systems is also given, as well as all other headers that should be included when that function is used.

Sample Code

Most functions that have been introduced by the POSIX.1 committee, or with semantics that have changed significantly from UNIX systems, are used in examples in the text. These examples illustrate how the functions are intended to be used.

Appendices for Reference

The body of this book is written in a "how-to" format. For those who wish to use the book as a reference, appendices are provided.

- Appendix A gives, for each POSIX.1 function that is not imported from the C standard, the function's headers, prototype, return values, possible errno values, and a brief description of the function's semantics.

- Appendix B does the same for the POSIX.1 functions that come from the C standard.

- Appendix C describes the 37 portable values of errno that are supported by POSIX.1.

- Appendix D lists the headers specified by either POSIX.1 or the C standard and the reserved name-space associated with each header. (See Chapter 1, Section 1.6.) This name-space includes functions, macros, typedefs, structures, and external variables.

- Appendix E lists those POSIX.1 functions that can be safely invoked from a signal-catching function.

- Appendix F gives references to other POSIX standards and proposed standards and to related documents.

Exercises

Exercises are provided at the end of most chapters. Every reader should try some of them to test his or her understanding. They can also be used in a classroom setting.

Glossary

A glossary defining some of the most important terms is included.

About Portability and This Book

Programmers face two different classes of problems when trying to write portable programs. One class deals with nonportabilities intrinsic to the language. For example, it's easy to write C programs that make implicit assumptions about byte order within integers, about the relative sizes of pointers and integers, or about the layout of fields within structures. Any of these assumptions can render the program unportable. One might term these *internal* portability issues. They arise in all programming languages, although C is particularly vulnerable to them. Internal portability has to do with the relationship of the program's own code to hardware; it is under the complete control of the programmer.

Another class of problems has to do with the choice of external interfaces (functions and macros) that a program uses, the semantics that the program assumes for these interfaces, and the types of arguments that the program passes and return values that it expects. These might be termed *external* portability issues. They deal with the code invoked by, but external to, the program: the libraries and system calls that the program depends on. Problems of external portability arise in many programming languages, but again C is particularly vulnerable, because of its heavy dependence on libraries. External portability is only under the control of the programmer if the external interfaces are standardized. Without standards, external portability is impossible.

This book deals with external portability in the context of POSIX conforming systems. If you've tried to move C programs from one UNIX system to another you may have noticed that, while some programs compile without change and behave identically, others either don't compile or don't run in quite the same way. Given the differences among UNIX systems, this is unavoidable. In principle, if you write a Strictly Conforming POSIX.1 Application program it should compile on all POSIX.1 systems (or on none) and should have, within certain constraints, the same semantics on all of them.

Structure

Chapter 1 presents an overview of POSIX.1 concepts. This is the sort of material that programmers like to skip, to get to the "real code", but in fact it's essential in order to understand the issues that shaped the standard. Chapters 2 through 8 present the POSIX.1 C-language application programming interface (API). The API is the set of programming interfaces specified in the standard. Chapter 9 describes the data interchange formats specified by the standard. Chapter 10 describes the current state of proposed future extensions to POSIX.1. Chapter 11 discusses related standards, draft standards, and specifications, including the work of other POSIX groups and the *X/Open Portability Guide*. Finally, Chapter 12 discusses some general portability considerations for C programs. The six appendices were described above.

Acknowledgments

Only someone who has authored a book can know how much the book depends on the efforts of others. I have been fortunate to have the assistance of able reviewers, editors, and colleagues, without whose help this book could not have been written. Clarke Echols of Hewlett-Packard, Randolph Bentson of Colorado State University, Mark Sobell of Sobell Associates, and Claudia DeBlauw of Mindcraft all reviewed early portions of the manuscript. Robert Bismuth of DEC and Kathy Bohrer of IBM read portions of later drafts of the manuscript and made many valuable suggestions. Jim Isaak of DEC read two complete drafts of the manuscript, corrected many errors, and provided valuable advice and suggestions. I thank all of these people for their efforts. I also have had the good fortune to work with a very able editorial and production staff at Benjamin/Cummings: Alan Apt, John Thompson, Vivian McDougal, and Laura Kenney guided me through the complex process that ends in a published book. Anna Huff and Gary Palmatier did a thorough, capable job of copy editing and production.

I owe a special debt to my colleagues at Mindcraft, especially Bruce Weiner and Chuck Karish. Bruce introduced me to POSIX and to the standards way of thinking. Chuck read several drafts of this book with great care, pointing out many errors and making numerous worthy suggestions. He also helped me to read and interpret the POSIX.1 standard, with an attention to detail and subtlety that was invaluable. To all of these people I give sincere thanks.

Despite all this help, it is possible (and perhaps inevitable) that errors remain in the text. Of course, the responsibility for such errors is mine alone. Any reader who finds errors, or has suggestions, should notify me either through Benjamin/Cummings or, if desired, by electronic mail over the Internet. I can be reached at the Internet address *fred@mindcraft.com*.

Finally, I thank my wife, Linda Garfield, for giving me encouragement and putting up with the trials that are known only to authors' spouses, and my sons, Ben and Micah, who also encouraged me and (almost always) left me time and space to write when I asked them to, even when they were beset by the urgent needs of adolescence. And thanks, Flash, for curling up at my feet while I wrote.

Brief Contents

Detailed Contents

The POSIX Environment

In this book we describe the operating system interface standard informally known as POSIX or (more accurately) POSIX.1. This standard describes an operating system interface from the point of view of a C program. It is largely derived from the UNIX system. In fact, the adopted standard is fairly close to an amalgam of the core parts of AT&T UNIX System V.3 and 4.3BSD UNIX. The purpose of the POSIX.1 standard is to promote source code portability of application programs. UNIX system functions that were deemed to be of use only for system administration, and not for application programs, are not addressed in POSIX.1.

Some C programs that run portably on existing UNIX systems will also run, unchanged, on all systems that conform to the POSIX.1 standard. However, POSIX differs from UNIX in a number of significant ways. For example, UNIX system programs that catch signals, that control terminal attributes with *ioctl()*, that use certain "magic numbers" such as octal file modes, or that rely on file system parameters (like NAME_MAX) remaining constant across the entire file hierarchy—such programs will not be portable across all POSIX.1 systems. This is because POSIX has replaced these interfaces and features. In some cases the changes are based on features of historical versions of the UNIX system such as 4.2BSD. In other cases the 1003.1 committee chose to invent a new interface, either because two or more incompatible interfaces were already in wide use or because the existing interface was unsatisfactory for one reason or another.

This book concentrates on the new features of POSIX.1. If you are not experienced in C programming, this book is not the right place to start learning about POSIX; we assume knowledge of C. If you know C but are unfamiliar with any existing UNIX system, you can use this book to learn

1

about UNIX as well as POSIX, although it may be slow going. If you *are* an experienced UNIX programmer, then to write portable POSIX.1 programs you will have to learn both new function interfaces and new concepts. The function interfaces are detailed but straightforward, and their description constitutes the bulk of the remaining chapters. First, we discuss the environment in which POSIX.1 programs execute.

1.1   Our Goal

The purpose of this book is to teach you how to use the POSIX.1 standard. There are two distinctly different points of view from which you can look on the standard. From the viewpoint of a system implementor, the standard is a (partial) specification. It gives requirements that your system must satisfy. From that viewpoint, this book tries to clarify those requirements. From the viewpoint of an applications programmer, the standard is a guarantee. It describes interfaces and data structures with specified semantics on which you can rely, if your application runs on a conforming POSIX.1 system. From that viewpoint, this book tries to teach you how to write portable applications by using those interfaces and data structures. The standard, in keeping with this dichotomy, describes two types of conformance: implementation cconformance and application conformance.

1.1.1   Implementation Conformance

According to the POSIX.1 standard, a conforming implementation "shall support all required interfaces defined within this part of ISO/IEC 9945. These interfaces shall support the functional behavior described herein." The phrase "this part of" refers to the fact that other POSIX standards will eventually be adopted as parts of ISO/IEC 9945. Thus, it simply means POSIX.1.

A conforming implementation may, and in practice certainly will, support additional functions. It may even support nonstandard extensions that change the semantics of the functions defined in the standard. However, if it does so, it must define an environment in which an application can be run with the semantics given in the POSIX.1 standard. Thus an implementation can support alternate forms of some functions for backward compatibility and still conform to the POSIX.1 standard.

Every conforming implementation must be accompanied by a document called the *conformance document*. The conformance document must have a structure modeled on the structure of the standard. For example, signals are described in Chapter 3 of the standard, so information about signal handling must be given in Chapter 3 of the conformance document. The conformance document also must specify the full name, number, and date of the standard to which it applies. It must give the values of the system limits specified in the headers <limits.h> and <unistd.h>.* It must specify the behavior of the implementation in all situations where the behavior is specified by the standard to be implementation-defined.

If you are writing an application for a particular implementation, the conformance document for that implementation is an invaluable reference. It will tell you the behavior of many aspects of the system interface that the POSIX.1 standard leaves up to the implementation. However, if you are writing an application that must be portable among many POSIX systems, you must not rely on the unique characteristics described in any one system's conformance document.

Certain common terms are used with technical meaning by the standard, and we shall use them in the same way. Here are some definitions.

- *Implementation-defined.* This describes a value or behavior that the standard does not specify, but that the implementation is required to document, for correct programs and data. For example, a POSIX.1 system supports a signal mechanism in which processes can block signals, which are then left pending until they are unblocked. If a particular signal is blocked by a process, two or more instances of that signal are then generated for the process, and the signal is then unblocked, is the signal delivered just once or more than once? That is, are blocked signals queued? The standard allows either behavior, but an implementation must document which choice it makes.

- *Unspecified.* This describes a value or behavior for which the standard imposes no requirements for correct programs and data. For example, suppose a process has blocked two different signals, and both are pending. Suppose that the process then unblocks both of them simultaneously. The order in which the signals are delivered is unspecified. A conforming implementation need not document its behavior in this situation. (Indeed, the behavior might be indeterminate.)

- *Undefined.* This describes a value or behavior for which the standard imposes no requirements for erroneous programs or data. For example, if an application chooses to ignore the SIGSEGV signal and such a signal is generated for the process by a reference to an invalid memory address, the behavior of the process after the signal is generated is undefined. A portable application must not do this; do not rely on undefined behavior.

- *Shall.* This word, whether referring to implementations or applications, describes a requirement.

---

* See Sections 1.3 and 1.4 below for an explanation of these values.

- *Should.* This word, when referring to implementations, describes a recommendation. When referring to applications, it describes a requirement for a Strictly Conforming POSIX.1 Application.

- *May.* This word, when referring to implementations, describes an optional feature that need not be present. A Strictly Conforming POSIX.1 Application must not depend on such a feature. It may make use of such a feature, as long as it can still work in the absence of the feature.

1.1.2   Application Conformance

The POSIX.1 standard specifies a hierarchy of levels of application conformance. The levels are:

- *Strictly Conforming POSIX.1 Application.* Such an application "requires only the facilities described in this part of ISO/IEC 9945 and the applicable language standards. Such an application shall accept any behavior described in this part of ISO/IEC 9945 as *unspecified* or *implementation-defined*, and for symbolic constants shall accept any value in the range permitted by this part of ISO/IEC 9945." This is the strictest level of application conformance. The phrase "applicable language standards" refers to those parts of a language standard that are referred to by the POSIX.1 standard. At this writing, only C language interfaces for POSIX.1 have been standardized. (FORTRAN and Ada interfaces should be standardized by 1992.) We describe those parts of the ANSI C standard that are supported by POSIX.1 in Chapter 8.

- *ISO/IEC Conforming POSIX.1 Application.* Such an application "uses only the facilities described in this part of ISO/IEC 9945 and approved Conforming Language Bindings for any ISO or IEC standard. Such an application shall include a statement of conformance that documents all options and limit dependencies, and all other ISO or IEC standards used." This level of conformance is less strict in two ways. First, it allows applications to rely on other standards. Thus, an ISO/IEC conforming POSIX.1 application could make use of the facilities in the GKS or the PHIGS standards, both of which have been adopted by the ISO. Second, this level of conformance allows applications to require POSIX.1 options or limit values beyond the minimum. For example, such an application could require job control or could require that the implementation support file names of at least 32 characters. (The POSIX.1 minimum is 14 characters.)

- *<National Body> Conforming POSIX.1 Application.* This is just like an ISO/IEC Conforming POSIX.1 Application, except that this type of application can also use standards adopted by a single member body of the ISO/IEC, such as ANSI or BSI (British Standards Institute). These two levels of conformance are grouped by the standard under the term *conforming POSIX.1 application.*

- *Conforming POSIX.1 Application Using Extensions.* Such an application uses nonstandard facilities that are consistent with the POSIX.1 standard. Such facilities must be documented. For example, any C program that uses the POSIX.1 interface but also uses the interfaces in the UNIX "curses" library is a conforming POSIX.1 application using extensions. This is a very weak level of conformance; almost every C program could satisfy it with suitable documentation.

Figure 1.1 illustrates the relationship between these levels of conformance. It is a hierarchy; stricter conformance categories are shown above less strict categories.

1.1.3 Our Goal, Restated

Now that we have defined enough terms, we redefine our goal: it is to teach you to write Strictly Conforming POSIX.1 Applications. When conforming POSIX.1 implementations are common (which will be very soon!), such programs will be among the most portable of C programs.

An important impetus for the rapid development of conforming POSIX.1 implementations is the POSIX.1 FIPS. A FIPS is a federal information processing standard. We discuss the POSIX.1 FIPS in Chapter 11, Section 11.1.

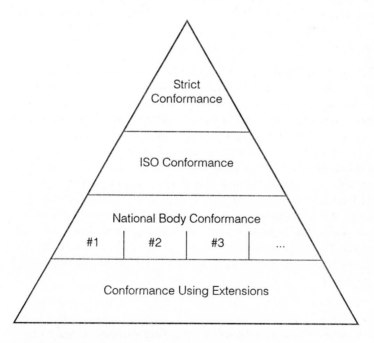

Figure 1.1

Levels of Application Conformance

Here we will briefly state that it is a procurement specification of the U.S. government. This happens to be an organization that buys a lot of computers. For this and other reasons, most major computer vendors have declared their intention to conform to the POSIX.1 FIPS.

Incidentally, the requirements of the POSIX.1 FIPS are somewhat stricter than those of the POSIX.1 standard itself. The differences are detailed in Chapter 11. As it is likely that most POSIX.1 systems will be FIPS conforming, an application program can—with a possible slight loss of portability—assume a FIPS-conforming environment. We discuss this in Section 11.1.1.

There is not currently a FIPS for the procurement of application software. Nevertheless, a software developer who wishes to sell programs to the U.S. government would be wise to write his or her programs as strictly conforming POSIX.1 applications. Failure to do so may eventually result in exclusion from a significant portion of the market.

1.2   The POSIX.1 Environment

POSIX describes an interface, not an implementation. The description consists largely of a series of specifications of functions callable from C programs,* of headers, and of data structures. No distinction is made between system calls and library functions. In fact, a system call in one implementation may quite possibly be a library function in another. Processes execute concurrently and have largely the same attributes—process IDs, real and effective user IDs, current directories, etc.—that UNIX system processes have. The file system is a hierarchy—not really a tree, because (as in UNIX systems) links can exist—and files have pathnames that are formed precisely as in UNIX systems.

Yet, POSIX is not UNIX. One way to think about their relationship is to think of POSIX as a generalization of UNIX. A number of concrete UNIX system concepts are replaced by abstractions in POSIX. An example is a *file system*. In the UNIX system a file system has a specific structure. It can be created (via *mknod()*), mounted and unmounted, made read-only, and so forth. A UNIX system file is uniquely specified by its file system and i-number within the file system. In POSIX.1 a file system is simply a name-space in which file serial numbers (the equivalent of i-numbers) are unique. Nothing is specified about how file systems are created or maintained. Thus, a UNIX file system is one example, but not necessarily the only one, of a POSIX.1 file system.

This sort of abstraction occurs for a number of reasons. One is that all system administrative issues were deemed outside the scope of the POSIX.1

---

*   Although the current POSIX.1 standard is written in terms of the C language, work is
    proceeding on a language-independent description, which will be accompanied by
    language-specific interfaces for several languages.

standards effort. Another, perhaps more central, is that the abstraction can encompass a number of existing, incompatible systems (to say nothing of systems not yet designed). For example, nothing prevents a POSIX.1 system from simultaneously providing a System V.3 file system, a BSD file system, and even non-UNIX file systems from environments like VMS, OS/2, or MVS. Some of these might have to be "disguised" by a layer of software.

The fact that some systems unrelated to UNIX will eventually conform to POSIX.1 has implications for the applications programmer. In particular, you should not rely on the availability of functions that are not part of POSIX.1 but that have historically been present in most or all UNIX systems. For example, *mknod()* has been present in most UNIX systems, but it is not included in the POSIX.1 standard. Thus a portable program must not use *mknod()*.

The POSIX.1 standard has a special relationship to the ANSI C standard, X3.159–1989. POSIX directly incorporates 110 functions from the ANSI C standard library. You will find them listed in Appendix B. POSIX.1 specifies extra semantics for nine of these functions. POSIX also takes from the C standard a number of headers, typedefs, and macros (e.g., <stdio.h>, time_t, NULL). However, a POSIX.1 system need not support full ANSI standard C; most of the included functions are part of existing "common C" libraries. We discuss the relationship between the POSIX.1 and C standards in Chapter 8.

Like UNIX system functions, POSIX.1 functions report errors by returning –1 or NULL and by setting the value of the external int variable errno. The identifiers used for the values of errno referenced by POSIX.1 functions are defined as macros in the header <errno.h>, just as in UNIX systems. You can find a list of these identifiers in Appendix C. (You may notice that the list differs somewhat from the corresponding list for System V.3 or the list for 4.3 BSD.) Implementations are free to add values to this list and to use the given values or others for errors not described in the POSIX.1 standard. However, they must use the specified values of errno to report those errors that are explicitly described in the standard. No POSIX.1 function ever sets errno to zero to indicate an error. However, the value of errno can only be relied upon if the most recently called function has returned an error. Functions may modify errno as a side effect when they are successful. Thus, the procedure is:

- Call the function.

- Examine the return value. If it indicates an error, then . . .

- Examine the value of errno to determine the error.

The errno mechanism is part of the C standard, although that standard only specifies two errno values (EDOM and ERANGE). However, the POSIX.1 specification of errno is more strict. POSIX.1 requires that errno be an int variable. The C standard simply requires that errno be defined and evaluate to a modifiable lvalue of type `int`. A number of C constructs satisfy this requirement.*

Every POSIX.1 implementation must claim one of two types of conformance to the standard: C standard support or common usage C support. If an implementation claims C standard support, then it must provide a function prototype declaration for every POSIX.1 function in an appropriate header. If common usage C support is claimed, then every function that does not return a "plain" `int` must have an external declaration in the specified header. Two consequences of these facts are the following rules:

- When you use a POSIX.1 function in a program, include all of its associated headers.

- Do not give a prototype or external declaration of the function.

We suggest these rules because if your program is compiled on a C standard system, including the appropriate header will automatically include a prototype for the function. And if your program is compiled on a common usage C system, either the function has type `int`—in which case no external declaration is needed—or the function has an external declaration in the included header.

Appendix A gives a prototype for each POSIX.1 function, except those taken from the C standard (for which you can find prototypes in Appendix B), and describes the header in which such a prototype must be found. In the body of this book we do not discuss the details of every POSIX.1 function, because we are principally concerned with differences between POSIX.1 and UNIX. However, we do give the prototype, associated headers, and semantics of all POSIX.1 functions, and we discuss the details of those functions that are new or significantly different in POSIX.

1.3　Some Differences between UNIX and POSIX Systems

A number of UNIX system constructs exist in somewhat altered form in POSIX. For many programs the differences will be inconsequential, but occasionally they are crucial. Two of the more significant ones involve process

---

* For example,
```
#define errno *(_errno())
```
where `_errno()` is a function that returns a pointer to an `int` in which an error code is stored.

privileges and configuration constants (which, in POSIX, are more properly termed *configuration variables*).

A familiar UNIX system concept is that of the *superuser*. Certain functions require privileges that are reserved for processes whose effective user ID is zero. POSIX replaces the superuser with the concept of *appropriate privileges*. Each action that may require special privileges can, in principle, have its own way of defining and assigning those privileges. The method of determining which processes have which privileges is implementation-defined: it is not specified in the POSIX.1 standard. This is a generalization of the superuser; that is, it is in conformance with the POSIX.1 standard to associate all appropriate privileges with effective user ID zero. However, it is also conforming to have a completely different, non-monolithic method for determining privileges. For example, in the UNIX system a process with superuser authority can change the mode of any file and can send signals to any process. A POSIX.1 process with appropriate privileges can perform either of these actions, but the required privileges might not be the same; that is, a process might have the privilege to change any file mode but not to send signals to any process, or vice versa. This generalization of the privilege mechanism allows POSIX.1 systems the option of having a more stringent security mechanism than that of UNIX systems. Such more stringent mechanisms are required for conformance with the higher levels of security specified in the Department of Defense's "Orange Book."

A crucial difference regarding privileges is that, in the UNIX system, a process can determine if it is privileged by calling *geteuid()* (see Chapter 2, Section 2.2) and checking whether the result is zero. There is no portable way for a process executing on a POSIX.1 system to determine if it has any privileges, or what they might be, short of trial and error.

UNIX System V.3 specifies a list of implementation-specific constants that may vary from one implementation to another. These values may or may not be available in a header file that can be included in an application program. For example, OPEN_MAX, the maximum number of files that a process can have open at any one time, is an implementation-specific constant. Another is LINK_MAX, the maximum number of links to a file. These and other limits are documented, but need not be available for programs to use. This can be inconvenient to application developers who want to release object code only and don't want to build implementation-specific constants into their code. For example, suppose you wish to allocate enough space to hold the longest possible filename, with room for a null byte at the end. The maximum length of a filename (a pathname component) is given by the value of the symbol NAME_MAX. You can use an array of NAME_MAX + 1 characters:

```
char    filename[NAME_MAX + 1];
```

If NAME_MAX isn't defined in a header, you could look it up in the system documentation (where it is guaranteed to appear) and define it in one of your program's private headers. But this is not a portable construction. For this reason, the second edition of AT&T's *System V Interface Definition (SVID)* states that "a portable application should not refer to these constants in its code." But then, how much space do you allocate?

The problem the application programmer faces is: how can I write programs that will run on as many systems as possible but will take advantage of facilities that are not available on all of these systems? Historically, three approaches have been widely used.

- Maintain two or more versions of the program. This is horrible. Eventually the different versions will diverge in function and in correctness.

- Write for the lowest common denominator. In other words, give up: don't use any facilities that are not present on all systems, and use the lowest limits that any of the systems support (e.g., no job control, short filenames). This typically results in a program with fewer features than you would like. Worse, in some cases there is no lowest common denominator. That is, systems have different, mutually incompatible features, and you simply have to choose one.

- Maintain one version of the program, with conditional compilation (using preprocessor tools like #ifdef) of the features that are not portable. This has probably been the best alternative of the three. However, it requires that you know in advance the features of the systems for which you are writing code. Each time a new system comes along, you may have to add more conditionally compiled code.

The POSIX.1 standard provides a fourth alternative: determine the system's limits and attributes at run time and take appropriate action. POSIX makes information about these limits and attributes available to application programs, both at compile time and at run time, in a very flexible way. First, POSIX specifies minimum values for the implementation-specific limits. These minimum values must be met or exceeded by any conforming POSIX.1 system. Although these minimum limits are absolute constants (specified in the POSIX.1 standard), they have symbolic names and are defined in the header <limits.h>. The identifier for the minimum is the same as the identifier for the value in question, preceded by _POSIX_. For example, the minimum possible value of NAME_MAX on any POSIX.1 system is 14; on any POSIX.1 system, the symbol _POSIX_NAME_MAX will be defined as 14 in <limits.h>. The actual value of NAME_MAX can be any value 14 or greater. Figure 1.2 shows the symbols and their values. Note that the _POSIX_ symbols are "minimum maxima"; that is, a POSIX.1 system must support a maximum value for the configurable parameter that is *at least* the value of the corresponding _POSIX_ constant. Thus, ARG_MAX represents a limit, or maximum, imposed by a system, and it will vary from one POSIX.1 system to another, but no conforming POSIX.1 system can have a value of ARG_MAX that is less than _POSIX_ARG_MAX, which is 4,096.

Symbolic Name	Minimum Value	Description
ARG_MAX	_POSIX_ARG_MAX = 4096	Maximum length of all arguments + environment strings to exec().
CHILD_MAX	_POSIX_CHILD_MAX = 6	Maximum number of simultaneous processes per real user ID.
LINK_MAX	_POSIX_LINK_MAX = 8	Maximum link count of a file.
MAX_CANON	_POSIX_MAX_CANON = 255	Maximum number of bytes in a terminal canonical input queue.
MAX_INPUT	_POSIX_MAX_INPUT = 255	Maximum number of bytes of space in a terminal input queue.
NAME_MAX	_POSIX_NAME_MAX = 14	Maximum number of bytes in a filename.
NGROUPS_MAX	_POSIX_NGROUPS_MAX = 0	Maximum number of simultaneous supplementary group IDs per process.
OPEN_MAX	_POSIX_OPEN_MAX = 16	Maximum number of simultaneous open files per process.
PATH_MAX	_POSIX_PATH_MAX = 255	Maximum number of bytes in a pathname.
PIPE_BUF	_POSIX_PIPE_BUF = 512	Maximum number of bytes in an atomic write to a pipe.
STREAM_MAX	_POSIX_STREAM_MAX = 8	The number of streams that one process can have open at one time.
SSIZE_MAX	_POSIX_SSIZE_MAX = 32767	The value that can be stored in an object of type ssize_t.

Figure 1.2

Minimum Values of Configurable Constants

It is the minima, the _POSIX_ values, that are guaranteed to be defined in <limits.h>. Whether or not the actual limits are defined in <limits.h> is complicated by two facts: (1) on a POSIX.1 system, some of these values need not be constants, which means they can vary at different points in the file hierarchy, and (2) some of these values are permitted to be indeterminate, which means they may not be defined at all. To understand this we have to classify the limits from Figure 1.2 into four groups.

The first group consists of the single limit NGROUPS_MAX. This limit *will* be defined in <limits.h> and thus is available at compile time. Application programs can also query the system for this value at run time. The value returned at run time will be at least as great as the value defined in the header; it may be greater. Note that the minimum required value, _POSIX_NGROUPS_MAX, is zero. Implementations in which the value of NGROUPS_MAX is zero effectively do not support supplementary group IDs. (See Chapter 2, Section 2.2.1.) On systems that conform to the POSIX.1 FIPS, NGROUPS_MAX must be at least 8.

The second group of limits includes ARG_MAX, CHILD_MAX, STREAM_MAX, and OPEN_MAX. These values are permitted to be indeterminate. For example, a system might allow a user ID to own as many processes as the system has memory for (but it must allow at least 6, the value of _POSIX_CHILD_MAX). In this case, a limit will exist, but it may vary among specific instances (e.g., machines) of a particular POSIX.1 implementation. If one of these four values is indeterminate, the corresponding symbol is not defined in <limits.h>. However, the value supported by the current instance of the implementation is available to the application at run time.

The third group of limits includes LINK_MAX, MAX_CANON, MAX_INPUT, NAME_MAX, PATH_MAX, and PIPE_BUF. These are the *pathname-variable* limits. Their values may differ from place to place in the file hierarchy. If so, they will not be defined in <limits.h>. Applications can query the system for their values relative to a given pathname at run time. For example, suppose a POSIX.1 system has both System V.3 and BSD file systems mounted at the same time, either locally or via a network. The value of NAME_MAX is 14 on most System V.3 systems but is 255 on BSD systems. POSIX provides an application with the ability to determine during execution the limits appropriate for any file or directory in the file hierarchy, either by pathname or (for open files) by file descriptor.

The final group consists of the single limit SSIZE_MAX, which is invariant. It will be defined in <limits.h>. There is no way to determine it at run time and no need for a portable application to ever do so.

An application determines these values by using the POSIX.1 functions *sysconf()*, *pathconf()*, and *fpathconf()*. These functions can be used to query the system for a number of configuration variables, of which the twelve listed in Figure 1.2 are only a part. We discuss the use of these functions in Section 1.5 of this chapter.

You may have noticed that we have been referring to *headers* rather than *header files* when we talk about POSIX. A POSIX.1 header need not be a file. The idea of an abstract header originated in the ANSI C standard and has been adopted by POSIX. Under this scheme, a header is something that, when included in a C source file, behaves as if it were an ASCII file whose text is now part of the source. But the header need not exist as a physical file. It can be built into the compiler, or be in ROM, or be a traditional file in the traditional /usr/include directory, or exist in some other form. Some POSIX headers have names that look like portions of UNIX pathnames, e.g.,

<sys/types.h>. However, this does not imply that a file named types.h exists in a directory named sys somewhere. Appendix D contains a list of all the required POSIX.1 and C standard headers along with the types, macros, and data structures that are defined in each one.

1.4   Configuration Options

Although one major goal of the POSIX standardization process was to resolve incompatibilities among different versions of the UNIX system, some differing features could not easily be unified. The committee decided that for certain features a POSIX system would simply have to implement one of two historical alternatives and arrange for programs to know which choice applied to the current implementation. Every POSIX.1 implementation has to make such a choice for five features:

- Job control. A system can either implement a modified form of Berkeley-style job control or not and still conform to the POSIX.1 standard. Job control allows a user to stop and restart "jobs" (command pipelines). From the point of view of an executing process, job control appears as an extra set of signals, a modified idea of process groups and additional control of the user's terminal. Job control is required by the POSIX.1 FIPS.

- Saved set-user-IDs. If a process with an effective user ID that differs from its real user ID uses *setuid()* to change its effective user ID to its real one, can it later change back—i.e., is the set-user-ID saved somewhere for later use by *setuid()*? Some UNIX systems, including System V.3, save the set-user-ID; others, including 4.3BSD, do not. Either behavior is POSIX.1 conforming. However, saved set-user-IDs are required by the POSIX.1 FIPS.

- Restricted use of *chown()*. On System V.3 systems, a user can use *chown()* to "give away" his or her files. On Berkeley-style and some older AT&T systems, the use of *chown()* to change the owner of a file is limited to the superuser. A POSIX.1 system can either allow *chown()* to be used as in System V.3 or require appropriate privileges. Moreover, this can vary within the file hierarchy; that is, whether or not *chown()* of a file is privileged can depend not only on the system but also on the file. On systems that conform to the POSIX.1 FIPS, *chown()* must be restricted (i.e., require appropriate privileges) everywhere in the file hierarchy.

- Truncation of long names. On some UNIX implementations, path components longer than NAME_MAX bytes are simply truncated. On others, such components cause an error. Either behavior is POSIX.1 conforming. This can also vary within the file hierarchy. On systems that conform to the POSIX.1 FIPS, long path components must cause an error everywhere in the file hierarchy.

- Disabling of special characters. The UNIX system terminal driver recognizes certain characters that have special behavior, e.g., to erase the previous input character or to cause an interrupt. The values of these special characters are under program control. Some UNIX systems provide a special value that, when assigned to a special character, disables that special function. A POSIX.1 system may, but need not, have such a value. The presence or absence of such a value can vary from one terminal device to another. On systems that conform to the POSIX.1 FIPS, every terminal device must have such a value defined.

The header <unistd.h> can be used to determine if the job control or saved set-user-ID options are present. If the symbol _POSIX_JOB_CONTROL is defined in this header, then the system supports job control, and otherwise it does not. If the symbol _POSIX_SAVED_IDS is defined in <unistd.h>, then the system supports saved set-user-IDs (and saved set-group-IDs as well).

Symbol	Description
_POSIX_JOB_CONTROL	If defined, job control is supported. System-wide.
_POSIX_SAVED_IDS	If defined, saved set-user-IDs and set-group-IDS are supported. System-wide.
_POSIX_CHOWN_RESTRICTED	If defined in <unistd.h>, then: if –1, *chown()* is not restricted; otherwise, *chown()* is restricted. If not defined in <unistd.h>, then evaluated with the same meaning on a per-file basis or on a per-directory basis that applies to all nondirectory files in that directory.
_POSIX_NO_TRUNC	If defined in <unistd.h>, then: if –1, long pathname components are truncated to NAME_MAX bytes; otherwise, long components are an error. If not defined in <unistd.h>, then evaluated with the same meaning on a per-directory basis that applies to all pathname components in that directory.
_POSIX_VDISABLE	If defined in <unistd.h>, then: its value (if not –1) is the disabling value for special characters for all terminal special files. If defined as –1, then there is no such disabling value. If not defined, then evaluated with the same meaning on a per-terminal-device basis.

Figure 1.3

Symbolic Constants Describing Implementation Options

An application can also use the *sysconf()* function to determine at run time if either of these options is in effect.

Determining if the three pathname-dependent options are present is slightly more complex. If _POSIX_CHOWN_RESTRICTED is defined in <unistd.h> and has the value –1, then the restricted use of *chown()* does not apply to any file in the system. If it is defined and has any value other than –1, the restriction of *chown()* applies to all files. If this symbol is not defined in the header, then the *pathconf()* and *fpathconf()* functions must be used on a per-file or per-directory basis to determine if use of *chown()* is restricted. Similarly, if _POSIX_NO_TRUNC is defined in <unistd.h> and its value is –1, long names are truncated; if its value is not –1, long names are an error. If it is not defined at all, then applications must use *pathconf()* and *fpathconf()* on a per-directory basis.

The special character disabling feature behaves a bit differently. If the symbol _POSIX_VDISABLE is defined in <unistd.h> as any value other than –1, then its value is the character value used to disable a special character. If it is defined to be –1, then there is no such disabling value. If it is not defined, then applications must use *pathconf()* and *fpathconf()* on a per-terminal-file basis. Figure 1.3 summarizes the constants and their meanings.

The ability of an application to determine at run time which options apply can be crucial. Suppose that an application uses a filename given on the command line and creates a new file with a suffix appended to the original name. (For example, some UNIX systems have a utility named compress that, with an input file named <filename>, creates the file <filename>.Z.) Consider the following code fragment:

```
char filename[NAMESIZE];      /* To hold new filename */
int fd;                       /* File descriptor */
mode_t mode;                  /* Mode of newly created file */
    /* ... */
(void)strcpy(filename, argv[1]);  /* Copy first argument */
(void)strcat(filename, ".Z");     /* Append ".Z" */
errno = 0;
if ( (fd = creat(filename, mode)) < 0 )
{
    if ( errno == ENAMETOOLONG )
        fprintf(stderr,"Cannot create %s; name too long.",
                    filename);
    else
        fprintf(stderr,"Cannot create %s; errno = %d.", errno);
}
```

This code is unsafe! If the system generates ENAMETOOLONG for over-long filenames, then the fragment will work. But if the system truncates filenames silently, then the call to *creat()* might destroy the original file. Alternatively, it might create a new file whose name has only the " . " appended. (The "Z" gets truncated.) What makes this a particular problem is that this code might be executing on a networked file system, in which different nodes have different behavior. Without the ability to determine the behavior locally at each directory, there is no way that the application can know what will happen. Of course, in this case the application can always test the new filename's length against the maximum permitted length. But this length, too, can vary across nodes in a networked file system and must be determined locally at run time.

1.5   Determining Configuration Values during Execution

The *sysconf()* function is used to determine configuration values that are not pathname-dependent. Its prototype is:

```
#include <unistd.h>
long sysconf(int name);
```

As promised, in this book we always show function declarations using the prototype format and always list the headers that should be included when a particular function is used. Even if you are unfamiliar with the prototype format, it should be self-explanatory. A traditional (parameter-list style) declaration of *sysconf()* would look like:

```
#include <unistd.h>
long sysconf(name)
int name;
```

The C standard, though it supports the traditional parameter-list method of defining C functions, has declared this method to be obsolescent.

The possible values of name are symbolic constants defined in <unistd.h>. They are shown in Figure 1.4. In this figure are two system-wide values that we have not yet discussed. One is _POSIX_VERSION, a long integer value that describes the version of the POSIX.1 standard with which the system conforms. It is 198808L for systems that conform to the original version of the standard. It is 199009L for systems that conform to the 1990 revision of the standard. _POSIX_VERSION is always a 6-digit (decimal) integer. The first 4 digits indicate the year and the last 2 indicate the month in which the version of the standard to which the system conforms was adopted.

The other new value is CLK_TCK. POSIX.1 requires this value to be defined in the header <time.h>. CLK_TCK is the number of intervals per second used in defining the type clock_t, which is used to measure process execution times. The value of CLK_TCK given in the <time.h> header and that returned by *sysconf()* are always the same.

When the POSIX.1 standard was adopted, CLK_TCK was a symbol defined in the then current draft of the ANSI C standard. Since then, the C

standard has dropped the symbol CLK_TCK. (This shows the dangers of relying on a draft version of a standard!) CLK_TCK is now a POSIX-defined
symbol and is considered obsolescent. CLK_TCK is now defined as simply a
synonym for sysconf(_SC_CLK_TCK), and a portable program should always use the latter construct.

The value returned by *sysconf()* is the current value for the requested
parameter on the system. If the parameter is undefined, *sysconf()* returns a
value of –1. *Sysconf()* also returns –1 if an error occurs. You can distinguish
between these cases by examining errno. When an error occurs, errno is set,
but when a parameter is undefined, errno is unchanged. The only error that
POSIX recognizes for the *sysconf()* function is use of an invalid value for
name, in which case errno will be set to EINVAL. Here is an example of the
use of *sysconf()*.

```
#include <unistd.h>
#include <errno.h>

main()
{
    extern int errno;
    long open_max;

    errno = 0;
    if ( (open_max = sysconf(_SC_OPEN_MAX)) == -1 )
    {
        if ( errno != 0 )
            printf("sysconf error: _SC_OPEN_MAX not recognized\n");
        else
            printf("On this system, OPEN_MAX is indeterminate\n");
    }
    else
        printf("On this system, OPEN_MAX = %ld\n", open_max);
    exit(0);
}
```

Note that we do not need an external declaration of *sysconf()*, even though
it returns a type other than int. Such a declaration will be found in
<unistd.h>.

The *pathconf()* and *fpathconf()* functions are similar to *sysconf()*, but each
takes an extra parameter:

```
#include <unistd.h>
long pathconf(const char *path, int name);
long fpathconf(int fildes, int name);
```

The path parameter points to a string that is a (relative or absolute)
pathname for the file or directory for which you wish to know the configurable
value. A process may want to know a value for an open file for which it does
not know a path (e.g., standard input). In that case you should use *fpathconf()*

Configurable Value	**Value of name Argument**
ARG_MAX	_SC_ARG_MAX
CHILD_MAX	_SC_CHILD_MAX
CLK_TCK	_SC_CLK_TCK
NGROUPS_MAX	_SC_NGROUPS_MAX
OPEN_MAX	_SC_OPEN_MAX
_POSIX_JOB_CONTROL	_SC_JOB_CONTROL
_POSIX_SAVED_IDS	_SC_SAVED_IDS
_POSIX_VERSION	_SC_VERSION

Figure 1.4

Configurable System Values and *sysconf()* Arguments

---

with the open file descriptor for the `fildes` argument. Figure 1.5 shows the values of `name` that correspond to the path-dependent configurable parameters.

There are a number of points to clarify about the semantics of *pathconf()*. For example, the `path` parameter (or the `fildes` parameter of *fpathconf()*) may refer to a directory or to a nondirectory file. Does the return value refer to the directory itself or to the filenames in that directory? The answer is governed by a rather complicated set of rules. Here they are:

- If the query is for the value of LINK_MAX and `path` refers to a directory, the value returned applies to the directory itself. Files within the directory might have different values of LINK_MAX.

- If the query is for the value of NAME_MAX or _POSIX_NO_TRUNC, `path` must refer to a directory, and the value returned applies to filenames within the directory.

- If the query is for the value of MAX_INPUT, MAX_CANON, or _POSIX_VDISABLE, then `path` must refer to a terminal file. If not, the behavior is undefined.

- If the query is for the value of PATH_MAX, `path` must refer to a directory, and the value returned is the maximum length of a *relative* pathname when the specified directory is the working directory. Thus, to find the maximum length of an *absolute* pathname, you would call `pathconf("/", _PC_PATH_MAX)` and add 1. (The extra 1 is for the leading '/', because a pathname relative to the root directory differs from an absolute pathname in that it lacks a leading '/'.)

Configurable Value	Value of name Argument
LINK_MAX	_PC_LINK_MAX
MAX_CANON	_PC_MAX_CANON
MAX_INPUT	_PC_MAX_INPUT
NAME_MAX	_PC_NAME_MAX
PATH_MAX	_PC_PATH_MAX
PIPE_BUF	_PC_PIPE_BUF
_POSIX_CHOWN_RESTRICTED	_PC_CHOWN_RESTRICTED
_POSIX_NO_TRUNC	_PC_NO_TRUNC
_POSIX_VDISABLE	_PC_VDISABLE

Figure 1.5

Path-Dependent Configurable Values and *(f)pathconf()* Arguments

- If the query is for the value of PIPE_BUF, then path must refer to a directory or FIFO (or, in the case of *fpathconf()*, fildes must refer to a directory, FIFO, or pipe). If the parameter refers to a directory, then the returned value refers to any FIFOs created in that directory. Neither path nor fildes may refer to any other type of file.

- If the query is for the value of _POSIX_CHOWN_RESTRICTED and path refers to a directory, then the returned value applies to all nondirectory files within that directory.

Each consideration applies to *fpathconf()* and the fildes parameter as well. Here is an example of the use of *pathconf()* and *fpathconf()*.

```
#include <unistd.h>
#include <errno.h>

main()
{
    extern int errno;
    long name_max;
    long disable_char;

    /* Determine NAME_MAX for current directory */
    errno = 0;
    if ( (name_max = pathconf(".", _PC_NAME_MAX)) == -1 )
    {
        if ( errno != 0 )
            printf("pathconf error: _PC_NAME_MAX not recognized\n");
```

```
        else
            printf("In the current directory, NAME_MAX is \
indeterminate\n");
    }
    else
        printf("In the current directory, NAME_MAX = %ld\n",
                        name_max);

    /* Determine _POSIX_VDISABLE for standard input */
    if ( ! isatty(0) )
        printf("Standard input is not a terminal\n");
    else
    {
        errno = 0;
        if ( (disable_char = fpathconf(0, _PC_VDISABLE)) == -1)
        {
          if ( errno == EINVAL )
            printf("pathconf error: _PC_VDISABLE not recognized\n");
          else
            printf("_POSIX_VDISABLE undefined for standard \
input\n");
        }
        else
            printf("For standard input, _POSIX_VDISABLE is 0x%lx\n",
                        disable_char);
    }
    exit(0);
}
```

1.6   Standard Types

UNIX System V.3 uses a number of defined types, such as time_t, to define
the types of some function parameters and data structure members. POSIX
makes even more extensive use of such types. Many System V.3 functions
that return a standard C type are replaced by virtually equivalent POSIX.1
functions that return a defined type. For example, the *SVID* specifies that the
function *lseek()* returns a long. In POSIX, *lseek()* returns an off_t. Figure 1.6
shows the simple (nonstructured) types that must be defined on a POSIX.1
system and the headers in which their definitions can be found.

All of these types must be arithmetic. (This includes chars, ints and
floats, signed or unsigned, short or long, and enumerated types.) The
types off_t, pid_t, and ssize_t must be signed types. POSIX requires
that user IDs and group IDs be nonnegative, and uid_t and gid_t are

Type Name	Header	Use In POSIX.1
cc_t	<termios.h>	Terminal special characters
clock_t	<time.h>	Times in CLK_TCKths of a second
dev_t	<sys/types.h>	Device numbers
gid_t	<sys/types.h>	Group IDs
ino_t	<sys/types.h>	File serial numbers
mode_t	<sys/types.h>	Various file attributes
nlink_t	<sys/types.h>	Link counts
off_t	<sys/types.h>	File sizes
pid_t	<sys/types.h>	Process IDs and process group IDs
size_t	<sys/types.h>	Byte counts
speed_t	<termios.h>	Asynchronous line speeds
ssize_t	<sys/types.h>	Signed byte counts
tcflag_t	<termios.h>	Terminal control modes
time_t	<time.h>	Times in seconds
uid_t	<sys/types.h>	User IDs

Figure 1.6

Defined Simple Types Used in the POSIX.1 Standard

usually defined as unsigned types. The types size_t and ssize_t were not required in the originally adopted POSIX.1 standard; they were added in the 1990 revision. The type size_t is also required by the C standard and must be defined in the <stdlib.h> header required by that standard. The header <sys/types.h> is permitted to contain definitions of other types, but all must have names ending in _t.

1.7   Name-Space Pollution

A typical POSIX program will include a significant number of headers with contents that the programmer has no control over. This presents a potential problem, because in theory these headers can define all sorts of symbols, which possibly would clash with symbols that the programmer has defined. There are two solutions to this problem: *reserved symbols* and *feature test macros*.

Reserved symbols are simply symbols that the application programmer is not permitted to use. They are reserved for use by the system implementors. POSIX, by reference to the C standard, reserves the following symbols:

- All external identifiers that begin with an underscore.

- All identifiers that begin with two underscores.

- All identifiers that begin with an underscore followed by an upper-case letter.

These requirements are adopted from the C standard. In addition, all other identifiers reserved by the C standard are reserved by POSIX, including all external identifiers found in any of the C standard library headers. Unfortunately, there is no particular pattern to these identifiers, which include such macros as BUFSIZ and FILE. This reserved name-space is shown in Appendix D.

The POSIX.1 standard reserves some other name-spaces as well. All identifiers ending in _t are reserved for the implementation (for use as defined names in <sys/types.h> or other headers). In addition, the prefixes and suffixes shown in Figure 1.7 are *reserved with respect to their corresponding headers*. Implementations are free to add symbols to the headers as long as those symbols begin with one of the prefixes or end with one of the suffixes reserved for that header. This means that no identifier with any of the given prefixes or suffixes should be used by the application until after the last inclusion of the corresponding header.

After the last such inclusion, the prefixes and suffixes shown in boldface in the figure may be used with no constraints. Other prefixes may be used if the corresponding symbol is first undefined with #undef. For example, the following is permitted:

```
#include  <sys/stat.h>
#define   st_filler st_mode
int       st_mode;
```

After the (last) inclusion of <sys/stat.h>, the st_ prefix is no longer reserved.

The following is also permitted:

```
#include  <signal.h>
int d_size; /* <dirent.h> is not included at all */
#undef    SIG_IGNORE
#define   SIG_IGNORE      SIG_IGN
```

The d_ prefix is not reserved if the <dirent.h> header is not included, and the SIG_ prefix is not reserved after the inclusion of <signal.h> *as long as the symbol is first undefined*. However, the following is not permitted:

```
#define   st_filler st_mode
#include  <sys/stat.h>
```

The problem here is that a conforming implementation may have a field named `st_filler` in its `stat` structure. The definition of `st_filler` shown will cause the structure to have two `st_mode` fields. If the definition occurs after the header is included, the effect will be different: the `st_filler` field of the structure will simply be inaccessible (all references to it will be interpreted as references to the `st_mode` field).

The reason that some identifiers need to be undefined and others do not is that in C each structure or union has its own name-space for structure members. Thus the following two instances of the identifier `snark` do not conflict:

```
struct {
    int snark;
} x;
char snark[16];           /* A different "snark" */
```

When a name-space has been reserved for members of a structure or union, use of the name-space after the structure or union has been defined can be unrestricted. But identifiers that occupy the "top level" name-space may conflict with identifiers that are defined or declared later. The boldface prefixes in Figure 1.7 are prefixes of structure members.

Feature test macros are macros that control the scope of symbols defined in a header. A feature test macro is a symbol that you `#define` in your program *before* any headers to which you want it to apply. It must begin with

Header	Reserved Prefix	Reserved Suffix
<dirent.h>	**d_**	
<fcntl.h>	**l_**, **F_**, **O_**	
<grp.h>	**gr_**	
<limits.h>		**_MAX**
<locale.h>	**LC_**, **n_**, **p_**	
<pwd.h>	**pw_**	
<signal.h>	**sa_**, **SIG**, **SIG_**, **SA**	
<sys/stat.h>	**st_**, **S_**	
<sys/times.h>	**tms_**	
<termios.h>	**c_**, **V**, **I**, **O**, **TC**, **B**[0-9]	

Figure 1.7

Name-Spaces Reserved for Corresponding Headers

an underscore character. Its exact meaning depends on whether or not the POSIX.1 implementation claims C standard support:

- If an implementation claims such support and no feature test macros are present in your program, then only the symbols specified by the C standard are made visible by including the header. That is, even if other symbols are defined in the header, they will not appear as so defined to your program. (Typically, such symbols are protected by #ifdefs.)

- If the feature test macro _POSIX_SOURCE is defined in your program, then for every header defined in the POSIX.1 standard, all symbols defined by that standard *or* the C standard will be visible.

- If no other feature test macros are present then no other symbols are made visible from these headers, except possibly symbols whose names are constrained by rules in the POSIX.1 standard (e.g., other types in <sys/types.h> whose names end in _t) and members of structures or unions in addition to those members specified in one of the two standards.

- Other feature test macros can cause other symbols from these headers to become visible. For example, the current (as of this writing) draft of the POSIX.2 standard specifies the feature test macro _POSIX2_SOURCE. If this symbol is defined in a program, it causes other symbols to be made visible from the header <unistd.h>.

What does all this mean? For the programmer, it means that if you're careful to avoid using documented symbols or reserved symbols, and if you use the feature test macro _POSIX_SOURCE, you don't have to worry about your identifiers clashing with surprises from a header. So a good rule to follow is:

The first non-comment line of every POSIX program should be

    #define _POSIX_SOURCE

If an implementation of POSIX.1 supports common usage C, the rules are almost the same: if _POSIX_SOURCE is not defined before any headers are included, then the symbols visible to an application are implementation-defined. However, if this feature test macro is defined, then the same set of symbols is visible as in the C standard support case: the symbols from the C standard, those from the POSIX.1 standard, and possibly some symbols whose names are restricted by the POSIX.1 standard.

The exception regarding restricted names allows implementors to include and make freely visible reserved symbols or to define symbols such as other types in `<sys/types.h>` that end in `_t`. The easiest rule to follow regarding reserved identifiers is:

> Avoid using prefixes or suffixes that are reserved for use by the C standard or for any POSIX.1 header.

Generally, these rules are easy to follow. The exception is the `_t` rule. Many application programs have followed the convention of naming their own `typedefed` types with names that end in `_t`. Such names are now nonportable, as they may conflict with implementation-defined names. Of course, the possibility of conflict has always existed. The difference is there was never anything you could do about it before.

1.8   Environment Strings

Executing POSIX.1 processes have access to an array of strings known as the process *environment*. These environment strings are identical in form to the environment strings available to UNIX processes: they are of the form *name=value*. However, UNIX programs access their environment strings in at least three ways:

- via the *getenv()* function.
- via the external variable `extern char **environ`.
- via a third argument to *main(argc, argv, envp)*.

Only the first two of these methods are portable in POSIX. The C standard requires that *main()* be declared with either zero or two arguments and that it have a return type of `int`.

No environment strings are required by POSIX.1. However, a number of environment strings are constrained, in the sense that if they are defined, they must have a particular meaning. These include HOME, LOGNAME, PATH, TERM, and TZ. All of these have the usual UNIX system meaning, although the format of TZ (the time zone string) is governed by extensions to the UNIX rules. Other environment strings will be discussed in the section on internationalization in Chapter 8.

Exercises for Chapter 1 _____

1. Write a strictly conforming POSIX.1 application that reports the values of the following configurable options for the host system on which it runs:

   - Whether job control is supported.

   - Whether saved set-user and set-group IDs are supported.

   - Whether the use of *chown()* is always restricted to privileged processes, is never restricted, or may or may not be restricted on a per-file basis.

   - Whether long pathname components are always truncated, are never truncated, or may or may not be truncated depending on the pathname.

   - Whether terminal special characters can be disabled and, if so, the hexadecimal value of the disabling character for the current terminal.

   - What version of the POSIX.1 standard the system conforms to.

2. Write a strictly conforming POSIX.1 application that reports the values of the following characteristics of its host:

   - The length of the longest permissible absolute pathname.

   - The length of the longest permissible pathname relative to the current directory in which the program is executing.

   - The length of the longest possible directory entry in the root directory.

   - The length of the longest possible directory entry in the current directory.

3. Suppose you want to implement a version of the UNIX cp utility on a POSIX.1 system. The syntax of cp is:

   ```
   cp file [file ...] target
   ```

   where, if more than one file is specified, target must be a directory. Suppose that one or more of the files to be copied are in a part of the file hierarchy in which NAME_MAX is 255, while target is in a part of the file hierarchy in which NAME_MAX is 14.

   (a)   What kinds of problems can arise?

(b)   If _POSIX_NO_TRUNC is in effect for target and the command

```
cp veryverylongfilename target
```

is issued, what should happen?

(c)   If _POSIX_NO_TRUNC is not in effect for target and the same command is issued, what should happen?

(d)   If _POSIX_NO_TRUNC is not in effect for target and the command

```
cp veryverylongfilename1 veryverylongfilename2 target
```

is given, what would you expect to happen?

(e)   Write the portable POSIX function

```
int clash(char *name1, char *name2, char *target)
```

which will determine if the filenames name1 and name2 can exist in directory target and if they will be truncated to the same name. Your function should return 0 if both filenames can exist without being truncated, 1 if one or more of the names will be truncated but they will remain distinct, and –1 if name1 and name2 will be truncated to the same name in target. The function should behave reasonably if either name1 or name2 is NULL or points to an empty string. You may use the UNIX string functions such as *strlen()* and *strcmp()*, all of which are POSIX.1 portable.

Process and System Attributes

A **program in execution** is referred to as a *process*. A POSIX.1 system associates with every process a number of attributes, most of which the process can determine by calling appropriate functions. In this chapter we discuss the ways a process can determine and control the values of these attributes.

Figure 2.1 shows some of the process attributes that we are concerned with. All of these should be familiar to UNIX System V.3 programmers except the supplementary group IDs, signal mask, and session. Supplementary groups and signal masks are taken from the Berkeley's BSD UNIX system. The idea of a session also comes from BSD, as part of job control, but the term is new with POSIX. A process's session is unusual among attributes in that it is anonymous. That is, a process does not have a session ID.

2.1 Determining Current Process Attributes

A process can interrogate the system for the current value of most of its attributes, using the functions shown in Figure 2.1. The *getpid()* and *getppid()* functions return the caller's process ID and parent process ID, respectively. They are unchanged from the UNIX system, except for their return types (which are int in System V.3). Moreover, a process has no control over its process ID or its parent process ID. Prototypes for these functions are:

```
#include <sys/types.h>
#include <unistd.h>
pid_t getpid(void);
pid_t getppid(void);
```

Attribute	Type	Function to Get Current Value	Function to Set New Value
Process ID	pid_t	getpid()	—
Parent process ID	pid_t	getppid()	—
Process group ID	pid_t	getpgrp()	setpgid()
Login user name	char *	getlogin()	—
Real user ID	uid_t	getuid()	setuid()†
Effective user ID	uid_t	geteuid()	setuid()
Real group ID	gid_t	getgid()	setgid()†
Effective group ID	gid_t	getegid()	setgid()
Supplementary group IDs	gid_t[]	getgroups()	—
Current directory	char *	getcwd()	chdir()
File mode creation mask	mode_t	umask()	umask()
Signal mask	sigset_t	sigprocmask()	sigprocmask()
Set of pending signals	sigset_t	sigpending()	—
Process times	struct tms	times()	—
Controlling terminal	char *	ctermid()	—
Session	none—session is anonymous		setsid()

† Only with appropriate privileges

Figure 2.1

Process Attributes

The process group ID is another matter. Here, AT&T UNIX and Berkeley UNIX have historically diverged because of job control. To avoid conflict with either one, POSIX has introduced some new terminology and a new function, *setpgid()*. The ideas, however, correspond to Berkeley UNIX. To understand them, we need a brief overview of job control.

2.1.1 BSD Job Control Concepts

On BSD UNIX systems, a *job* is a command pipeline. At any moment, a user can be executing one or more jobs. (If no command is executing, the shell is the only current job.) At any moment, a user has one foreground job and zero or more background jobs. For example, suppose you type the command line

```
ls -s | sort -rn > f_list & grep "x" *.log | grep -v "y" | wc
```

This command line launches two jobs: a foreground job (the one with the two greps and the wc) and a background job (the one with ls and sort). The foreground job consists of three processes connected by pipelines. The background job has two processes connected by a single pipe. If you had followed the entire line with another &, both jobs would be background jobs and the shell would be in the foreground.

A user can stop active jobs, restart stopped jobs, move jobs from the foreground to the background or vice versa, and control whether terminal output from background jobs should or should not mingle with output from the foreground job. Clearly, if you want to stop a job, you should stop all the processes in it together. Because the system controls jobs by using signals, it needs to somehow group together processes in the same job. Moreover, processes that are not part of the same job (such as ls and grep in the example above) should not be signalled together; they should not be grouped. In BSD UNIX, all the processes that belong to a given job are members of the same *job control process group*.

2.1.2   System V Process Groups

In System V.3, which does not support job control, processes are also organized into groups—principally so that they can be signalled together. For instance, if a user logs on over a phone line, launches a number of processes, and then hangs up, the system can send the SIGHUP signal to all the processes by sending it (via *kill()*) to the process group. A System V.3 process inherits its process group from its parent and can change it with a call to *setpgrp()*: a successful call to *setpgrp()* changes the caller's process group ID to its own process ID. Typically, the login shell calls *setpgrp()* and no other user process does so during the login session, so that all the processes that are descendants of the login shell will have the same process group ID—namely, the process ID of the shell.

2.1.3   POSIX Process Groups, Sessions, and Controlling Terminals

In POSIX.1, every process is a member of a process group, and every process group is a member of a session. Conceptually, a session corresponds to a login session at a terminal—that is, everything a user does between the time he or she logs on and logs off. In this respect a session is like a System V.3 process group. However, there is no such thing as a session ID. Sessions are anonymous: they have no names visible to a user process. A consequence of this is that, in general, there is no way to send a signal to every process in a session. POSIX process groups correspond to Berkeley UNIX job control process groups. They have IDs of type pid_t.

In every process group there is one process whose process ID (PID) is the same as the process group ID (PGID). That process is called the *process group leader.* We will see below how a process becomes a process group leader. Similarly, in every session there is one process that is the *session leader.* Figure 2.2 illustrates the relationship of sessions, process groups, and processes.

A session may be, but need not be, associated with a *controlling terminal.* The controlling terminal for a session—and there can be at most one per session—is the terminal from which special characters (like `interrupt` and `quit`) can be sent to processes in the session. POSIX does not specify any way in which a session acquires a controlling terminal. On UNIX systems, if a process that has no controlling terminal opens a terminal file, that terminal becomes the controlling terminal for the process. In POSIX, controlling terminals are acquired in an implementation-defined manner. In practice, the terminal on which you log in will be the controlling terminal for your session.

An application program rarely needs to change its process group or session. Typically, only the shell needs to worry about manipulating these attributes. However, for those rare occasions, we include an explanation of the *setsid()* and *setpgid()* functions.

When a process is created, it is a member of the same session as its parent. A process can detach itself and start a new session by calling *setsid()*.

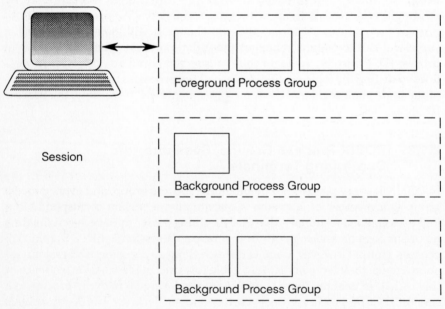

Figure 2.2

Sessions and Process Groups

Typically, a login shell or the process that invokes it will do this when the shell starts up. Here is the prototype of *setsid()*:

```
#include <unistd.h>
#include <sys/types.h>
pid_t setsid(void);
```

When a process calls *setsid()* successfully, it becomes the only member of a new process group, which in turn is the only process group of a new session. The PGID of the new process group will be the PID of the caller; this is the return value of *setsid()*. Thus, a successful caller of *setsid()* becomes a process group leader. It also becomes the session leader. In fact, as it is the only member of the new process group, which is the only member of the new session, it must be the leader of both. A process that is already a process group leader may not call *setsid()*. If it tries, the call will fail with errno set to EPERM.

An important consequence of a successful call to *setsid()* is that the caller becomes detached from its controlling terminal. It either remains without a controlling terminal or acquires one in an implementation-defined way. Disposing of a controlling terminal is one reason that an application might wish to call *setsid()*.

A POSIX.1 process can detach itself from its process group by calling *setpgid()*. In early draft versions of POSIX this function was called *setpgrp()*. However, that name is used both in System V.3, where it roughly corresponds to POSIX *setsid()*, and in 4.3BSD, where it corresponds to *setpgid()*. To avoid confusion, the POSIX.1 committee chose the new name. The function that a process calls to learn its PGID is still named *getpgrp()*. (There were no semantic differences between the BSD and System V versions of this function.) Prototypes for *setpgid()* and *getpgrp()* are:

```
#include <unistd.h>
#include <sys/types.h>
pid_t setpgid(pid_t pid, pid_t pgid);
pid_t getpgrp(void);
```

An implementation of POSIX.1 is required to support *setpgid()*, but only in a limited way: if the implementation does not support job control, then the *setpgid()* function must be present, but it is permitted to always fail. If the POSIX.1 implementation supports job control, then the consequences of a successful call to *setpgid()* are:

- If pid and pgid are nonzero, then the process whose PID is pid becomes a member of process group pgid. Process group pgid must either be an existing process group within the session of the caller or be equal to pid (in which case a new process group is created, with process pid as its sole member). As we will see below, a process can only change the process group ID of itself or one of its children.

- If `pid` is zero, the same semantics apply, except that the PID of the caller is used in place of `pid`.

- If `pgid` is zero, the same semantics apply, except that the PID of the caller is used in place of `pgid`.

Thus, on a system that supports job control, if the call

```
setpgid(0, 0);
```

succeeds it places the caller in a new process group whose PGID will be its own PID. The process becomes the process group leader, and sole member, of a new process group within its original session.

A call to *setpgid()* might fail for a number of reasons. We have already mentioned that, on systems that do not support job control, it is permitted for *setpgid()* to always fail. In such a case `errno` will be set to ENOSYS. In any case, you can only change your own PGID, or that of one of your children, if it is still in the same session and *if it has not yet successfully called an* exec() *function*. If the value of the `pid` argument does not match the PID of the caller or of any of the caller's children, then *setpgid()* fails with `errno` set to ESRCH. If `pid` is the PID of a child of the caller but the child has already *exec()*ed, then `errno` is set to EACCES. (This is an unusual meaning for EACCES.) If the value of `pid` describes a session leader, or if it describes a child of the caller that is no longer in the same session, then `errno` is set to EPERM. If there is no process group in the caller's session with PGID equal to `pgid`, then `errno` also is set to EPERM. Finally, if the value of `pgid` is negative or otherwise invalid, then `errno` is set to EINVAL.

From these rules you can get an idea of how a job control shell uses the *setsid()* and *setpgid()* functions. The login shell or one of its ancestors calls *setsid()* at startup. No other process need call the function. When a job is launched, one process in the job becomes the process group leader of the new job. (Usually it's the last process in the pipeline.) Each process in the job, as soon as it has *fork()*ed and before it *exec()*s, calls *setpgid()* with the process group ID of the process group leader. Alternatively, some shells arrange for the last command in the pipe to be the parent of all the others. In that case, the process for that command can *fork()* first, call *setpgid()*, and then *fork()* again to create the other processes. They will inherit the PGID of their parent.

A process group also can become *orphaned*. An orphaned process group is one for which the parent of every member of the process group is either itself in the same process group or is not a member of the same session. This rather complex definition is not terribly meaningful at first glance. Before we explain it, let's explain the problem that it is intended to solve.

Suppose that, on a system with job control, a job is started. The processes in the job constitute a process group. Typically, the parent process of at least one of the processes in the job is the user's shell. The shell is not a member of this job. Thus, by the above definition, this process group is not orphaned. Commands issued to the shell can move the process group from the foreground to the background or vice versa and can stop all the processes in the process group. Thus, this process group is under the control of the shell.

Now suppose that the shell exits and the job continues to execute. Processes that were children of the shell are inherited by an implementation-defined system process that is not a member of the current session. Thus, this process group becomes orphaned. This situation must be treated specially as there is no longer a process that can exercise control over the job. This is not a problem as long as the job is running, but it could be a problem if the job is stopped: there would be no way to restart it. If it is executing in the background, there is no process that can move it to the foreground. As we will see in Chapter 7, POSIX.1 places restrictions on access to the terminal by processes in orphaned background process groups and prevents such processes from stopping in response to terminal signals.

Typically, the shell itself is a member of an orphaned process group. It is the only member of a process group, and its parent is in a different session. This guarantees that the shell itself will not be stopped by an interactive signal.

2.2   Process User and Group IDs

As in UNIX systems, each POSIX.1 process has a real and an effective user ID and a real and an effective group ID. These IDs are all available to the process through the functions *getuid()*, *geteuid()*, *getgid()*, and *getegid()*, which are unchanged from UNIX systems except for their return types. All of these functions return `unsigned short` in both UNIX System V.3 and 4.3BSD. Their POSIX.1 prototypes are:

```
#include <sys/types.h>
#include <unistd.h>
uid_t getuid(void);
uid_t geteuid(void);
gid_t getgid(void);
gid_t getegid(void);
```

If the symbol `_POSIX_SAVED_IDS` is defined, then each process also has a saved set-user-ID and a saved set-group-ID. (There is no POSIX.1 function to determine a process's saved IDs, if they are supported.) In discussing all these IDs, we will focus on the user ID. Everything we say applies to process group IDs as well.

The real user ID of a process is inherited from its parent and can only be changed if the process has appropriate privileges. The effective user ID is also inherited but can be changed by an *exec()* function call: if the mode of the process image file has the set-user-ID bit set, then the effective user ID is changed to the owner ID of the new process image file. On systems where `_POSIX_SAVED_IDS` is defined, when a process does an *exec()*, the new effective user ID is copied to the saved set-user-ID.

In case you are unfamiliar with the concept of an effective user ID, we review it briefly. The attributes associated with objects that the process creates (such as directories and files) are associated with its effective user ID. On UNIX systems, the privileges of a process are also associated with its effective user ID; a process with an effective user ID of zero has super-user privileges. This may be true on some POSIX systems as well, although the POSIX.1 standard leaves the acquisition of privileges up to the implementation.

An example of a program that makes use of effective user IDs is the UNIX system `mail` program. The problem in sending mail is that you need to be able to write to another user's mailbox file. However, you should not be allowed to write to it indiscriminately. Otherwise, you could truncate it to zero length, overwrite other letters, or otherwise interfere with the file contents. UNIX systems solve the problem by making the `mail` program a set-user-ID program owned by the superuser. Thus, when a user invokes the `mail` command, the shell *fork()*s a process that *exec()*s `mail`. The `mail` program then executes with the effective user ID of the superuser. This user ID carries with it the right to write to any file and, in particular, to any mailbox, but the program (if it is written without any security loopholes) only appends to the file. The real user ID of the `mail` process remains your user ID.

If you have used `mail` on UNIX systems, you may know that you can interrupt the mailing of a letter to get a shell prompt and issue commands. This may seem like a security loophole: will the shell started up by `mail` run with privileges? It would if no care were taken, and this would indeed be a problem. But in fact, `mail` invokes a shell by calling *fork()* to create a new process, which then changes its effective user ID back to its real user ID—that is, your user ID—before calling *exec()* to become a shell. Thus, some method of changing the effective user ID back to the real user ID is essential for this scheme.

If the real and effective user IDs of a process differ, or if the process is privileged, it is possible for the process to change its effective user ID by calling the *setuid()* function. The prototypes for *setuid()* and *setgid()* are:

```
#include <unistd.h>
#include <sys/types.h>
int setuid(uid_t uid);
int setgid(gid_t gid);
```

Both of these functions return 0 on success, −1 on failure. The semantics of *setuid()* are:

- If a process has appropriate privileges, then the call

    ```
    setuid(uid);
    ```

    changes the process's real and effective user IDs, and (if defined) the saved set-user-ID, to `uid`. Typically, when a user logs on the system login program calls this function with the user's ID before *exec()*ing a shell. This is how the user's processes initially acquire their user IDs.

- If the process does not have the appropriate privilege but `uid` equals the real user ID of the process, then the effective user ID of the process is set to `uid`.

- If the process does not have the appropriate privilege but `_POSIX_SAVED_IDS` is defined and `uid` is equal to the saved set-user-ID of the process, then the effective user ID of the process is set to `uid`.

- If the process does not have the appropriate privilege and `uid` is neither the real nor the saved user ID, the *setuid()* call fails with `errno` set to EPERM.

So apparently, `_POSIX_SAVED_IDS` allows you to change your effective user ID to your real user ID and later change it back again. There's a catch, however. If your process has the appropriate privilege, then a call to *setuid()* will change your saved set-user-ID. If, as a result of the call to *setuid()*, your process no longer has the appropriate privileges, it will not be able to call *setuid()* to change any of its user IDs. Thus, you cannot toggle back and forth between privileged and nonprivileged user IDs. In particular, on UNIX System V.3 systems (which support saved set-user-IDs), a process with an effective user ID of zero cannot give up superuser privileges and then reclaim them. But a process with real and effective user IDs that differ and that are both unprivileged can toggle its effective user ID back and forth.

The situation is even more confusing in POSIX.1 than on UNIX systems: on a traditional UNIX system, in which privileges are monolithic and vested in the superuser, a process can determine if it is privileged by calling *geteuid()*. On a POSIX system there's no portable way for a process to determine if it has any privileges and what they might be. Thus a process calling *setuid()* cannot generally know what the effect of the call will be! The only guarantee is that

```
setuid(getuid());
```

will change the caller's effective user ID to its real user ID.

If `_POSIX_SAVED_IDS` is not defined, then once you've changed your effective user ID to your real user ID you can't change back (unless, after the *setuid()* call, you still have the appropriate privileges). The semantics of *setgid()* are similar; the above rules apply if you replace `uid` with `gid` and the word *user* with the word *group*.

Both *setuid()* and *setgid()* will fail if the values of their respective arguments are invalid, i.e., not supported by the implementation. In such a case, `errno` is set to EINVAL. Precisely what constitutes an invalid ID is implementation-defined.

2.2.1   Supplementary Group IDs

Not only processes have user and group IDs; users do as well. Every POSIX.1 system maintains a *user database* in which a user's login user ID and group ID are stored. In addition, each POSIX.1 system maintains a *group database* in which information about membership in groups is stored. These databases correspond roughly to the files /etc/passwd and /etc/group on a UNIX system; they are discussed in more detail later in this chapter. What is relevant for the present discussion is this: each user has a single group ID in the user database, but each user can be a member of several groups. This fact gives rise to the concept of *process supplementary group IDs*.

A POSIX.1 process can have up to NGROUPS_MAX supplementary group IDs. The idea of these group IDs comes from Berkeley UNIX. In BSD systems, the group IDs of the groups that a user belongs to (as listed in /etc/group) are made available to any of the user's processes. Although a user may in principle be listed in any number of groups, there is a limit—NGROUPS—to the number of such group IDs that the process has access to. This idea has been adopted in POSIX, with the following changes:

- A POSIX.1 implementation is free to have a limit NGROUPS_MAX of zero. Such an implementation effectively does not support supplementary groups.

- It is not specified anywhere in the POSIX.1 standard that any relationship exists between the entries in the group database and a process's supplementary group IDs. The way in which a process acquires supplementary group IDs is not specified.

Supplementary group IDs are of limited usefulness. For example, a process cannot change its group ID to one of its supplementary group IDs. However, on systems where changing the ownership and group of files is restricted (systems where _POSIX_CHOWN_RESTRICTED is in effect; see Chapter 3), a process can change the group ID of its files to one of its supplementary group IDs. A process can query the system for its supplementary group IDs by means of the *getgroups()* function. Here is a prototype of *getgroups()*:

```
#include <sys/types.h>
#include <unistd.h>
int getgroups(int gidsetsize, gid_t grouplist[]);
```

The grouplist argument, an array of type gid_t, should have enough space to hold all the supplementary groups. The gidsetsize argument should specify the number of elements in grouplist. When a process calls *getgroups()* the return value is the actual number of supplementary group IDs associated with the process. These are filled into the grouplist array. If the value of gidsetsize is not zero but is less than the actual number of supplementary group IDs, then *getgroups()* returns –1 and sets errno to EINVAL.

There are two ways to ensure that you have enough space in your `grouplist` array. One is to use *sysconf()* to determine the value of `NGROUPS_MAX` at run time and allocate that much space. (Recall from Chapter 1, Section 1.3, that the value of `NGROUPS_MAX` available at compile time may not be the same as the value determined at run time. Use the run-time value.) The other method depends on the following special case when calling *getgroups()*: if the value of `gidsetsize` is zero, then *getgroups()* returns the actual number of supplementary group IDs associated with the process and does not modify the array pointed to by `grouplist`. Figure 2.3 illustrates both methods.

When a process gets its list of supplementary group IDs by calling *getgroups()*, is its current effective group ID in that list? The answer is that POSIX.1 leaves this unspecified. Thus, for example, if you want a list of all your possible group IDs, you must get the supplementary group list, see if your effective group ID is on the list, and, if not, append it. A proposed revision to the standard addresses this issue (see Chapter 10, Section 10.1.3).

2.3   Who and Where Am I?

The procedure for logging on to a POSIX.1 system is unspecified and may differ widely among systems. Nevertheless, most user processes are associated with a login name and have a controlling terminal. A process can query the system for the value of its login name. It can also, in a somewhat convoluted way, find out if it has a controlling terminal.

The function to determine the login name associated with a process is *getlogin()*. Its prototype is:

```
#include <unistd.h>
char *getlogin(void);
```

The return value is a pointer to the name under which the user logged in. If this name cannot be determined, then NULL is returned, but that should only happen under the most unusual conditions. Even if several login names are associated with a single user ID, *getlogin()* returns the name with which the login session of the calling process was started.

A related function is *cuserid()*. The *cuserid()* function returns a name associated with the current value of the process's *effective* user ID. It has the following prototype:

```
#include <unistd.h>
#include <stdio.h>
char *cuserid(char *s);
```

Although the *cuserid()* function was in the original POSIX.1 standard, it was removed by the 1990 supplement. The reason is that the adopted semantics differed from the semantics of the *cuserid()* function in UNIX System V, in

```
#include <sys/types.h>
#include <unistd.h>
#include <limits.h>
#include <stdlib.h>

gid_t   *grouplist;
extern int errno;

/********************** Method 1 **************************/
/*
** This function determines NGROUPS_MAX, allocates an array of
** NGROUPS_MAX gid_t slots, and uses it to call getgroups().
** The actual number of supplementary group IDs is returned.
*/
method_1()
{
    int ngroups_max;
    int actual_ngroups;

    errno = 0;
    if ( (ngroups_max = sysconf(_SC_NGROUPS_MAX)) < 0 )
    {
        fprintf(stderr, "Cannot determine NGROUPS_MAX (error %d)\n",
                errno);
        exit(1);
    }
    if ( ngroups_max == 0 )
    {
        grouplist = (gid_t *)NULL;
        return(0);
    }
    if ( (grouplist = (gid_t *)malloc(ngroups_max * sizeof(gid_t)))
            == NULL )
    {
        fprintf(stderr, "Cannot allocate space for grouplist\n");
        exit(1);
    }
    errno = 0;
    if ( (actual_ngroups = getgroups(ngroups_max, grouplist)) < 0 )
    {
        fprintf(stderr, "getgroups returns %d (error %d)\n",
                actual_ngroups, errno);
        exit(1);
    }
    return (actual_ngroups);
}
```

Figure 2.3 *(continued on facing page)*

Two Ways of Using *getgroups()*

```
/*********************** Method 2 ***************************/
/*
** This function uses getgroups() to determine the actual number
** of supplementary group IDs and allocates that much space.
** The actual number of supplementary group IDs is returned.
*/
method_2()
{
    int gidsetsize;

    errno = 0;
    if ( (gidsetsize = getgroups(0, grouplist)) < 0 )
    {
        fprintf(stderr, "getgroups returns %d (error %d)\n",
                gidsetsize, errno);
        exit(1);
    }
    if ( gidsetsize == 0 )
        return(0);                /* No supplementary group IDs */
    if ( (grouplist = (gid_t *)malloc(gidsetsize * sizeof(gid_t)))
            == NULL )
    {
        fprintf(stderr, "Cannot allocate space for grouplist\n");
        exit(1);
    }
    return(getgroups(gidsetsize, grouplist));
}
```

Figure 2.3   *(continued from facing page)*

Two Ways of Using *getgroups()*

which the name associated with the real rather than the effective user ID is returned. This was simply a mistake. As this function has been dropped from the standard you should not use *cuserid()*.

In POSIX, as in UNIX, terminals are associated with pathnames. In UNIX System V the special pathname /dev/tty can be used to refer to the current terminal in any function where a pathname is required. The UNIX system function *ctermid()* returns a pointer to this string. The *ctermid()* function is defined in POSIX.1, but with slightly different semantics: it generates an unspecified string that "when used as a pathname, refers to the current controlling terminal for the current process".[1] A prototype for *ctermid()* is:

```
#include <unistd.h>
#include <stdio.h>
char *ctermid(char *s);
```

Note that *ctermid()* does not tell a process whether or not it actually has a controlling terminal. It may simply return a constant string such as /dev/tty (or some other string appropriate for the implementation). The argument to *ctermid()*, if NULL, is ignored and a pointer to a (possibly static) area is returned. If the argument is not NULL, it is presumed to point to an array of at least L_ctermid bytes (where the constant L_ctermid is defined in <stdio.h>) and the string is placed in this array, whose address is returned.

A process can attempt to determine whether or not it has a controlling terminal (CTTY) by using the *ctermid()* function along with *open()*. Figure 2.4 shows a function that does this. The idea is to call *ctermid()* and try to open the file named by the returned string. If the open succeeds, the process has a CTTY. If it fails, then you have to figure out why. If errno is equal to ENOENT then the process does not have a CTTY. If errno is some other value, then the function cannot determine whether or not the process has a CTTY; for example, if errno is equal to EMFILE the process already has as many files open as it can have, and the *open()* fails regardless of whether or not the process has a CTTY.

A function related to *ctermid()*, but somewhat more useful, is *ttyname()*. This function requires a file descriptor, and it returns a pointer to the name of the character special file associated with the file descriptor, if the special file refers to a terminal device. If the file is not associated with a terminal, then NULL is returned. A prototype for *ttyname()* is:

```
#include <unistd.h>
char *ttyname(int fildes);
```

2.4   System Databases and Security

We mentioned above that every POSIX.1 system has two system databases, referred to as the *user* and *group* databases. These databases have a partially specified structure. The user database has objects of type struct passwd, which contain at least the following members:

```
struct passwd {
    char    *pw_name;     /* Login name */
    uid_t   pw_uid;       /* User ID */
    gid_t   pw_gid;       /* Group ID */
    char    *pw_dir;      /* Initial working directory */
    char    *pw_shell;    /* Initial user program */
    /* ... */             /* Possibly other entries */
};
```

This structure is defined in the header <pwd.h>. Note that the order of the members need not be as shown. Although this structure obviously has its origin in the UNIX /etc/passwd file, it does not include encrypted

```
#include <unistd.h>
#include <stdio.h>
#include <sys/types.h>
#include <sys/stat.h>


/*
** has_control() - returns 1 if the process has a controlling
** terminal, 0 if not, -1 if it can't decide.
*/
has_control()
{
    char *p;
    int fd;
    extern int errno;

    p = ctermid((char *) NULL);
    if ( (fd = open(p, O_RDONLY)) < 0 )
    {
        if ( errno == ENOENT )
            return 0;                   /* No controlling tty */
        else
            return -1;          /* Can't tell */
    }
    else
    {
        close(fd);
        return 1;                       /* Controlling tty exists */
    }
}
```

Figure 2.4

Determining If a Process Has a Controlling Terminal

passwords and is not a password database. Moreover, it cannot be portably "browsed".

Two POSIX functions read the user database: *getpwnam()* and *getpwuid()*. These are similar to their UNIX counterparts. Each takes a parameter—respectively, a pointer to a name and a user ID—and searches the user database for an object with the corresponding entry, returning a pointer to a passwd structure if found. Their prototypes are:

```
#include <pwd.h>
struct passwd *getpwnam(const char *name);
struct passwd *getpwuid(uid_t uid);
```

What most distinguishes this database and interface from its UNIX counter-part is the absence of the functions *setpwent()*, *getpwent()*, and *endpwent()*. These can be used in UNIX systems to search the password file linearly. For reasons of security, such a facility is not provided in POSIX.

Note that there *is no* portable way for a process to get access to the encrypted version of any password of any user. There is no guarantee that such passwords exist. Application programs should not attempt to implement their own security or authentication mechanisms. The responsibility for system security lies with the system. For this reason, POSIX.1 makes no provisions for functions related to password encryption or verification.

Similar access restrictions apply to the group database. The `struct group` data structure, defined in the header `<grp.h>`, includes the members:

```
struct group {
    char    *gr_name;    /* Group name */
    gid_t   gr_gid;      /* Group ID */
    char    **gr_mem;    /* Vector of pointers to member names */
    /* ... */            /* Possibly other members */
};
```

As before, the above entries need not be present in the given order. The gr_mem vector is guaranteed to be terminated by a NULL pointer. A process can get access to a group database entry by using the functions *getgrnam()* and *getgrgid()*. They have the prototypes:

```
#include <grp.h>
struct group *getgrnam(const char *name);
struct group *getgrgid(gid_t gid);
```

Again, browsing is not possible. In particular, the UNIX system functions *setgrent()*, *getgrent()*, and *endgrent()* are not supported by POSIX.

The information in the system databases does not constitute an attribute of any process. However, it can be used by a process to get the process's attributes. For example, suppose you want to know the user name associated with your real user ID. You can call `getpwuid(getuid())` and use the pw_name entry from the returned data structure:

```
struct passwd *pwd;
errno = 0;
if ( (pwd = getpwuid(getuid())) != NULL )
    printf("My real name is %d\n", pwd->pw_name);
else
    printf("Cannot determine name associated with user ID %u. \
errno = %d.", (unsigned int)getuid(), errno);
```

However, if several entries in the user database have the same pw_uid value, there is no way to determine which of these will be returned by *getpwuid()*. Thus, the name returned in this way might not be the name under which the user logged in (which you can determine with *getlogin()*).

The above code fragment checks for errors. Your code should always do the same, even though the POSIX.1 standard does not document any circumstances under which *getpwnam()*, *getpwuid()*, *getgrnam()*, or *getgrgid()* sets errno.

2.5 Current Working Directory

Every process has a current working directory and can learn its absolute pathname by calling *getcwd()*. The semantics of the POSIX *getcwd()* function differ very slightly from its UNIX counterpart. A prototype for *getcwd()* looks like this:

```
#include <unistd.h>
char *getcwd(char *buf, size_t size);
```

(This prototype is actually the one given in the revised standard. In the original standard the type of the size argument is int. This change should not affect the portability of programs that use *getcwd()*.) The buf argument is a pointer to an array of at least size bytes, in which an absolute pathname of the current working directory is stored. (Note that we cannot refer to *the* absolute pathname. Because implementations may permit links between directories, a directory may have more than one absolute pathname.) If size is less than or equal to zero, then *getcwd()* fails (returning NULL) and errno is set to EINVAL. If size is positive but not sufficient to allow space for the pathname, then *getcwd()* fails and errno is set to ERANGE. All this is just as in UNIX System V.3.

The *getcwd()* function may also fail because some ancestor of the current working directory is not readable by the process. (Whether this condition causes failure depends on how *getcwd()* is implemented.) If such a failure occurs, then errno is set to EACCES. This is a minor difference from System V. Two other differences refer to the size argument. In System V, size must be at least two greater than the actual length in bytes of the absolute pathname returned. POSIX only requires that size be one greater than this length. More interesting is deciding how large size has to be. In System V, a size of PATH_MAX will always suffice. In POSIX this is also true, except that PATH_MAX need not be defined. A POSIX.1 implementation may support arbitrarily long pathnames. If so, how does a process know what size array to provide?

There is no simple answer. The best procedure is probably as follows: use *pathconf()* to find out if PATH_MAX is defined for the root directory. If so, this value plus 1 is the length of the largest possible absolute pathname. (See Chapter 1, Section 1.4.) If PATH_MAX is not defined then try using some arbitrary size such as _POSIX_PATH_MAX to start, and if it is insufficient keep increasing the size. Figure 2.5 illustrates this method by showing a possible implementation of the UNIX pwd utility.

Note that the ANSI standard C function *realloc()* is supported by POSIX. Instead of using *free()* and *malloc()* repeatedly in this example, we could have used *realloc()* inside the loop.

The code in Figure 2.5 is clumsy. Unfortunately, the generality of the POSIX.1 environment makes some such clumsiness inevitable. On the other hand, this code will run successfully on systems with tight restrictions on pathname lengths and on systems with no restrictions whatsoever.

A POSIX.1 process can change its current working directory with the *chdir()* function. This function is identical to its UNIX system counterpart. Its prototype is:

```
#include <unistd.h>
int chdir(const char *path);
```

The pathname given by path can be absolute or relative. If *chdir()* fails (which can happen if path is invalid or the process lacks the required permission), it returns –1 and the process's current directory is unchanged.

2.6   Environment Strings

Each POSIX.1 process, when it begins execution, has access to an array of strings called its *environment strings*. Each of these strings is of the form "name=value", where name and value are sequences of characters that do not contain null bytes or '=' characters. The string name is referred to as an *environment variable*, and value is referred to as the *value* of that variable. The addresses of these strings are collected into an array, which is terminated by a NULL address. The address of the array (and hence, the address of the first of the string addresses) is stored in the external variable environ, which is of type char **. Figure 2.6 illustrates the relationship of environ to the environment strings.

A process can get access to its environment strings through environ, but this is not easy. Modifying the environment strings is particularly difficult; for example, deleting an environment string may require deleting an address in the middle of the array. Changing the value of an environment variable is also tricky, as it typically involves allocating space and changing a pointer somewhere in the environ array. This is a common source of programming errors. Nevertheless, the POSIX.1 standard provides no portable way for a process to modify its environment strings.*

---

*   See Chapter 10, Section 10.1.5, for a proposed modification to POSIX.1 that includes the functions *putenv()* and *clearenv()* to manipulate the environment strings.

```
/*
** Display an absolute pathname of the current working
** directory on standard output.
*/
#define _POSIX_SOURCE
#include <unistd.h>
#include <limits.h>
#include <errno.h>

#define CHUNK 64;       /* Number of bytes to increase each try */

extern int errno;
int path_max;
char    *cwd;

main()
{
    errno = 0;
    if ( (path_max = (int) pathconf("/", _PC_PATH_MAX)) < 0 )
    {
        if ( errno != 0 )     /* Cannot determine PATH_MAX */
            err_exit();
        path_max = _POSIX_PATH_MAX;
    }
    path_max += 1;                /* Room for leading '/' */
    if ( (cwd = (char *)malloc(path_max)) == NULL )
        err_exit();
    while ( getcwd(cwd, path_max) == NULL && errno == ERANGE )
    {
        free(cwd);
        path_max += CHUNK;
        errno = 0;
        if ( (cwd = (char *)malloc(path_max)) == NULL )
            err_exit();
    }
    if ( errno !=0 )
        err_exit();
    printf("%s\n", cwd);
    exit(0);
}

err_exit()
{
    perror("pwd");
    exit(1);
}
```

Figure 2.5

Displaying the Current Working Directory

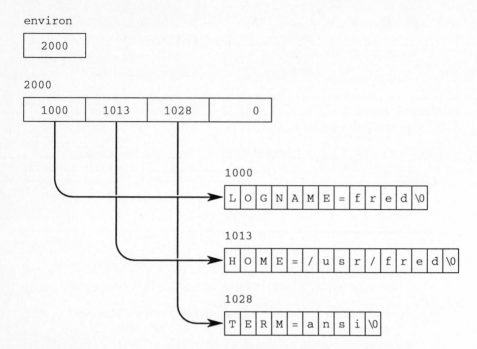

Example of an environment in which the strings `"LOGNAME=fred"`, `"HOME=/usr/fred"`, and `"TERM=ansi"` are defined and located at addresses 1000, 1013, and 1028, respectively. The array of string addresses is located at address 2000.

Figure 2.6

Environment Strings in Memory

It's much simpler for a process to determine the value of its environment variables. This can be done directly through `environ`, but such an approach is error-prone. POSIX.1 provides the *getenv()* function for this purpose. The POSIX *getenv()* is essentially identical to its UNIX system counterpart. It has the following prototype:

```
#include <stdlib.h>
char *getenv(const char *name);
```

The argument `name` is the name of an environment variable. If the variable is defined (i.e., if there is an environment string whose initial portion is `"name="`), then *getenv()* returns the value associated with name. If the variable is not defined, then *getenv()* returns a NULL pointer. For example, if there is an environment string of the form `"HOME=/usr/fred"`, then the call

```
p = getenv("HOME");
```

will make p point to the string /usr/fred. It is unspecified whether the pointer returned by *getenv()* points into the actual environment string or into a copy. The standard specifically allows an implementation to return a pointer to a static location that will be overwritten by subsequent calls to *getenv()*.

2.7 Process Times

Every POSIX.1 system keeps track of the elapsed CPU time that a process uses. In fact, it does so rather elaborately. The data is kept in a struct tms, a data structure that contains at least the following four members:

```
struct tms {
    clock_t tms_utime;  /* User mode CPU time */
    clock_t tms_stime;  /* System mode CPU time */
    clock_t tms_cutime; /* Terminated childrens' user time */
    clock_t tms_cstime; /* Terminated childrens' system time */
    /* ... Possibly other members */
};
```

Note that these four members are of type clock_t, a change from the UNIX System V structure, in which they are of type time_t. In POSIX, all times that are measured in CLK_TCKths of a second are stored in clock_t objects, while times measured in whole seconds are stored in time_t objects. The tms_utime member gives the number of CLK_TCKths of a second charged for the execution of the process's instructions. The tms_stime member gives the time charged for execution by the system on behalf of the process.

A process can determine its process times by calling the *times()* function, whose prototype is:

```
#include <sys/times.h>
clock_t times(struct tms *buffer);
```

A call to *times()* stores the contents of a struct tms that has the caller's elapsed times in a tms buffer pointed to by the argument to *times()*. In addition, *times()* returns the elapsed real (wall clock) time, in CLK_TCKths of a second, since an arbitrary point in the past. This is useful only if you call *times()* more than once; the difference between the two return values gives the elapsed time between the calls. Note that the return value can wrap around the maximum value of a clock_t object.

2.8 System Time

Every POSIX.1 system also keeps track of the current system time. Of course, this is not a per-process attribute, but a system attribute. A process can determine the current system time with the *time()* function, which is taken from the C standard. A prototype for *time()* is:

```
#include <time.h>
time_t time(time_t *tloc);
```

The type `time_t` is defined in `<time.h>`. A call to *time()* returns the current system time. In addition, if the `tloc` argument is not a NULL pointer, the time is stored in the location pointed to by `loc`. POSIX.1 imposes semantics on *time()* in addition to those given by the C standard: the C standard specifies that the time will be returned and stored in an implementation-defined manner. POSIX.1 defines this manner as the number of seconds since January 1, 1970, 0:00 Greenwich Mean Time (GMT). This date and time are referred to as "the Epoch". UNIX systems, and POSIX systems, measure time in seconds since the Epoch. (Incidentally, though the phrase *Greenwich Mean Time* and the abbreviation *GMT* are still correct, they have been replaced in international standard usage by *Coordinated Universal Time* and *UTC*, respectively.)

2.9   System Name

The POSIX.1 standard provides a way for a process to get information about the name of the system on which it is running. This information is kept in the `utsname` structure. The contents of all of the fields of this structure are implementation-defined. The `utsname` structure is defined in the header `<sys/utsname.h>` and has the following members:

```
struct utsname {
     char    sysname[];    /* Name of OS implementation */
     char    nodename[];   /* Name of this node in a network */
     char    release[];    /* Release level of OS implementation */
     char    version[];    /* Version level of release */
     char    machine[];    /* Hardware name */
};
```

Each member of the structure is a null-terminated character array of unspecified length. A process can retrieve a copy of the system's `utsname` structure with the *uname()* function, whose prototype is:

```
#include <sys/utsname.h>
int uname(struct utsname *name);
```

As the contents of this structure are implementation-defined, the most useful thing a portable application can do with the structure is to display its contents in the hope of providing identification of when and

where the program ran. For example, a program might usefully have a
fragment like this:

```
#include <stdio.h>
#include <sys/utsname.h>
#include <time.h>

int show_time_and_place(void)
{
    struct utsname ut;

    if (uname(&ut) < 0)
        return(1);
    printf("%s\nExecuted under %s Version %s Release %s on %s\n",
        ctime(time(NULL), ut.sysname, ut.version, ut.release,
        ut.nodename));
    return(0);
}
```

The *ctime()* function used here prints an ASCII formatted version of the date
and time. It is included in the POSIX.1 standard from the C standard library.
We discuss this function in Chapter 8, Section 8.4.2.

Processes have other attributes besides those we have discussed. In
Figure 2.1 we listed the file mode creation mask, which we discuss in Chapter 3. We also listed the signal mask and the set of pending signals; we
discuss these in Chapter 5. Other process attributes, such as open file descriptors and pending alarms, are discussed in the context of their related
functions.

Exercises for Chapter 2 _____

1. The POSIX.2 draft standard specified a utility named id that writes the
   user's name followed by the user's real user ID in parentheses, followed
   by the group name and parenthesized group ID. If the effective user ID
   is different from the real user ID, then it and the name associated with it
   are displayed; similarly for the effective and real group IDs. Write a
   version of this utility.

2. Modify the program from Exercise 1 to print a list of the supplementary
   groups (both names and IDs) as well. Make sure that you do not print
   the same group twice in your output.

3. Suppose you want to write a program that displays its own process ID
   and its parent process ID on the standard output. What difficulty will
   you have in writing this in a portable manner? (Hint: what are the types
   of these values?)

4. Take any program for which you have access to the source code and modify it so that when it completes it displays the amount of user and system time that it consumed. This will involve two calls to *times()* and some arithmetic.

5. Write a program that detaches itself from the current session and then prompts for input, reads a single line of input from the standard input, and writes this line to a file. Run this program. In your line of input use the interactive interrupt character. What do you expect to happen?

6. Explain what happens if a process calls

    ```
    setsid(); setpgid(0,0);
    ```

    or if it makes the same calls in the reverse order:

    ```
    setpgid(0,0); setsid();
    ```

    or if a process calls *setpgid()* twice:

    ```
    setpgid(0,0); setpgid(0,0);
    ```

7. Determine what string is returned by a call to *ctermid()* on your system. Take the function *has_control()*, given in the chapter to determine if your process has a controlling terminal, and call it in a program twice, before and after a call to *setsid()*. Modify *has_control()* so that it displays the value of errno if the *open()* call fails.

3

Files and Directories

P OSIX.1 systems support a file hierarchy that, to executing processes, appears very similar to the UNIX file system. Note that, in discussing POSIX, we avoid using the term *file system* to describe the file hierarchy. UNIX literature uses the term in two different ways: to describe the general scheme by which files are maintained on the system and to describe a portion of the entire hierarchy with its own data structures, such as the superblock, inodes, and free list. A POSIX.1 file system corresponds to the latter use of the term, although its structure is more abstract.

We briefly review the structure of the file hierarchy. It is a directed graph (not necessarily a tree, because of links) with a root. Nodes in the graph that can be the parents of other nodes are *directories*. Directories are considered to be files. In fact, POSIX.1 systems recognize five types of files:

Regular files

Directory special files

FIFO special files

Block device special files

Character device special files

All of these file types are derived from the UNIX system. (Some UNIX systems recognize other types of special files as well.)

Figure 3.1 illustrates a portion of a POSIX.1 file system. Except for the root directory, whose name is ' / ', the filenames shown in this figure are not special to POSIX. Some of them are traditional on UNIX systems.

In many cases, the same functions (such as *open()* and *close()*) can be used to manipulate all types of files. However, the behavior of these functions

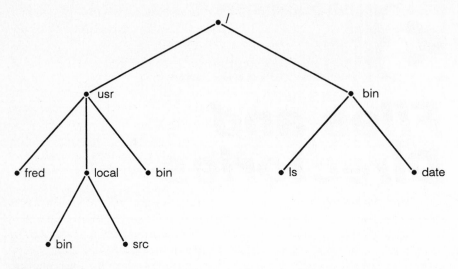

Figure 3.1

Part of a POSIX.1 File Hierarchy

may differ substantially depending on the type of file being manipulated. In this chapter we discuss the functions POSIX uses to create files and to read directories. Chapter 4 deals with input from and output to files.

3.1   Pathname Resolution

POSIX systems form pathnames according to the same rules as the UNIX system: a pathname consists of components separated by slash (/) characters. The components (filenames) should be constructed out of the characters in the *portable filename character set*. This set consists of the following characters:

```
a b c d e f g h i j k l m n o p q r s t u v w x y z

A B C D E F G H I J K L M N O P Q R S T U V W X Y Z

0 1 2 3 4 5 6 7 8 9

. _ -
```

A portable filename must not begin with a '-' (hyphen). (Such filenames are hard to use with utilities that, like traditional UNIX system utilities, use '-' to indicate command line options.) Upper- and lower-case letters are guaranteed to be distinct on all conforming implementations. Thus, the names `datafile` and `Datafile` refer to different files.

POSIX.1 systems can support other characters in filenames, including 8- or 16-bit characters from non-Latin character sets such as Chinese or

Arabic. The characters in the portable character set are simply those that must be supported by *all* POSIX.1 systems. Clearly, portable applications should only create files whose names are portable.

Pathnames beginning with a leading `'/'` are *absolute pathnames* and describe how to find a file starting at the root directory. For example, the file named `src` in Figure 3.1 has the absolute pathname `/usr/local/src`. Other pathnames are *relative pathnames* and describe how to find a file starting at a process's current working directory. For example, if a process has as its current directory the directory `/usr` in Figure 3.1, then the relative pathname of `src` for this process is `local/src`. The pathname of the root directory is simply `'/'`. The process of determining which file is referred to by a pathname is called *pathname resolution*.

The special path components *dot* (.) and *dot-dot* (..) refer, as in the UNIX system, to the current directory and the parent of the current directory, respectively. There is no requirement that entries for dot and dot-dot be present in a directory. However, this makes no difference to pathname resolution. Even if the current directory has no entry for dot-dot, the pathname `../prog.c` refers to the file `prog.c` in the parent directory of the current directory. Multiple contiguous slash characters are permitted and are considered to be equivalent to a single slash, with one exception: if a pathname begins with exactly two slashes, its meaning is implementation-defined. This exception is made to accommodate some existing network file system implementations.

3.2   Determining File Characteristics

Files have attributes. Certain attributes are meaningful for all POSIX.1 file types. For example, every POSIX.1 file has an owner ID and a group ID.* Other attributes may only be meaningful for certain file types. For example, regular files and FIFO special files have a file size: the number of bytes currently in the file. File size is not necessarily meaningful for directories or for block or character special files. The following file attributes are defined by POSIX.1:

- The file type (regular, directory, FIFO, block, or character special).

- The file's access permissions.

- The file's device number and serial number. The serial number corresponds to the UNIX system's i-number, or inode-number. A file is uniquely determined by its device number and serial number.

---

*   Proposed extensions to POSIX.1 will add the symbolic link file type (see Chapter 10, Section 10.1.1). Symbolic links do not have owner or group IDs.

- The file's link count, explained below.

- The file's owner ID and group ID.

- The file's length in bytes, if it is a regular file.

- The last time the file was accessed.

- The last time the file was modified.

- The last time the file's status was changed (e.g., a change to the access permissions).

A process can learn about these attributes if it knows the file's name or if it has the file open. The attributes, which are referred to as the file's *status*, are described in struct stat, a data structure defined in <sys/stat.h>. This data structure has at least the following members:

```
struct stat {
    mode_t  st_mode;   /* File type and access permissions */
    ino_t   st_ino;    /* File serial number */
    dev_t   st_dev;    /* File device number */
    nlink_t st_nlink;  /* File link count */
    uid_t   st_uid;    /* File owner's user ID */
    gid_t   st_gid;    /* File group's group ID */
    off_t   st_size;   /* File size in bytes
                              (regular files only) */
    time_t  st_atime;  /* Time of last file access */
    time_t  st_mtime;  /* Time of last file modification */
    time_t  st_ctime;  /* Time of last file status change */
    /* ... */          /* Possibly other members as well */
};
```

(Note that the order of the members in the data structure is unspecified and need not be the order shown above.) An implementation is free to add members to this structure; if present, such additional members must have names that begin with st_.

If you compare this structure to the corresponding System V.3 data structure, you'll see that the principal difference between them lies in the types of the structure members. In the POSIX.1 version, every member is of a defined type. This allows source compatibility across a wider variety of machine architectures, but it may lead to some pitfalls. Some of the types may be signed on some POSIX.1 systems and unsigned on others. The sizes of the types will vary between architectures, so using hard-coded constants for what you think is the highest word of some variable will lead you astray. You should use *sizeof()* to determine the sizes of objects of any type, defined or otherwise.

The attributes have the familiar meanings from the UNIX system. In particular, the file mode encodes several different attributes, including the file's type, the set-user-ID and set-group-ID bits, and the permissions assigned to the file. As in UNIX, every process is in exactly one of three classes with respect to each file: a process is in the *file owner class* if its effective user ID matches the file user ID; it is in the *file group class* if it is not in the file owner class but its effective group ID or one of its supplementary group IDs matches the file group ID; it is in the *file other class* if it is not in either of the first two classes.

The encoding of attributes within the mode is unspecified. Therefore, programs *must* use macros defined in <sys/stat.h>, not octal constants, to manipulate the mode. The following macros are bit masks that encode the file's permissions:

S_IRUSR	Read permission for file owner class
S_IWUSR	Write permission for file owner class
S_IXUSR	Execute permission for file owner class
S_IRGRP	Read permission for file group class
S_IWGRP	Write permission for file group class
S_IXGRP	Execute permission for file group class
S_IROTH	Read permission for file other class
S_IWOTH	Write permission for file other class
S_IXOTH	Execute permission for file other class

For convenience, three other bit masks are defined:

```
S_IRWXU = S_IRUSR | S_IWUSR | S_IXUSR
S_IRWXG = S_IRGRP | S_IWGRP | S_IXGRP
S_IRWXO = S_IROTH | S_IWOTH | S_IXOTH
```

The portion of the st_mode member that corresponds to the bitwise or of these masks, S_IRWXU | S_IRWXG | S_IRWXO, constitutes the file's *permission bits*. Two more macros encode the set-user-ID and set-group-ID bits:

S_ISUID	Set the effective user ID to the file owner ID on execution
S_ISGID	Set the effective group ID to the file group ID on execution

These are meaningful only for regular files. Implementations are free to use these bits in the modes of special files with implementation-defined meanings.

The file type is also encoded in an unspecified way. The following five macros, when applied to the st_mode field of a file's stat structure, each return true (nonzero) if the file is of the corresponding type, and zero otherwise:

S_ISDIR(mode)	True if the file is a directory
S_ISBLK(mode)	True if the file is a block special file

S_ISCHR (mode)   True if the file is a character special file

S_ISFIFO (mode)   True if the file is a pipe or FIFO special file

S_ISREG (mode)   True if the file is a regular file

A process can determine a file's status by using the *stat()* or *fstat()* functions. These functions, which are essentially identical to the corresponding UNIX system functions, have the following prototypes:

```
#include <sys/types.h>
#include <sys/stat.h>
int stat(const char *path, struct stat *stat_buf);
int fstat(int fildes, struct stat *stat_buf);
```

To query the system for a file's status with *stat()*, a process must be able to search each component of the path prefix of the file, but it needs no permissions for the file itself. To use *fstat()*, the process must have a file descriptor associated with an open file description for the file. Here is an example of the use of *stat()* to determine the type of a file:

```
struct stat st;
errno = 0;
if (stat(filename, &st) < 0)
    fprintf(stderr, "Can't stat %s. errno = %d.\n",
        filename, errno);
else if (S_ISREG(st.st_mode))
    printf("%s is a regular file.\n", filename);
else if (S_ISDIR(st.st_mode))
    printf("%s is a directory.\n", filename);
else if (S_ISFIFO(st.st_mode))
    printf("%s is a FIFO.\n", filename);
else if (S_ISBLK(st.st_mode))
    printf("%s is a block special file.\n", filename);
else if (S_ISCHR(st.st_mode))
    printf("%s is a character special file.\n", filename);
else
    printf("Cannot determine file type of %s.", filename);
```

3.2.1   File Access Permission

The access control mechanism described by a file's permission bits can be overridden by an *additional file access control mechanism*. This is up to the implementation and allows POSIX.1 implementations to provide extra security. Any such mechanism can only further restrict file access. For example, if the permission bits indicate that a process does not have read access to a file, an additional access control mechanism cannot grant the process read access.

Thus, such a mechanism, if it is in place, supplements but does not replace the traditional file access scheme.

A POSIX.1 implementation is also permitted to have an *alternate file access control mechanism*. Such a mechanism, if present, is subject to the following three restrictions:

- It must be enabled explicitly, on a per-file basis, either by the owner of the file or by a user with appropriate privileges.

- It must specify access permission for the same classes of processes as the basic POSIX.1 mechanism: the file owner, file group, and file other classes. These permissions must be specified by an alternate setting of the permission bits in the st_mode field associated with the file, which will be returned by a call to *stat()* or *fstat()*. Thus, such an alternate mechanism can simply be viewed as a second set of permission bits, which effectively replaces the original set when the mechanism is enabled.

- If the file access permission bits of a file are modified by a call to *chmod()* (see Section 3.9, below), then any alternate access control mechanism for that file is automatically disabled.

What does all this mean for the application programmer? The bottom line is that if your process needs to know whether or not it has read, write, or execute access to a file, there are two definitive ways to find out:

- Try it and see what the results are.

- Use the *access()* function.

These methods are not necessarily interchangeable. Using *access()* allows a process to determine the access permissions associated with its *real* user ID. Trying to get file access and seeing if you succeed allows a process to determine the permissions associated with its *effective* user ID.

The *access()* function has the following prototype:

```
#include <unistd.h>
int access(const char *pathname, int mode);
```

The value of the mode argument must be either F_OK or the bitwise or of one or more of the values R_OK, W_OK, or X_OK. These values are all defined in <unistd.h>. The F_OK flag is used to test for the existence of a file: the call

```
access(path, F_OK);
```

returns zero if a file named path exists, and –1 otherwise. However, a return value of –1 can also indicate an error. For example, if search permission is denied for the process on a component of the prefix of path, then *access()* will return –1 with errno set to EACCES.

If mode is the bitwise or of some non-empty combination of R_OK, W_OK, and X_OK, then the call

```
access(path, mode);
```

returns zero if the process would have the indicated access to the file with its real user ID in place of its effective user ID, and nonzero otherwise. The test performed by *access()* takes into account any alternate or additional access control mechanism. Note that when you combine flags in the mode field, you are inquiring about combined access. Thus, the call

```
access(path, R_OK | W_OK);
```

returns zero only if the process has both read access *and* write access for the file.

The *access()* function is useful for a process that has an effective user ID that differs from its real user ID. Typically, such a process is privileged. It may need to know what access permissions it will have after a call to

```
setuid(getuid());
```

Such a call changes its effective user ID to its real user ID (see Chapter 2, Section 2.2), typically giving up privileges. The *access()* function allows a process to know what file access permissions it will have after such a call, without the process having to make the call (whose effects are generally irreversible).

There is a historical problem with the UNIX system version of *access()* that POSIX does not solve. In many UNIX system implementations of *access()*, if the calling process's real user ID is that of the superuser, *access()* always indicates any type of access permission for any file. This includes execute permission for a file even if the file is not executable. The POSIX.1 standard allows but does not require this behavior: a process with appropriate privileges may report success for X_OK for a file even when none of the file's execute permission bits is set and the file is not an executable file.

3.3   File Descriptors and Open File Descriptions

When a process has a file open, it refers to the file via a nonnegative integer associated with the file—the *file descriptor*. Typically, this association is made via a call to *open()* (see Section 3.5, below), but that is not the only possible way. Here are the ways for a process to get a file descriptor:

- via a call to *open()* (possibly disguised as a call to *fopen()*).

- by inheriting it from a parent process, via *fork()*. (UNIX system processes inherit their standard input, output, and error file descriptors in this way.)

- via a call to *dup()*, *dup2()*, or *fcntl()*.

- possibly by a call to *fdopen()*.

A POSIX system maintains information about files currently open for each process. This information includes the current file offset (the place where the next read or write associated with the file will take place), the file's access mode (whether it is open for reading, or writing, or both), and a couple of status flags (O_APPEND and O_NONBLOCK) that we discuss below. Together, this information constitutes an *open file description* for the file. An open file description is always created by a call to *open()*, and every file descriptor is implicitly associated with an open file description.

An important feature of POSIX systems, as of UNIX systems, is that this association need not be one-to-one; several file descriptors can refer to the same open file description. These file descriptors can be in one process or in several. This has important consequences. For example, if two processes share an open file description, each *read()* by one process advances the file offset for both processes. Clearly the association of multiple file descriptors with a single file description can cause problems. On the other hand, it can be very useful.

Associated with a file descriptor is a flag called the descriptor's *close-on-exec* flag. If this flag is set, then when one of the *exec()* functions is successfully executed the file descriptor is closed. (See Chapter 6 for a description of the *exec()* family of functions.) This flag is an attribute of the file descriptor rather than of the open file description; thus, it is possible for two file descriptors to refer to the same open file description, yet have different settings for the flag.

3.4   Regular Files

Regular files are both opened and created using the *open()* function. (The *creat()* function is also supported, for purely historical reasons, but is entirely superfluous.) The *open()* function can also be used with special files, but its behavior with such files can be quite different: a program cannot portably create special files with *open()*, and some flags used with *open()* only apply to special files, while others apply only to regular files. In this section we are only concerned with regular files. For regular files, the behavior of the POSIX.1 *open()* function is very similar to that of the UNIX system's *open()*, so our discussion is brief. A prototype for *open()* is:

```
#include <sys/types.h>
#include <sys/stat.h>
#include <fcntl.h>
int open(const char *path, int oflag, ...);
```

Note that the number of arguments is variable. In fact, there are always two arguments, unless the file is being created. In that case, there are three arguments, with the third being the mode of the new file, an argument of type `mode_t`.

The semantics of *open()*—as applied to regular files—are essentially the same as those of System V.3. The `oflag` argument is the bitwise or of a number of flags. Exactly one of the three flags

O_RDONLY	open for reading only
O_WRONLY	open for writing only
O_RDWR	open for reading and writing

must be included in `oflag`. In addition, any combination of the following flags may be included:

O_APPEND	set offset to end-of-file before each *write()*
O_CREAT	create the file if it does not exist
O_EXCL	fail if the file does exist and O_CREAT is set
O_TRUNC	if the file exists, truncate it to zero length
O_NOCTTY	
O_NONBLOCK	

The O_NONBLOCK and O_NOCTTY flags have no portable use with regular files; we discuss them in the sections on the relevant file types.

To create a regular file with *open()*, you must set the O_CREAT flag in `oflag` and must supply a mode argument. The mode *must* be constructed as the or of the symbolic values defined in <sys/stat.h>. Only use permission bits in the mode argument. The use of other mode bits (e.g., S_ISUID and S_ISGID) has implementation-defined meaning and is not portable; use *chmod()* (see Section 3.9, below) if you need to set those bits. The mode is modified by the process's file mode creation mask: bits that are set in the file mode creation mask are cleared in the mode. Thus, if the value of the file mode creation mask is umask, the effective mode is not mode but rather (mode & (~umask)). A process can control its file mode creation mask with the *umask()* function, described in Section 3.9.

The owner ID of a newly created file is always the effective user ID of the creating process. POSIX allows two kinds of behavior for the file's group ID. It may be set equal to the effective group ID of the creating process (this is the behavior of System V.3), or it may be set equal to the group ID of the directory in which the file is first created (this is the behavior of 4.3BSD). POSIX does not specify that the file group ID should be set in the same way everywhere in the file hierarchy, so presumably an implementation could use the System V.3 method in some places and the BSD method in others. There is no flag that a program can query, via *sysconf()* or *pathconf()*, that describes which method is used. Your applications should not rely on either behavior. Instead, explicitly set the group ownership if it is important, using *chown()* (see Section 3.9, below).

The POSIX.1 FIPS requires that the group ID of a newly created file be that of its parent directory, as in 4.3BSD.

If the O_CREAT flag is set but the file already exists, this flag and the mode are ignored, unless the O_EXCL flag is also set. Setting O_EXCL means that you want to create a new file, not use an existing one of the same name. If O_CREAT and O_EXCL are both set and the file already exists, then the *open()* call fails.

If O_CREAT is not set in oflag, then *open()* attempts to open an existing file. In this case, do not use O_EXCL (whose meaning is then implementation-defined).

If O_TRUNC is set, and the file already exists and is a regular file, and it is opened for writing (i.e., either O_RDWR or O_WRONLY), then the file is truncated to zero length. O_TRUNC has no effect on FIFOs or directories, and its meaning is implementation-defined for other file types. Only use O_TRUNC with regular files.

A successful call to *open()* creates a new (i.e., not shared) open file description associated with the file and returns a nonnegative file descriptor associated with the open file description. As in the UNIX system, the returned file descriptor is guaranteed to be the smallest nonnegative integer not currently used as a file descriptor by the process. The file offset is set to the beginning of the file (even if O_APPEND is set).

The *creat()* function can be defined in terms of *open()*. Its prototype is:

```
#include <sys/types.h>
#include <sys/stat.h>
#include <fcntl.h>
int creat(const char *path, mode_t mode);
```

Calling

```
creat(path, mode);
```

is the same as calling

```
open(path, O_CREAT | O_WRONLY | O_TRUNC, mode);
```

In particular, mode is modified by the process's file mode creation mask.

Open files are closed with the *close()* function, which is identical to its UNIX system counterpart. A prototype for *close()* is:

```
#include <unistd.h>
int close(int fildes);
```

When a process exits normally, or is terminated by *abort()* or by a signal, all of its open file descriptors are closed.

A *link* to a file is a directory entry for the file. When a file is created, one link is created for it—the link identified by `path`, the pathname given to *open()*. Additional links to existing files are created with the *link()* function. For regular files, *link()* behaves just like its UNIX system counterpart. A prototype for *link()* is:

```
#include <unistd.h>
int link(const char *path1, const char *path2);
```

If a call to *link()* succeeds, the directory entry `path2` is created and refers to the same file as `path1`. If `path1` and `path2` are on different file systems, the call to *link()* may fail; POSIX.1 implementations are permitted, but not required, to support links across file systems. You can tell if *link()* fails for this reason, because `errno` will be set to `EXDEV`. If `path2` names an already existing file, *link()* will fail, with `errno` set to `EEXIST`. A call to *link()* can fail for other reasons as well; these are listed in Appendix A.

Consider the file hierarchy shown in Figure 3.1. Suppose that a process makes the call

```
link("/bin/ls", "/usr/bin/list");
```

Suppose further that this call succeeds. The file hierarchy would then look as shown in Figure 3.2. Note that the newly linked file has two names and two absolute pathnames. However, there is only one copy of this file.

On some UNIX systems, including those based on Berkeley UNIX, another special file type called a *symbolic link* can be created. A symbolic link

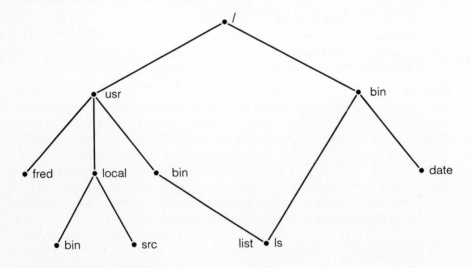

Figure 3.2

Part of a POSIX.1 File Hierarchy, with a Link

shares some, but not all, of the properties of a link (which on these systems is sometimes called a *hard link*). The advantage of symbolic links is that they can cross file systems. POSIX.1 does not currently support symbolic links, but such support has been suggested in a proposed future extension to the standard. As of this writing, that extension is just in the beginning stages of the POSIX standards process, but it is likely that future versions of POSIX.1 will support some form of symbolic links. We discuss symbolic links in Chapter 10, Section 10.1.1.

Regular files can be removed with the *unlink()* function. A prototype for *unlink()* is:

```
#include <unistd.h>
int unlink(const char *path);
```

The POSIX.1 *unlink()* function behaves like its UNIX system counterpart: it merely removes the directory entry and decrements the file's link count. If a call to *unlink()* causes the link count to reach zero, and no process has the file open, then the space occupied by the file is freed. If a process has the file open, then the link is removed but the file contents are preserved until all references to the file are closed.

3.5   Directories

A POSIX.1 process can create a directory with the *mkdir()* function. This replaces the UNIX system *mknod()* function, which is not defined by POSIX.1, for creating directories. A prototype of *mkdir()* is:

```
#include <sys/types.h>
#include <sys/stat.h>
int mkdir(const char *path, mode_t mode);
```

Calling *mkdir()* creates the directory named `path`, with permission bits set to `mode` as modified by the process's file creation mask. The new directory is owned by the effective user ID of the calling process. The group ID of the directory is either the process's effective group ID or the group ID of the parent directory; implementations may choose which of these policies to adopt. The directory will be empty. An empty directory is one that has no entries except possibly for dot and dot-dot.

POSIX implementations may, but need not, support links between directories. However, even on those systems where *link()* can be used to create a link to a directory, it requires appropriate privileges. Portable applications should never use *link()* with directories.

Directories can be removed using the *rmdir()* function, which originated in 4.2BSD and is also included in System V.3. Applications should not use *unlink()* to remove a directory. Support of such a use of *unlink()* by an implementation is not required, and even if this use is supported an application must have appropriate privileges. A prototype for *rmdir()* is:

```
#include <unistd.h>
int rmdir(const char *path);
```

The directory referred to by path must be empty. If it is the root directory of a process or the current working directory of a process, the result of the *rmdir()* call is implementation-defined. If the directory is empty but is currently opened by some process, and the call to *rmdir()* would remove the last link to the directory, then the following occurs: the entries dot and dot-dot, if present, are removed immediately, and creation of new entries in the directory is blocked. However, the directory's space is not freed until all references to it are closed.

The structure of a POSIX directory is unspecified. Thus, although it may be possible to *open()* and *read()* directories like files, a portable program can never usefully do so. Instead, POSIX provides four functions that manipulate directories abstractly, enabling a process to sequentially read the entries. These functions originated in 4.2BSD and are present in System V.3. They are modeled on the C library functions for manipulating FILE streams. Their prototypes are:

```
#include <sys/types.h>
#include <dirent.h>
DIR *opendir(const char *dirname);
struct dirent *readdir(DIR *dirp);
void rewinddir(DIR *dirp);
int closedir(DIR *dirp);
```

The type DIR, which represents a directory stream, is the analogue of the FILE type. It describes a sequence of directory entries. Implementations may use a file descriptor to implement the DIR type, in which case the total number of files and DIR streams open for a process at any one time cannot exceed OPEN_MAX. The structure struct dirent, defined in <dirent.h>, is required to have at least the single member char d_name[], a character array of unspecified size. Implementations may define other members of this structure, but a portable application cannot reference them.

The only safe way to use a struct dirent is to use one pointed to by the return value of *readdir()*. If you declare such a structure in your own code, there's no guarantee that the d_name member actually has enough space reserved to hold a directory name.

If a process wishes to read a directory, it opens a stream associated with the directory by calling *opendir()*. If the directory is opened successfully, *opendir()* returns a pointer to the corresponding DIR object. If *opendir()* fails (for example, because the process has no read permission for the directory), then NULL is returned and errno is set. The process can use the returned DIR pointer in successive calls to *readdir()*. Each call returns a pointer to a `dirent` structure whose d_name member contains the name of the next entry from the directory. (A successful call to *readdir()* on a `DIR` stream may overwrite the results of the previous call on the same stream; it is guaranteed not to overwrite data from a *readdir()* on a different stream.) After the last entry of the directory has been read, the next call to *readdir()* returns `NULL` and does not change `errno`. If a call to *readdir()* results in an error, then `NULL` is returned and `errno` is set.

Access to directory entries is strictly sequential. The functions *telldir()* and *seekdir()*, which are supported by 4.3BSD and can be used in that system to save and return to a place in a directory stream, are not part of POSIX.1. If a process calls *rewinddir()* on an open DIR stream, then the stream is repositioned at the beginning. A call to *closedir()* closes the stream, i.e., disassociates it from the directory. Note the following rules about the semantics of the directory operations:

- If the contents of a directory change after the most recent *opendir()* or *rewinddir()* for that stream, it is unspecified whether or not a subsequent *readdir()* call will reflect the change.

- In addition to repositioning the directory stream to the beginning, a call to *rewinddir()* causes the stream to refer to the current state of the directory (i.e., subsequent *readdir()* calls will reflect changes made before the *rewinddir()*).

- After a *fork()*, either the parent or the child—but not both—may continue to process the directory stream.

- If the implementation of the DIR type uses a file descriptor, this file descriptor is closed by the system when the process successfully executes an *exec()* function (see Chapter 6, Section 6.2).

Figure 3.3 illustrates the use of the directory operations. It shows a primitive version of an `ls`-type utility. This program simply lists all the entries in the requested directories (including dot and dot-dot if they are present).

3.6   Pipes

A *pipe* is a nameless file that only exists during the time that it is kept open. Even if you have not programmed with pipes, you've probably used them in the shell. The shell syntax

```
command1 | command2
```

creates a pipe, redirects the standard output of command1 (file descriptor 1)

```
#define _POSIX_SOURCE
#include <sys/types.h>
#include <dirent.h>
#include <stdio.h>
#include <errno.h>

extern int errno;

main(int argc, char *argv[])
{
    if ( argc == 1 )
        show(".");
    else
        while (--argc)
            show(*++argv);
    exit(0);
}


show(char *dir)
{
    DIR *dirp;
    struct dirent *direntp;

    if ( (dirp = opendir(dir)) == NULL )
    {
        fprintf(stderr, "%s: Cannot open\n", dir);
        return;
    }
    printf("%s:\n", dir);
    errno = 0;
    while ( (direntp = readdir(dirp)) != NULL )
        printf("%s\n",direntp->d_name);
    if ( errno != 0 )
        fprintf(stderr, "Error reading directory %s\n", dir);
    closedir(dirp);
    return;
}
```

Figure 3.3

Using Directory Operations

to the pipe, and redirects the standard input of command2 (file descriptor 0) from the pipe. Pipes have the following characteristics:

- As pipes are nameless, they are not associated with entries in any directory.

- Data can only be read from the beginning of a pipe: seeking in a pipe is not possible. Thus, data is always read from a pipe in the same order that it was written to the pipe. As data is read from a pipe, it is discarded.

- When all processes that have had the pipe open for reading have closed it, any data left in the pipe is discarded. A process that tries to write to a pipe that is not open for reading by any process will get a SIGPIPE signal, which by default will terminate the process. If the process is blocking, ignoring or catching SIGPIPE the *write()* will return an error (with errno = EPIPE). A process that tries to read from a pipe that is empty will get an end-of-file indication (return value of zero from *read()*).

- Two processes can only communicate via a pipe if the process that created the pipe is a common ancestor of both of those processes.

A process that creates a pipe receives two file descriptors that refer to the pipe. The pipe is open for reading with one descriptor and for writing with the other. These file descriptors are the only way of referring to the pipe. Because open file descriptors are inherited by child processes, descendants of the creating process can also refer to the pipe, but no other processes can.

POSIX supports pipes in a manner that is essentially unchanged from the UNIX system. Pipes are created with the *pipe()* function, whose prototype is:

```
#include <unistd.h>
int pipe(int fildes[2]);
```

The argument passed to *pipe()* must point to an array of two integers. File descriptors are returned in this array; the pipe is open for reading with fildes[0] and for writing with fildes[1]. Both file descriptors refer to open file descriptions in which the O_NONBLOCK flag (described in Section 3.7, below) is clear. In UNIX System V.3, it is an error to try to use fildes[0] for writing or fildes[1] for reading. POSIX.1 is silent on this issue; implementations are free to create "full-duplex" pipes in which each file descriptor can be used for both reading and writing. However, a portable program must not assume that this is possible.

Figure 3.4 illustrates the use of the *pipe()* system call to create a pipe between two processes. This example uses the *fork()* function. If you are not familiar with *fork()*, you will find it discussed in Chapter 6.

```
int fd[2];                      /* Pipe file descriptors */
extern int errno;
pid_t  pid;                     /* Child process ID */
/* ... */

errno = 0;
if (pipe(fd) < 0)
    fprintf(stderr, "pipe() failed; errno = %d\n", errno);
else
{
    if ( (pid1 = fork()) < 0 )
        fprintf(stderr, "Cannot fork(); errno = %d\n", errno);
    else if ( pid1 == 0 )
    {   /* Child 1 Process */
        close(fd[0]);           /* Close reading end */
        /* ... Child can now write the pipe ... */
    }
    else
    { /* Parent Process */
        close(fd[1]);           /* Close writing end */
        /* ... Parent can now read the pipe ... */
    }
}
```

Figure 3.4

Using *pipe()* to Communicate between Child Processes

In the code fragment shown in Figure 3.4, a process creates a pipe and then creates a child process. The child process will write the pipe, and the parent will read it, so the child closes fd[0] and the parent closes fd[1].

3.7   FIFO Special Files

FIFOs are named pipes. They are present in System V.3 (and even System III) but not in 4.3BSD. In POSIX, a FIFO (the name is an acronym for first-in-first-out) can be created with the *mkfifo()* function, whose prototype is:

```
#include <sys/types.h>
#include <sys/stat.h>
int mkfifo(const char *path, mode_t mode);
```

No bits in the mode argument other than the permission bits should be used by a portable program. The S_ISUID and S_ISGID bits may have implementation-defined meaning. As with *open()*, *creat()*, and *mkdir()*, the value of mode is modified by the process's file mode creation mask. A successful call to *mkfifo()* creates an empty FIFO with a directory entry named by path. The FIFO is *not* opened by this call; it is available for any process to open for reading or writing. Because it can be referred to by name, a FIFO can be used for communication between any two processes; they need not be related. To remove a FIFO, you can use *unlink()*.

Because FIFOs act like pipes, data read from a FIFO is removed as it is read. FIFOs are opened with *open()* and closed with *close()*, like ordinary files. While a FIFO is not opened by any process, it is empty. This is because closing the last open file descriptor associated with a FIFO causes any data left in the FIFO to be discarded. Thus, a process cannot open a FIFO for writing, write some data, close the FIFO, and expect the data to be there for another process to read later. FIFOs are designed for communication between two or more processes that are active concurrently.

Ordinarily, when a process opens a FIFO for reading, the process will block until some other process opens the FIFO for writing. Conversely, when a process opens a FIFO for writing, the process will block until some other process opens it for reading. This provides a limited form of process synchronization. For example, consider the following code fragment:

```c
#include <sys/types.h>
#include <sys/stat.h>
#include <fcntl.h>
#include <signal.h>
#define MODE_644 (S_IRUSR | S_IWUSR | S_IRGRP | S_IROTH)

int fd;     /* file descriptor */
pid_t pid;  /* process ID of child process */

    /* ... */
if ( mkfifo("myFIFO", (mode_t)MODE_644) < 0 )
    exit(1);
if ( (pid = fork()) == 0 )
{   /* CHILD PROCESS */
    /* Child part A */       /* Preliminary child processing */
    if ( (fd = open("myFIFO", O_RDONLY)) < 0 )
        exit(1);
    /* Child part B */
}
else
{   /* PARENT PROCESS */
    /* Parent part A */      /* Preliminary parent processing */
    if ( (fd = open("myFIFO", O_WRONLY)) < 0 )
    {
        kill(pid, SIGKILL);  /* Error; get rid of child */
        exit(1);
    }
    /* Parent part B */
}
```

In this fragment, a process creates a FIFO and then *fork()*s to create a child process. The parent and child each open the FIFO, one for reading, the for writing. These processes execute asynchronously. That is, although one of them will run first (unless the host has multiple processors), it is indeterminate which one it will be. However, neither call to *open()* will return until the other has been issued, so neither parent nor child will get beyond the *open()* call until the other has reached it. This guarantees that the code marked Child part A will execute before the code marked Parent part B and that the code marked Parent part A will execute before the code marked Child part B. There are a number of ways that POSIX.1 processes can perform this kind of synchronization, but this is one of the most general, as it can be done between unrelated processes.

A process also can choose to open a FIFO for reading without blocking. It does so by using the O_NONBLOCK flag in its *open()* call:

```
if ( (fd = open("myFIFO", O_RDONLY | O_NONBLOCK)) < 0 )
    . . .
```

This call opens the FIFO and returns without delay, whether or not a process has the FIFO open for writing. A process can also choose to open a FIFO for writing without blocking. However, the behavior is different: if no process has the FIFO open for reading, then the *open()* call fails, with errno set to ENXIO. If a process attempts to open a FIFO for both reading and writing with O_NONBLOCK set, the result is unspecified. Portable programs should avoid this practice. Note that System V.3 supports a flag named O_NDELAY whose behavior is similar, but not identical, to that of O_NONBLOCK. Note also that the use of O_NONBLOCK affects more than just the behavior of *open()*. Read and write requests to a FIFO opened with O_NONBLOCK will behave differently. See Chapter 4, Section 4.4, for a discussion of the differences.

POSIX guarantees that any *write()* to a pipe or FIFO of PIPE_BUF or fewer bytes will be atomic—that is, data from this call will not be intermingled with data written by other calls to *write()* from other processes. This enables concurrent processes to avoid scrambling data being sent to standard output, to a logging file, or to some other destination: they funnel the output through a common FIFO. Consider the programs for reader and reporter processes shown in Figure 3.5. The reader processes read messages from some unspecified source and sends them to a FIFO. The reporter reads the FIFO and writes to standard output. All messages are assumed to be a single line, of size no more than PIPE_BUF (which must be at least 512). We assume that a FIFO named /tmp/funnel has been created previously.

A user could initiate a single reporter process and any number of reader processes, perhaps reading character special files. Note that the processes do not have to be related in any way. This illustrates the principal advantage of FIFOs over pipes: unrelated processes can share them.

In both of the programs in Figure 3.5, we used blocking *open()*s. Thus, if a reader process is initiated first, it waits until the reporter starts to run before it completes its *open()*. Conversely, if the reporter is initiated first, it

```
/**********************************************************/
/*          Reader Process Code                      */
/**********************************************************/
#define _POSIX_SOURCE
#include <fcntl.h>
#include <limits.h>
#include <unistd.h>

char *msgbuf;

main(argc, argv)
int argc;
char *argv[];  /* Argument is filename to read for messages */
{
    int fdin;   /* Message File Descriptor */
    int fdout; /* FIFO File Descriptor */
    int nbytes;
    int pipe_buf;

    if ( argc != 2 )     /* Must have one command line argument */
        exit(1);
    if ( (fdin = open(*++argv, O_RDONLY)) < 0 )
        exit(1);
    if ( (fdout = open("/tmp/funnel", O_WRONLY)) < 0 )
        exit(1);
    if ( (pipe_buf = (int)fpathconf(fdout, _PC_PIPE_BUF)) < 0 )
        exit(1);
    if ( (msgbuf = malloc(pipe_buf)) == NULL )
        exit(1);
    while ( (nbytes = read(fdin, msgbuf, pipe_buf)) > 0 )
        write(fdout, msgbuf, nbytes);
    close(fdin);
    close(fdout);
    exit(0);
}
```

Figure 3.5 *(continued on next page)*

Reader and Reporter Processes Sharing a FIFO

blocks until at least one reader starts to run. Note that the code in Figure 3.5
is only a sketch. A real application would do much more; for example, it
would perform error checking, specify message formats, and identify the
source of each message.

```
/***************************************************************/
/*          Reporter Process Code                           */
/***************************************************************/
#define _POSIX_SOURCE
#include <fcntl.h>
#include <limits.h>
#include <unistd.h>

char *msgbuf;

main(void)
{
    int fd;      /* FIFO File Descriptor */
    int pipe_buf;

    if ( (fd = open("/tmp/funnel", O_RDONLY)) < 0 )
        exit(1);
    if ( (pipe_buf = (int)fpathconf(fd, _PC_PIPE_BUF)) < 0 )
        exit(1);
    if ( (msgbuf = malloc(pipe_buf + 1)) == NULL )
        exit(1);
    while ( (nbytes = read(fd, msgbuf, pipe_buf)) > 0 )
    {
        msgbuf[nbytes] = '\0';              /* Null-terminator */
        printf("%s", msgbuf);
    }
}
```

Figure 3.5 *(continued from previous page)*

Reader and Reporter Processes Sharing a FIFO

3.8   Block and Character Special Files

Block and character special files usually are associated with devices. Therefore, POSIX.1 provides no way to create such files; this is not an appropriate activity for a portable application program. However, special considerations apply to the opening of these files. We discuss those here. There are many more considerations that are specific to character special files associated with terminals. These are discussed in detail in Chapter 7.

A process can attempt to *open()* a block or character special file. For some of these files, attempting such an *open()* will block the calling process until the device is ready or available. (For example, on most systems, attempting to open a tty line attached to a modem will block the caller until a connection is established.) You can use the O_NONBLOCK flag on such files. If you do, then the *open()* returns immediately, but the behavior of the opened file depends on the type of device associated with it.

Recall from Chapter 2 that a process may have a controlling terminal and that a process with a controlling terminal may choose to give it up, for instance by calling *setsid()*. In UNIX System V.3, if a process with no controlling terminal opens a character device file associated with a terminal, that terminal becomes the process's controlling terminal. This is not necessarily true for POSIX.1 systems. In fact, POSIX.1 provides no portable way for a process without a controlling terminal to acquire one. It does, however, provide a way to *prevent* a newly opened terminal file from becoming the process's controlling terminal: the O_NOCTTY flag. If set in oflag when *open()* is called, O_NOCTTY prevents the opened terminal device from becoming the controlling terminal of the calling process.

3.9   Controlling File Attributes

The *stat()* and *fstat()* functions allow you to determine a file's attributes. Some of those attributes are under program control. In particular, a process can—if permitted—change a file's mode with the *chmod()* function and change the file's owner or group ID with *chown()*. A prototype of *chmod()* is:

```
#include <sys/types.h>
#include <sys/stat.h>
int chmod(const char *path, mode_t mode);
```

There are two differences between the use of the POSIX version of this function and its UNIX counterpart. The first is the type of the second argument, mode_t rather than int. More significant is the way in which the mode argument is formed. You must use the symbolic mode bit masks defined in <sys/stat.h>, not octal constants. For example, the UNIX System V.3 call

```
chmod("myfile", 04751); /* Old method */
```

is replaced, in POSIX, by the call

```
chmod("myfile", (mode_t)S_ISUID | S_IRWXU | S_IRGRP | S_IXGRP | S_IXOTH);
```

This is somewhat cumbersome, but it's portable. Usually it's more convenient to define the modes you're going to use earlier in the program:

```
#include <sys/types.h>
#include <sys/stat.h>
#define MODE_RWSR_X__X (S_ISUID|S_IRWXU|S_IRGRP|S_IXGRP|S_IXOTH)
    /* ... */
chmod("myfile", (mode_t) MODE_RWSR_X__X);
```

For a process to change the mode of a file, the process must either have appropriate privileges or have an effective user ID equal to the owner ID of the file. Notice that no bit masks are defined for mode bits other that the S_ISUID, S_ISGID, and file permission bits. Attempts to set such bits (whose meaning, if any, is implementation-defined) may be ignored. In addition, implementations may impose restrictions on the setting of S_ISUID and S_ISGID. Because of this, attempts to set these bits may also be ignored. Some UNIX systems have special meanings for these bits in the mode of files other than regular files. For example, both System V.4 and IBM's AIX 3.1 use the S_ISGID bit in directories to indicate how group IDs of newly created files in the directory should be assigned. If the directory's S_ISGID bit is set, then files created in that directory have the same group ID as the directory. Otherwise, the files have the group ID that is the effective group ID of the creating process. (Recall that POSIX.1 allows both types of behavior.)

If you must change the mode of a file other than a regular file—for instance, a directory—then do it as follows: *stat()* the file to determine the current mode. Mask out the permission bits of the current mode, and then or the result with the permission bits you want set. Then set the file's mode to the resulting value. The effect is to preserve the values of the S_ISUID and S_ISGID bits and any other bits that may be part of the mode:

```
#include <sys/types.h>
#include <sys/stat.h>
#define PERM_BITS (S_IRWXU | S_IRWXG | S_IRWXO)
/*
** setmode() sets only the permission bits of the file named
** in special_file to the permission bits of mode.
*/
int setmode(char *special_file, mode_t mode);
{
    struct stat st;
    mode_t newmode;

    if (stat(special_file, &st) < 0)
        return(-1);
    newmode = st.st_mode & ~PERM_BITS; /* Mask out PERM_BITS */
    newmode |= (mode & PERM_BITS); /* Mask in PERM_BITS of mode */
    return (chmod(special_file, newmode));
}
```

Remember, however, that POSIX.1 implementations are free to ignore the settings of the S_ISUID and S_ISGID bits, even for regular files.

If a process successfully calls *chmod()* for a regular file whose group ID does not match its effective group ID or any of its supplementary group IDs, then the S_ISGID bit of that file is cleared. This protects against a possible security glitch.

Suppose that, while a process has a file open for reading or writing, it or another process changes the file's mode in such a way that if the first process would now try to open the file for reading or writing, it would be denied permission. For example, you open a file that you own for reading, and while it is open you clear the S_IRUSR bit in that file's mode. What happens? The answer, alas, depends on the implementation. Of course, your programs cannot control when other processes have files open. However, you should avoid changing the file mode of any file while your own processes have it open, as the results are unpredictable.

The process file mode creation mask is controlled and reported with the *umask()* function, whose prototype is:

```
#include <sys/types.h>
#include <sys/stat.h>
mode_t umask(mode_t cmask);
```

A call to *umask()* sets the file mode creation mask to the permission bits of cmask; other bits in cmask are ignored. Remember that the bits you *set* in cmask are the bits that will be *cleared* in the modes of files that you create. The return value of *umask()* is the previous file mode creation mask. It is unfortunate that there is no way to determine the existing file mode creation mask that does not involve setting it. Thus, to determine the value of your process's file mode creation mask and leave it unchanged, you must call *umask()* twice:

```
mode_t oldmask;
oldmask = umask((mode_t)0);  /* Get it... */
(void) umask(oldmask);       /* ...and restore it */
printf("umask = 0%o\n", (int)oldmask);
    /* Conventionally displayed in octal */
```

The *chown()* function can change the owner ID or group ID of a file. Here is a prototype for *chown()*:

```
#include <sys/types.h>
#include <unistd.h>
int chown(const char *path, uid_t owner, gid_t group);
```

This function has two distinct kinds of behavior in historical implementations of the UNIX system. In derivatives of System V, a process can use *chown()* to "give away" files that it owns, i.e., change their owner ID. In BSD-based versions of the UNIX system only privileged users can change the ownership of files. As we discussed in Chapter 1, POSIX accommodates both of these rules, based on the setting of the _POSIX_CHOWN_RESTRICTED configuration variable. If this symbol is in effect (has a value other than –1), then BSD-style rules apply. Otherwise, System V rules apply. More precisely:

- If _POSIX_CHOWN_RESTRICTED is in effect, then only a process with appropriate privileges can change the ownership of a file, and an unprivileged process can change a file's group only if the file's owner ID matches the process's effective user ID and the file's group ID matches either the process's effective group ID or one of its supplementary group IDs.

- If _POSIX_CHOWN_RESTRICTED is not in effect, then a process whose effective user ID matches the owner ID of the file can change the file's owner and group IDs; so can a process with appropriate privileges.

- In either case, a successful call to *chown()* for a regular file by a process without privileges causes both the S_ISUID and S_ISGID bits of the file's mode to be cleared. The effect of a successful call to *chown()* on these bits for a special file, or on a regular file when called by a privileged process, is implementation-defined.

Recall from Chapter 1 that the POSIX.1 FIPS requires the BSD behavior.

Recall that every file has three associated times, which in its stat structure are named st_atime, st_mtime, and st_ctime. These are, respectively, the time of last access to the file, the time of last modification of the file, and the time of the file's last status change (change of a member of the stat structure). Many POSIX functions update one or another of these times. For example, creating a file causes the st_mtime of the file's parent directory to be updated. The values in these fields are represented as seconds since January 1, 1970, 0:00 UTC. (UTC is Coordinated Universal Time. This used to be called GMT, or Greenwich Mean Time. The time January 1, 1970, 0:00 UTC is referred to as *the Epoch*, and times measured as seconds elapsed since this time are measured in *seconds since the Epoch*.)

A process can—with permission—explicitly set the st_atime and st_mtime fields associated with a file. The function used to do this is *utime()*, whose prototype is:

```
#include <sys/types.h>
#include <utime.h>
int utime(const char *path, const struct utimbuf *times);
```

This function is virtually identical to its UNIX system counterpart. The difference lies in the existence of the POSIX.1 header <utime.h>. On many UNIX systems, a program calling *utime()* is required to define struct utimbuf in its own code. POSIX includes the definition of this structure, which has exactly the following members, in <utime.h>:

```
struct utimbuf {
    time_t actime;
    time_t modtime;
};
```

Unlike most other POSIX.1 data structures, implementations are *not* free to add members to this structure. That is because this structure is used to set system values, not to return them to the calling program. If an implementation has additional fields in such a structure there is no way that a portable program can know about them or set their values.

There are two ways to call *utime()*. If you pass a NULL pointer as the times argument, then the file's access and modification times are set to the current time. To call *utime()* this way, a process must either have an effective user ID equal to the file's owner ID, have write permission for the file, or have appropriate privileges. If you pass a pointer to an actual utimbuf structure, then the times in the structure are used. Having write permission for the file is not sufficient in this case; the process must be the owner of the file or have appropriate privileges. A successful call to *utime()* causes the file's st_ctime field to be updated to the current time.

3.10 Renaming Files

The ANSI C standard has introduced a *rename()* function that can be used to change the name of an existing file. POSIX.1 supports *rename()*, with extended semantics to deal with the file hierarchy. Although we discuss most of POSIX's ANSI C functions in Chapter 8, *rename()* is appropriate here, because it is exclusively concerned with files and directories. A prototype for *rename()* is:

```
#include <stdio.h>
int rename(const char *old, const char *new);
```

The basic use of *rename()* is very simple. The call

```
rename("current_month", "previous_month");
```

changes the name of the existing file current_month to previous_month without changing the file contents. However, there are a number of semantic issues to deal with. Can *rename()* be used with directories? What if the file named by the new argument already exists? Can old and new be in different directories? On different file systems? What if old and new are links to the same file? The C standard semantics of *rename()* are only concerned with a flat file system. Here are POSIX.1's rules for *rename()*:

- If the file referred to by new exists, it is removed, and old is renamed to new. However, if old refers to a regular file, new cannot refer to an existing directory. Similarly, if old refers to a directory, new cannot refer to an existing regular file.

- With the above proviso, *rename()* can be used to rename directories. If old and new both refer to directories, then the directory named by new must be empty (have no entries other than dot and dot-dot).

- If old and new are on different file systems, *rename()* may or may not succeed; success depends on whether or not the implementation supports links across file systems.

- If old and new are existing links to the same file, *rename()* immediately returns zero (success) and does nothing else.

- The pathname old cannot be embedded as a prefix in the pathname new. Thus, a call such as

      rename("/usr/src/progs", "/usr/src/progs/Cprogs");

  is not permitted. Clearly, such a call is meaningless.

- In all cases, the calling process must have write permission for the parent directories of both old and new. If old refers to a directory, implementations are permitted to require write permission in old as well; similarly for new, if it refers to an already existing directory.

The operation of *rename()* is guaranteed to be atomic. That is, other processes will always recognize the existence of either old or new, and if new names a pre-existing file then a link named new will exist throughout the operation. This has a consequence for implementors of POSIX.1 systems: *rename()* must be implemented as a system call (or, at least, invoke a system call that does the actual renaming).

Exercises for Chapter 3 _____

1. Modify the program in Figure 3.3 so that it does not print directory entries that begin with the character ' . ' unless the flag –a was present on the command line.

2. Modify the program in Figure 3.3 so that after each filename it prints a space followed by a single character that indicates the file's type:

   R for regular files

   D for directories

   F for FIFOs

   B for block special files

   C for character special files

   O for files of any other type

3. Modify the program in Figure 3.3 by making it recursive: each time a filename is read that is the name of a directory, the contents of that

directory should be displayed, indented by a tab stop. A potential problem is that if *opendir()* uses a file descriptor, you may run out of file descriptors on a large hierarchy. How might you deal with this problem?

4. Write a function that determines whether or not the process's standard input is a pipe or FIFO. The function should return:

    −1   if standard input is not open.

     0   if standard input is not a pipe or FIFO.

     1   if standard input is a pipe or FIFO.

5. Write a program that goes through the process's current directory and changes the mode of each file owned by the process's effective user ID. The mode change should consist of masking out any bits that are currently set in the process's file mode creation mask (umask). For example, if the process's umask currently has the value:

    ```
    S_IWGRP | S_IWOTH | S_IXOTH
    ```

    then those three bits should be cleared in the mode of every file owned by the process's effective user ID in the current directory.

6. The POSIX.2 utility touch has the command line syntax:

    ```
    touch [-t time] filename ...
    ```

    The ellipsis (. . .) means that any number of filenames can be given. Any named files that do not exist should be created as empty regular files. Each of the named files should have its last access and last modification times (st_atime and st_mtime) changed to the value of the time argument, which should be an integral value of type time_t representing the time in seconds since the Epoch. If the −t option and its associated argument are not present, touch defaults to the current system time.

    Write a touch utility. If your touch is passed a filename for which it does not have permission to change the times, it should write a suitable message to standard error and continue processing any remaining files.

4

Input and Output

$\mathbf{P}$ OSIX provides two ways for processes to do input and output. One way, which might be termed *low-level I/O*, is inherited from UNIX system calls. It is based on the *read()* and *write()* functions and allows the process to have complete control over the passage of data between its own address space and the system. The other way is inherited from the C standard I/O Library, by way of the C standard. This is based on FILE streams. It is generally more efficient, but involves buffering between the process and the system that is not under the process's control. In this chapter we discuss low-level I/O. Because many C programmers, even on UNIX systems, rarely use low-level I/O, we briefly cover these features of POSIX.1, even though they are essentially unchanged from their UNIX system counterparts. In Chapter 8, we discuss the ANSI C portion of POSIX.1, including high-level I/O.

4.1 Controlling Open File Descriptions

Recall that when a POSIX.1 process opens a file, it creates an open file description (see Chapter 3, Section 3.3). This data structure keeps track of the current file offset, the file's access mode (whether it is open for reading, writing, or both), and the settings of the O_APPEND and O_NONBLOCK flags. (POSIX.1 does not support the O_SYNC flag defined in UNIX System V.3.) The process can determine the access mode and status flag settings after the file has been opened by using the *fcntl()* function. It can also change the status flag settings, but not the access mode. Thus, for example, you can open a file with O_NONBLOCK set and later clear it using *fcntl()*, but if you open a file for reading only you cannot later use *fcntl()* to change that open file description to be open for both reading and writing. A prototype for *fcntl()* is:

```
#include <sys/types.h>
#include <unistd.h>
#include <fcntl.h>
int fcntl(int fildes, int cmd, ...);
```

The *fcntl()* function uses a variable number of arguments. The cmd argument describes the request being made with *fcntl()*. POSIX supports eight values for cmd: F_DUPFD, F_GETFD, F_SETFD, F_GETFL, F_SETFL, F_GETLK, F_SETLK, and F_SETLKW. Both the number of arguments and the type of the optional third argument are determined by the value of cmd. The values of cmd with their meanings are summarized in Figure 4.1.

　　　To determine the status flags and access mode, use the command F_GETFL. The return value of *fcntl()* will have the same flags set or cleared that the file description does:

```
int flags;
int append_flag;
int nonblock_flag;
int access_mode;
int fd;                     /* File descriptor */
    /* ...Suppose that fd is open... */
flags = fcntl(fd, F_GETFL);
append_flag = flags & O_APPEND;
nonblock_flag = flags & O_NONBLOCK;
access_mode = flags & O_ACCMODE;
```

Because O_APPEND and O_NONBLOCK are flags (1-bit masks), they can be tested directly in the return value of *fcntl()*. For example, a program could more briefly test the setting of the O_NONBLOCK flag with

```
if (fcntl(fd, F_GETFL) & O_NONBLOCK)
    /* ...Whatever should be done if O_NONBLOCK is set... */
```

However, the access modes O_RDONLY, O_WRONLY, and O_RDWR are not necessarily flags. In particular, on many UNIX systems the value of O_RDONLY is zero. On such systems a test of the form

```
if (fcntl(fd, F_GETFL) & O_RDONLY)
    /* ...Oops! Code here will NEVER be executed... */
```

does not work; the condition in the if statement will always be false (zero). For this reason POSIX.1 defines the O_ACCMODE bit mask in <fcntl.h>. This mask picks out the bits that encode the access mode. A correct version of the above test is:

```
if ( (fcntl(fd, F_GETFL) & O_ACCMODE) == O_RDONLY )
    /* ...Code to be executed if file is opened O_RDONLY... */
```

Command	Description
F_DUPFD	Duplicate file descriptors.
F_GETFD	Get values of file descriptor flags. The FD_CLOEXEC flag is the only flag of this type specified by POSIX.1.
F_SETFD	Set values of file descriptor flags.
F_GETFL	Get values of flags and access mode associated with open file description.
F_SETFL	Set values of flags associated with open file description.
F_GETLK	Get file lock information.
F_SETLK	Set or clear file lock. If not possible, return immediately.
F_SETLKW	Set or clear file lock. If not possible, block until it is possible.

Figure 4.1

Commands Recognized by *fcntl()*

To change a file status flag, use the F_SETFL command. This command takes a third argument, of type int, which should have precisely the flag settings that you want. For example, if you wish to turn on the O_APPEND flag and turn off the O_NONBLOCK flag for a particular open file, you would issue the command

```
fcntl(fd, F_SETFL, O_APPEND);
```

As the O_NONBLOCK bit is not set in the third argument (which is treated as an int), the corresponding flag is cleared.

The *fcntl()* function does not control one aspect of an open file description: the file offset. A process can determine or change the file offset in a regular file by using the *lseek()* function. A prototype for *lseek()* is:

```
#include <sys/types.h>
#include <unistd.h>
off_t lseek(int fildes, off_t offset, int whence);
```

This is almost, but not quite, identical to the System V.3 version of *lseek()*. In System V.3 the type of the offset argument and the return type of *lseek()* are both long rather than off_t. Also, in System V.3 the valid values for the whence argument are 0, 1, or 2. In POSIX.1 they are SEEK_SET, SEEK_CUR, and SEEK_END, symbols that are defined in <unistd.h>. The call

```
lseek(fd, offset, SEEK_SET);
```

sets the file offset to offset. The call

```
lseek(fd, offset, SEEK_CUR);
```

sets the file offset to its current value plus offset (which may be negative; the type off_t is required to be a signed type). The call

```
lseek(fd, offset, SEEK_END);
```

sets the file offset to the end of the file plus offset (which can be positive or negative). In all cases, the return value is the new file offset. Thus, a process can determine the file offset of an open file by calling

```
curr_pos = lseek(fd, (off_t) 0, SEEK_CUR);
```

Figure 4.2 illustrates the three different kinds of *lseek()*s.

Remember to cast the offset argument to type off_t! On many systems, off_t is defined as long, and if ints are shorter than longs on such a system the arguments to *lseek()* will be passed incorrectly.

You cannot change the file offset of a pipe or FIFO. You cannot portably change the file offset of a block or character special file, as the meaning of such an offset (if any) will be hardware dependent. Thus, a portable POSIX.1 program should only use *lseek()* on regular files.

A process may set the file offset to a point beyond the end of the file. This does not, by itself, extend the length of the file. However, if a *write()* is done past the end of the file, then the file is extended and a "gap" is created. For example, suppose that a certain file is 1,000 bytes long and a process *lseek()*s to offset 1,350 and then writes 20 bytes. This changes the file size to 1,370 bytes. Bytes number 1,000 through 1,349 (counting the first byte as byte 0) constitute the gap. An attempt to read data from this gap will behave as if null bytes had been written there. Subsequently, a program can write into the gap.

On UNIX systems, when an *lseek()* past the end of a file creates a gap with whole blocks, the blocks are not actually allocated to the file. This has advantages and disadvantages. The advantages are speed and conservation of space: the sequence

```
fd = creat("longfile", S_IRWXU);
if ( lseek(fd, (off_t)2000000L, SEEK_SET) == 0 )
    write(fd, "x", 1);
```

creates a file of length 2,000,001 bytes very quickly on such systems, as only one disk block is actually allocated and written. The disadvantage is that there is no way to pre-allocate space on UNIX systems, short of actually writing blocks of zeros (or whatever character you want to use to hold the space). Thus, the time penalty is paid later, if and when the first 2,000,000 bytes of the file are actually written.

The POSIX.1 standard does not address the issue of whether blocks are allocated for such a gap. Thus, the UNIX system behavior is conforming, but not required. A system that requires large, fast writes to a file (for example, one that stores video images in real time) might arrange to pre-allocate

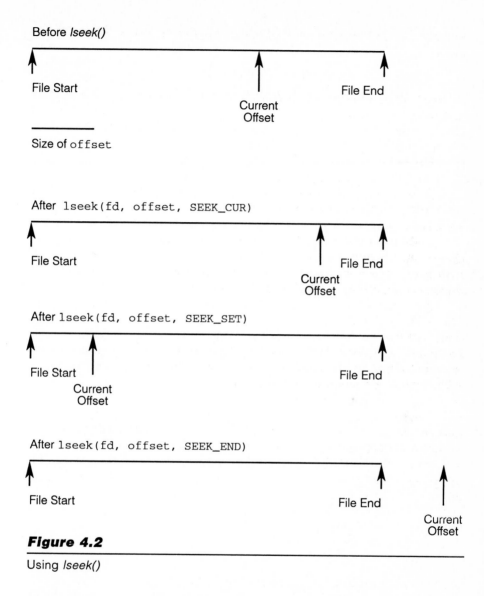

Figure 4.2

Using *lseek()*

contiguous blocks with an *lseek()* such as the one shown in the code fragment above. This, too, is conforming POSIX.1 behavior.

4.2 Controlling File Descriptors

We mentioned in Chapter 3 that it's possible to associate several file descriptors with the same open file description. This is called *duplicating* a file descriptor.

The *fcntl()* function can duplicate file descriptors, using the command F_DUPFD. The call

```
new_fd = fcntl(fd, F_DUPFD, min_fd);
```

returns a file descriptor associated with the same open file description as fd. The third argument, min_fd, which should be an int, tells *fcntl()* that the returned file descriptor should be the smallest available (i.e., unused) file descriptor that is greater than or equal to min_fd. For example, if a process currently has file descriptors 0, 1, 3, and 6 open, the call

```
new_fd = fcntl(1, F_DUPFD, 3);
```

will return the value 4, and file descriptors 1 and 4 will now share a common open file description. This means that changing the status flags or file offset for one of these file descriptors changes it for the other as well.

You may wonder why a program would ever want to duplicate a file descriptor. In fact, it's very handy; the UNIX shell does it all the time. For example, the UNIX system's Bourne shell supports the I/O redirection syntax

```
command n>&m
```

where n and m are integers. This runs command with file descriptor n duplicating file descriptor m. Suppose that you want to execute command, saving the standard output in a file, and you want to save the standard error output in the same file. The UNIX Bourne shell allows you to type:

```
command > file 2>&1
```

This redirects file descriptor 1 to refer to file and makes file descriptor 2 a duplicate of file descriptor 1. Note that this is *not* the same as simply opening file twice. Because file descriptors 1 and 2 are duplicates, they share a file pointer. This guarantees that no standard output will overwrite any standard error output, or vice versa.

The UNIX functions *dup()* and *dup2()* are also supported by POSIX. They have the following prototypes:

```
#include <unistd.h>
int dup(int fildes);
int dup2(int fildes, int fildes2);
```

The *dup()* function is entirely superfluous; its behavior can be obtained by using *fcntl()*. The call

```
new_fd = dup(fd);
```

is precisely equivalent to

```
new_fd = fcntl(fd, F_DUPFD, 0);
```

Thus, *dup()* always returns the lowest available file descriptor. POSIX.1 kept *dup()*, like *creat()*, to avoid making existing programs that use *dup()*

nonconforming. (Historically, *dup()* has been in UNIX much longer than *fcntl()*.) It's also true that *dup()* is simpler to call than *fcntl()*.

The *dup2()* function is almost, but not quite, equivalent to a sequence using *fcntl()*. The call

```
new_fd = dup2(fd1, fd2);
```

closes fd2 if it's already open and then duplicates fd1 as fd2. Thus (if no error occurs), fd2 is returned by *dup2()*. This call is virtually equivalent to:

```
close(fd2);
new_fd = fcntl(fd1, F_DUPFD, fd2);
```

The difference is that *dup2()* does a bit of error checking before performing the equivalent of this sequence and performs the steps atomically (without possibility of interruption). If fd1 and fd2 are equal, then *dup2()* simply returns fd2 and does nothing else. If fd2 is not a valid choice for a file descriptor (i.e., if it is negative or is greater than OPEN_MAX), then *dup2()* returns –1 and sets errno to EBADF. And if fd1 is not the file descriptor of an open file, then *dup2()* does not close fd2.

Another important attribute of a file descriptor is its inheritance across *exec()*s. We discuss this in Chapter 6, Section 6.2.

4.3   Reading Regular Files

A process can read from a regular file that has been opened O_RDONLY or O_RDWR by using the POSIX.1 function *read()*. A prototype for *read()* as given in the original POSIX.1 standard is:

```
#include <unistd.h>
int read(int fildes, char *buf, unsigned int nbytes);
```

This differs very slightly from the System V.3 version of *read()*, in that the nbytes argument is of type unsigned. In System V.3, it is of type int. This argument specifies the number of bytes to be read. The return value of *read()* is the actual number of bytes read. The fact that *read()* and nbytes are of different types can present a problem to programs that wish to read very large amounts of data in a single call. Consider the following program fragment:

```
char big_buffer[40000]; /* A very big buffer */
int fd;                 /* A file descriptor */
int bytes_read;             /* Return value from read() */
    /* ...Suppose fd has been opened... */
bytes_read = read(fd, big_buffer, 40000);
```

Suppose this fragment is executed on a machine on which ints are 16 bits long, and the *read()* is successful. What will the return value be? It can't be 40,000;

the largest value that *read()* can return is INT_MAX, which on a 16-bit machine is 32,767. The nbytes argument can be as large as UINT_MAX, which on such a machine is 65,535. In general, if nbytes is greater than INT_MAX but less than UINT_MAX and the *read()* is successful, the return value is implementation-defined. Portable programs should not attempt to read more than INT_MAX bytes at a time. Fortunately, there's hardly ever a need to do so.

The 1990 revision of the POSIX standard changed the prototype of *read()*. The new prototype is:

```
#include <unistd.h>
ssize_t read(int fildes, void *buf, size_t nbytes);
```

The changes are in the types of the buf and nbytes arguments and in the return type of the function. This change does not affect the issues in the preceding paragraph. There is still a difference between the maximum value representable as an ssize_t and the maximum value representable as a size_t. In practice, on most current systems size_t is unsigned int, and ssize_t, if implemented, is int. However, the change does raise a portability issue. Consider the following code fragment:

```
#include <unistd.h>
struct person {
    char   name[30];
    int    age;
    char   sex;
    /* ...etc. ... */
} myself;
unsigned int len;
int nbytes;
ssize_t Nbytes;
/* ... */
len = sizeof(struct person);
nbytes = read(fd, (char *)&myself, len);
Nbytes = read(fd, (void *)&myself, sizeof(struct person));
```

This code has two calls to *read()*, one conforming to each of the prototypes. To make things more difficult, remember that we want this code to work when compiled on an ANSI C conforming system, in which one of the prototypes for *read()* is present in <unistd.h>, and also when compiled on a common usage C system. Which call is right? Can both of them work on such a system? Possibly.

On a system that supports the C standard, both calls will work. The reason is that there's guaranteed to be a prototype declaration for *read()* in <unistd.h>. The C standard guarantees that, in the presence of a prototype for a function, the arguments in calls to that function will be promoted or converted to the correct types (as given in the prototype), in the same way that they would be converted by an assignment. (See Chapter 8, Section 8.1.)

Thus, the third argument, which is of integral type, will be converted to an `unsigned int` or to a `size_t` according to the prototype. There's really no conflict with the type of the second argument, `&myself`; the C standard specifies that pointers of type `void *` are compatible with all other pointer types.

On a common usage C system, difficulty could arise with the third argument. If the constant given by the evaluation of a `sizeof` is treated by the compiler as an object of the same size as an `int`, then no problem will occur. But suppose an implementation has 16-bit `int`s and 32-bit `long`s and `size_t` is `unsigned long`. (That is, the expression `sizeof(...)` is treated as a `long` constant.) On such an implementation, only one of the above calls will work. The only thing that can be said is that such an implementation will break lots of existing code and is therefore unlikely to be popular. Using `sizeof` expressions as the third argument to *read()* is quite common in existing code; so is the use of `int` constants.

A *read()* request reads data starting at the file offset of the open file description associated with `fildes`. If the *read()* returns successfully, the file offset has been advanced by the number of bytes actually read. As in the UNIX system, the number of bytes read can be fewer than the number requested. For *read()*s directed at a regular file, there are only two reasons that this should occur. One is that fewer than `nbytes` bytes are left in the file; in fact, *read()* indicates end-of-file by returning zero. The other is that the *read()* was interrupted by a signal. This is unlikely when the target is a regular file. However, if it does occur a POSIX.1 system can exhibit two different kinds of behavior: it can return –1, in which case `errno` will be set to `EINTR`. Or, it can return the number of bytes read when the interrupt occurred. (This behavior is required by the POSIX.1 FIPS.) If a *read()* has succeeded in transferring some data before being interrupted but returns –1, there is no reliable way for the reading process to know this or to re-read the data. This is unfortunate, but it is the historical behavior of many implementations, including UNIX System V.3. We discuss this further in Chapter 10.

4.4   Reading Special Files

When a process uses *read()* to read a pipe, a FIFO, or a character special file associated with a terminal, a number of considerations arise that do not apply to regular files. A *read()* from an empty pipe or FIFO that is not open for writing by any other process will return zero; this is a simple end-of-file condition. If the pipe or FIFO is empty but some other process has it open for writing, and the reading process opened it without setting the `O_NONBLOCK` flag, then the *read()* will block until either some data appears or the pipe or FIFO is closed by all processes that have it open for writing. This is the same as the behavior in UNIX System V.3 (in which the `O_NDELAY` flag takes the place of `O_NONBLOCK`). However, suppose that the reading process opened the pipe or FIFO with O_NONBLOCK set. In this case, a *read()* of an empty pipe or FIFO will not block; it will return –1, with errno set to EAGAIN. This behavior differs from UNIX System V.3 (in which the *read()* returns zero if O_NDELAY is set) and explains why POSIX uses a different flag. The reason for the change is illustrated in Figure 4.3.

The problem is that, in System V.3, a reading process cannot distinguish between an empty pipe that will stay empty, i.e., one that is not open for writing by any process, and an empty pipe that may eventually be filled by a writer process. In order not to change the semantics of existing programs, the POSIX.1 committee created a new flag. An implementation can support both the O_NONBLOCK flag and the O_NDELAY flag, with their different semantics. A portable POSIX.1 program should never use O_NDELAY.

As with regular files, a *read()* from a pipe or FIFO, if interrupted by a signal, may return –1 and set errno to EINTR. However, this will never occur if the *read()* has actually transferred any data. This must be guaranteed, because reading data from a pipe or FIFO removes that data, and the data would be lost if the *read()* did not then return a value indicating that it had been read.

A POSIX.1 system can provide other file types that support nonblocking *read()*s. The typical example, familiar from UNIX systems, is a terminal. The semantics of reading from such a file are similar to those for a pipe or FIFO:

- If no data is available and O_NONBLOCK is clear, the *read()* blocks until data is available.

- If no data is available and O_NONBLOCK is set, the *read()* returns –1 immediately and sets errno to EAGAIN.

- If data is available, the setting of O_NONBLOCK is irrelevant. If less data is available than was requested, the *read()* returns the number of bytes it was able to read.

A key phrase here is *if data is available.* As in the UNIX system, a POSIX process can control when data typed at a terminal becomes available. (For instance, each character can be made available as it is typed, or the system can buffer entire lines.) We discuss this mechanism in Chapter 7.

4.5 Writing Regular Files

A process can write to a regular file that has been opened O_WRONLY or O_RDWR by using the POSIX.1 function *write()*. The prototype for *write()* based on the original POSIX.1 standard is:

```
#include <unistd.h>
int write(int fildes, char *buf, unsigned int nbytes);
```

System V Version

```
#include <stdio.h>
#include <sys/types.h>
#include <sys/stat.h>
#include <fcntl.h>

char  *fifoname = "msgFIFO";    /* Name of some existing FIFO */
int   fd;                       /* FIFO file descriptor */
char  msg_buf[BUFSIZ];          /* For data from FIFO */
int   bytes_read;               /* Return value from read() */

/* ... */
    if ( (fd = open(fifoname, O_RDONLY | O_NDELAY)) < 0 )
        exit(1); /* Can't open FIFO for nonblocking read */
    if ( (bytes_read = read(fd, msg_buf, BUFSIZ)) == 0 )
        /* Now what?  Is the FIFO open for writing by a process? */
```

POSIX Version

```
#include <stdio.h>
#include <sys/types.h>
#include <sys/stat.h>
#include <fcntl.h>
#include <errno.h>

char  *fifoname = "msgFIFO";    /* Name of some existing FIFO */
int   fd;                       /* FIFO file descriptor */
char  msg_buf[BUFSIZ];          /* For data from FIFO */
int   bytes_read;               /* Return value from read() */

/* ... */
    if ( (fd = open(fifoname, O_RDONLY | O_NONBLOCK)) < 0 )
        exit(1); /* Can't open FIFO for nonblocking read */
    errno = 0;
    if ( (bytes_read = read(fd, msg_buf, BUFSIZ)) == 0 )
        exit(2); /* Nobody has it open for writing */
    else while ( bytes_read == -1 && errno == EAGAIN )
    {   /* It's open for writing; try once per second */
        sleep(1);
        errno = 0;
        bytes_read = read(fd, msg_buf, BUFSIZ);
    }
```

Figure 4.3

Comparing System V O_NDELAY and POSIX O_NONBLOCK

This differs from the System V.3 version of *write()* in the same way that *read()* differs: the nbytes parameter is unsigned. The *write()* function returns the actual number of bytes written. As with *read()*, you should not try to write more than INT_MAX bytes of data to a file with a single call to *write()*. Moreover, the same change made in the 1990 revision for *read()* has been made for *write()*. The new prototype, with different argument and return types, is:

```
#include <unistd.h>
ssize_t write(int fildes, void *buf, size_t nbytes);
```

The portability considerations regarding the type of the third argument apply to *write()* as they do to *read()*.

When you write to a regular file, the data is written beginning at the file offset of the open file description associated with fildes. If the *write()* returns successfully, the file offset has been incremented by the number of bytes actually written. In general, this should be nbytes. It is possible to open a regular file with the O_APPEND flag set. If so, then the file offset is set to the end of the file before every *write()*. In other words, all *write()*s to the file will extend it. As long as O_APPEND is set, you won't write over existing data.

If a *write()* requests the writing of more bytes than there is room for, only the number of bytes that can fit will be written. This can occur if the file system runs out of room or if the implementation imposes limits on file sizes. If a *write()* request to a regular file is interrupted by a signal, it will either return –1 and set errno to EINTR or—if it has successfully written some data—it may return the number of bytes written. (The latter behavior is required by the POSIX.1 FIPS.) As with *read()*, implementations that return –1 after interrupted partial *write()*s don't provide the calling process with enough information to reliably determine the current state of the file.

4.5.1 A Simple Example

To illustrate the use of low-level I/O, we write a simple program that copies its standard input to its standard output. In Chapter 8, we will write the same program using high-level I/O. The program is shown in Figure 4.4. Note that it reads and writes 1 byte at a time.

This program will work on any POSIX.1 system. However, it might be quite slow. Type it into your computer and run it, comparing its performance with that of the program in Figure 8.5. You might also compare its performance with that of the program in Figure 4.5. This program reads and writes 32,000 bytes at a time.

4.5.2 I/O Synchronization

When a process writes to a regular file and the *write()* call returns, will a subsequent *read()* of the file by another process show the effects of the *write()*? Is the data already on the file's physical storage medium? These are two

```
#define _POSIX_SOURCE
#include <unistd.h>

char    ch;                      /* The byte being read */

main()
{
    while(read(0, &ch, 1) == 1)
        if(write(1, &ch, 1) != 1)
            exit(1);
    exit(0);
}
```

Figure 4.4

A Simple Copying Program

```
#define _POSIX_SOURCE
#include <unistd.h>

#define BIGBUF_SIZE    32000

char    buf[BIGBUF_SIZE];      /* The bytes being read */

main()
{
    int bytes_read;

    while ( (bytes_read = read(0, buf, BIGBUF_SIZE)) > 0 )
        if ( write(1, buf, bytes_read) != bytes_read )
            exit(1);
    exit(0);
}
```

Figure 4.5

Another Simple Copying Program

different questions, to which the answers are, respectively, "yes" and "not necessarily". Typically, a *write()* arranges for the transfer of data from the buffer named as the second argument to *write()* to the system's address space. The system has its own buffers, and the data in them can remain there until something happens to force it out to the physical file. However, a *read()* from the file—whether via the same file descriptor used by the *write()* or by another

file descriptor open on the same file—will look in the system's buffers if
necessary. Consider the following code:

```
#include <unistd.h>
#include <fcntl.h>
#include <sys/types.h>
#include <sys/stat.h>

#define    BUFFER_SIZE 512
#define    MODE ((mode_t)(S_IRUSR | S_IWUSR | S_IRGRP | S_IROTH))

main()
{
    int    fdin, fdout;   /* File descriptors */
    int    nbytes;        /* Return value from write() */
    int    len;
    char   buf[BUFFER_SIZE];
    char   *string = "Hello, world";

    if((fdout=open("myfile",O_WRONLY | O_CREAT | O_EXCL,MODE))< 0)
        exit(1);
    if( (fdin = open("myfile", O_RDONLY)) < 0 )
        exit(1);
    len = strlen(string);
    if( (nbytes = write(fdout, string, len)) != len )
        exit(1);
    nbytes = read(fdin, buf, len);
    buf[nbytes] = '\0';
    printf("%s\n", buf);
    close(fdin);
    close(fdout);
    exit(0);
}
```

This may be the silliest way to print "Hello, world" yet devised, but that's
what it will do. In particular, the *read()* will read what the *write()* wrote immediately before it. Even after the program terminates, however, there's no
guarantee that the contents of myfile are actually on disk. They may remain
in the system's buffers indefinitely.

Most UNIX systems provide a system call, *sync()*, which is automatically called periodically, to flush system buffers to disk. This guarantees that
data does not wait indefinitely in the buffers. In practice, *sync()* on most UNIX
systems returns after the I/O has been scheduled, but perhaps before it
completes. This is not really what is desired. The POSIX.1 committee felt that
specifying a function with these semantics would not help; on the other
hand, specifying a *sync()* that did not return until all buffers had been physically written would have made virtually all existing implementations of
sync() nonconforming. Thus, there is no *sync()* function in POSIX.1. Moreover, some versions of the UNIX system allow a process to open a file for

writing with a synchronization flag set. A *write()* to such a file will not return until the data is physically written to the storage medium. Again, POSIX has no such mechanism.

Ordinarily, this is not the concern of the application programmer, who has to rely on the integrity of the system in any case. However, under some circumstances great confusion can result. Suppose that you're running a program that writes a file and the program terminates successfully. A few seconds later, for unrelated reasons, the system crashes. Your first reaction might be, "I'm glad my program finished before the crash." But the data still might not have been written to disk. If that's the case, it's probably lost. It would be nice if a process could call something like a reliable *sync()* at appropriate moments.

A proposed revision to the POSIX.1 standard provides for a function, *fsync()*, that takes as argument a file descriptor and forces the flushing of output buffers associated with the corresponding open file description. The POSIX committee charged with developing a standard interface for real-time applications (IEEE 1003.4) will also provide some form of *synchronous I/O* that will solve this problem. (A synchronous I/O call is one that does not return until the data has been written to permanent storage.) But the interfaces of 1003.4, even when adopted as a standard, will be options that an application writer for POSIX.1 systems cannot rely on. This is what prompts the proposal for *fsync()*.

4.6   Writing Special Files

When a process writes to a pipe or FIFO, a number of considerations apply that do not apply to regular files. One, mentioned in the previous chapter, is that any *write()* of fewer than `PIPE_BUF` bytes is guaranteed to be atomic—that is, to behave as if it constitutes a single operation. Thus, if several processes are writing to the same pipe or FIFO but each *write()* requests that no more than `PIPE_BUF` bytes be written, the data from individual write requests will not be intermingled. If a process writes more than `PIPE_BUF` bytes to a pipe or FIFO in a single request, the system is free to interleaf the data with other data written to the file on arbitrary boundaries.

Historically, pipes and FIFOs have been implemented with size limits. For example, on some UNIX systems both file types hold a maximum of 4,096 bytes. This is quite convenient for process synchronization. Thus, if the command line

```
command1 | command2
```

is given to the shell, `command1` will not run indefinitely before `command2` starts to run. When the pipe is full, `command1` will block. This is because a pipe is always opened with `O_NONBLOCK` clear, and a *write()* to a full pipe or FIFO with `O_NONBLOCK` clear will block the writing process. Eventually, `command2` will run, emptying the pipe and allowing `command1` to continue.

If the O_NONBLOCK flag is set on a pipe or FIFO, then *write()* behaves somewhat differently. (You can set O_NONBLOCK on an open pipe by using *fcntl()*.) In no circumstance will such a *write()* block the process. A *write()* of fewer than PIPE_BUF bytes either transfers all nbytes bytes, returning nbytes, or transfers nothing, returning –1, with errno set to EAGAIN. It will not do a partial transfer. A *write()* of more than PIPE_BUF bytes either transfers whatever fits (returning the number of bytes transferred) or transfers nothing and returns –1. If the pipe or FIFO is empty, a *write()* of greater than PIPE_BUF bytes always transfers at least PIPE_BUF bytes.

Just as with *read()*, a *write()* to a pipe or FIFO that is interrupted by a signal will not return –1 or set errno to EINTR if it has actually transferred any data.

Requests to *write()* to a terminal special file are governed by a number of conditions, especially if the terminal is the process's controlling terminal and the implementation supports job control. We discuss these in Chapter 7. Here it suffices to mention that, if O_NONBLOCK is set for the file and the data cannot all be accepted immediately, *write()* transfers as many bytes as it can, returning that number. If it cannot transfer anything, then, as with writes to pipes and FIFOs, it returns –1 and sets errno to EAGAIN. This could occur, for example, on systems that buffer output to terminal special files, if all buffers are full.

4.7   File Locking

POSIX.1 supports advisory file locking, using the *fcntl()* function in a manner similar to System V.3. Mandatory (or enforcement-mode) file locking, as provided by System V.3's *lockf()* function, is not supported by POSIX.1. This can be a problem: advisory locking is only useful if all processes that use a file cooperate. If you write an application that consists of several concurrent processes and these processes share files that are unlikely to be used by any other concurrent processes, then advisory locking is useful; you can ensure that no data will be lost through concurrent updates to your files by your processes. However, if your application shares files with concurrent processes over which you have no control, you can only hope that these processes set locks and respect locks set by other processes.*

To help deal with this problem, you should arrange for your application to be installed in such a way that it can prevent access to its private files by unauthorized processes. There are a number of ways to do this. One is to

---

* On the other hand, mandatory locking is dangerous, because an uncooperative process can set a mandatory lock on a file and effectively prevent access to that file by other processes. Thus, mandatory file locks present serious security problems — one reason that they are not included in POSIX.1.

have the system administrator create a special user ID as part of the application installation. Arrange for your application's programs to be installed as owned by this user ID, with the set-user-ID bit set. Make sure that the modes of the files created by the application deny access to any processes that do not have the same effective user ID (or appropriate privileges).

In case you have not used file locking with *fcntl()*, we briefly review it. The following discussion only applies to regular files. A process can set a *read lock*, also called a *shared lock*, on any portion of a file that it has open for reading. It can also set a *write lock*, also called an *exclusive lock*, on any portion of a file that it has open for writing. These locks do not actually prevent any process from doing anything (except setting overlapping locks). They simply arrange so that, if a process inquires, it will learn that a certain portion of the file is locked. Thus, you can write your programs in such a way that, before they do any I/O, they check to see if a lock is there. If no lock is set, they lock the portion of the file against other processes, do the required I/O, and then unlock the file.

If a part of a file has a read lock set, other processes may set overlapping read locks, but no process may set an overlapping write lock. Setting a write lock on any part of a file prevents other processes from setting any kind of lock on an overlapping part of the file.

To control file locks, *fcntl()* uses the flock data structure, defined in <fcntl.h>, and the three commands F_GETLK, F_SETLK, and F_SETLKW. When calling *fcntl()* with any of these commands, you must pass a third argument that is a pointer to an flock structure. This structure has at least the following members:

```
struct flock {
    short l_type;    /* One of F_RDLCK, F_WRLCK, F_UNLCK */
    short l_whence;  /* One of SEEK_SET, SEEK_CUR, SEEK_END */
    off_t l_start;   /* Start offset in bytes from l_whence */
    off_t l_len;     /* Length of locked portion. 0 = to EOF */
    pid_t l_pid;     /* Proc ID that set lock; a return value */
};
```

This structure is the same as that used by UNIX System V.3. The only difference lies in its use: in System V the l_whence member has possible values 0, 1, and 2. POSIX changes these, as it did the corresponding arguments to *lseek()*, to the macros SEEK_SET, SEEK_CUR, and SEEK_END. The l_whence, l_start, and l_len members together describe the "record" (i.e., the portion of the file) being locked. A length of 0 is interpreted as extending from the start of the lock to the end of the file.

The command F_GETLK is used to learn about existing locks on the file. F_SETLK and F_SETLKW are both used to set locks. All three require a third argument to *fcntl()*. Here's how you use *fcntl()* to learn whether a portion of a file is locked. Suppose you want to set a read lock on the file referred to by file descriptor fd, extending from the current file offset to the end of the file. First, you can find out if any lock is currently set:

```
#include <sys/types.h>
#include <unistd.h>
#include <fcntl.h>
struct flock lock;
    /* ... */
errno = 0;
lock.l_type = F_RDLCK;
lock.l_whence = SEEK_CUR;
lock.l_start = (off_t) 0;     /* From current offset... */
lock.l_len = (off_t) 0;       /* ...to end of file */
fcntl(fd, F_GETLK, &lock);
```

When this call returns, the lock structure has been modified in one of two ways. If no lock exists on any portion of the file that overlaps the portion specified by lock, then the l_type member is set to F_UNLCK and nothing else is changed. If an overlapping lock does exist, then all of its attributes overwrite the corresponding members of lock and the l_pid member is set to the process ID of the process that set the lock.

You set or remove locks with either the F_SETLK or F_SETLKW commands. They differ in that, if the lock cannot be set, *fcntl()* with F_SETLK returns immediately with errno set to either EACCES or EAGAIN (the implementation can choose either), while *fcntl()* with F_SETLKW blocks until the lock can be set or until interrupted by a signal. If you don't want *fcntl()* to block indefinitely, you can use the *alarm()* function to set a timeout; *alarm()* is discussed in Chapter 5.

Note that the F_GETLK command may not reliably tell you when you can lock a record; you can learn that a portion of a file is unlocked, but by the time you try to lock it another process may have beat you to it. Thus, you should always be prepared for F_SETLK to fail or for F_SETLKW to block.

4.7.1   File Locking and Deadlocks

It is possible that cooperating processes that share and lock files and respect each others' locks can create a deadlock. Here is an example of one way that it can happen. Process A needs to set locks (of any type; it doesn't matter) on bytes 100–199 and bytes 500–599 of file. Process B needs to lock the same parts of the same file. Both processes are using fcntl(fd, F_SETLKW, ...) to set their locks. However, events happen in the following order. Process A locks bytes 100–199. Then process B runs, and locks bytes 500–599. Then process B tries to lock bytes 100–199. Because there is already a lock on these bytes, process B blocks. Then process A runs again and tries to lock bytes 500–599. Because there is already a lock on these bytes, process A blocks, and now each process will wait for the other forever.

This is a special case of a well-known problem that can occur whenever concurrent processes need exclusive access to a shared resource. It has well-known solutions. In this case, one good solution is to use a semaphore, and a good way to implement the semaphore is to use a write (exclusive) lock on byte 0 of the file. More precisely, if any process needs to set a lock on a portion of a file, and there is a possibility of a deadlock, the process should first do something like:

```
struct flock lock;
int fd;
    /* ... */
errno = 0;
lock.l_type = F_WRLCK;
lock.l_whence = SEEK_SET;
lock.l_start = (off_t) 0;
lock.l_len = (off_t) 1;
if (fcntl(fd, F_SETLKW, &lock) < 0)     /* Lock byte 0 */
    error();
else
{
    /* Lock other portions of file */
    /* Do whatever is necessary */
    /* Unlock remainder of file */
    lock.l_type = F_UNLCK;
    fcntl(fd, F_SETLK, &lock);          /* Unlock byte 0 */
}
```

This uses byte 0 (zero) of the file as the semaphore: if a process has locked byte 0, it can assume that it has the right to lock the rest of the file. It locks what it needs, does its file processing, removes the locks, and, finally, releases byte 0. If some other process has locked byte 0, this process waits until that other process releases it.

This solution will not work when a process needs to lock parts of several files, because the same sort of deadlock can occur: process A gets exclusive access to file1 while process B has gotten exclusive access to file2, and then each waits forever for the other to release the file. In a case like this, you have to follow a procedure of the following sort:

```
struct flock lock;
int   fd1,              /* For file1 */
      fd2;              /* for file2 */
int   got_both = 0;     /* Set to 1 if you can get both files */
      /* ... */
while (! got_both)
{
```

```
lock.l_type = F_WRLCK;
lock.l_whence = SEEK_SET;
lock.l_start = (off_t) 0;
lock.l_len = (off_t) 1;
    /* Try to get file1 */
if (fcntl(fd1, F_SETLKW, &lock) < 0)
    error();
else
{   /* Got the first file */
    /* Try to get file2. If not, release file1 */
    if (fcntl(fd1, F_SETLK, &lock) < 0)
    {   /* Release file1 */
        lock.l_type = F_UNLCK;
        fcntl(fd1, F_SETLK, &lock);
        sleep(1);
    }
    else
        got_both = 1;
}
}
/* Now have both files. Do whatever, then release */
/* them in reverse order. */
```

This can be generalized, with some pain, to work with any number of files. The key point is that when you are trying to lock byte 0 of any file after the first, do not use `F_SETLKW`. That is, don't block. Instead, if you can't get the file, release any files that you already have, wait a while, and then try again from the beginning.

Exercises for Chapter 4

1. Write a program that reliably renames files. It should attempt to rename a file by using the *rename()* function, but if this fails with `errno` set to EXDEV, then the program should copy the old file to the new name and (if the copy succeeds) delete the existing file. (If the program does not have permission to delete the old file, then it should fail and not create the copy.)

2. Suppose you want to implement a message logging system in which users can use a utility to log messages that can later be read by a system administrator. You decide to use a FIFO to hold the messages and a system program to read the FIFO and write to the log file. Once a message is written to the FIFO, it should remain there until read by the

system program. No unprivileged program should be able to remove any data from the FIFO.

(a) How should the ownership and permissions on the FIFO, the system program, and the message logging utility be arranged?

(b) How can you ensure that the utility will never block indefinitely when writing the FIFO?

(c) Write the utility program.

(d) Write the system program to do the actual logging.

3. Explain how you can create a pipe that is opened for reading and writing in nonblocking mode.

4. Write program ypoc, which copies its standard input to its standard output backwards. (Do not reverse each line; reverse the entire file.) You will need to create a temporary file.

5. The default action on opening a FIFO for reading is to block until a process opens it for writing, and vice versa. Explain how this can be used to synchronize unrelated processes. More specifically, suppose that processes P1 and P2 are executing concurrently and asynchronously. Suppose that you must reliably guarantee that P1 calls function $f1()$ before P2 calls $f2()$. How can you use a FIFO to do this? (Hint: no actual I/O to the FIFO is needed.)

5

Signals

The way in which **POSIX handles signals** is one of the greatest areas of change from the UNIX system. The original method of signal-handling in the UNIX system has a defect. Consequently, the Berkeley 4.2BSD distribution introduced a different method. Semantically, the POSIX.1 signal-handling functions are derived from Berkeley's, but their syntax and a few semantic features are inventions of the POSIX committee.

Even some very experienced programmers of UNIX systems may not have used signals extensively. Because of this, and because signals can affect the behavior of almost every other POSIX.1 function, we review the basic facts regarding signals and their historical implementation. Readers who are thoroughly familiar with programming with UNIX system signals can quickly skim the following section. Note also that a number of the examples in this chapter, and some of the exercises at the end of this chapter, make use of the *fork()* function. If you are not familiar with *fork()*, refer to Chapter 6, Section 6.1.

5.1   Review of Signal Concepts and Implementation

The POSIX.1 standard defines a signal as "a mechanism by which a process may be notified of, or affected by, an event occurring in the system".[2] When the event that causes the signal occurs, the signal is said to be *generated*. When the appropriate action for the process in response to the signal is taken, the signal is said to be *delivered*. In the interim, the signal is said to be *pending*. The most important feature of signals is that, from the program's point of view, they are asynchronous; that is, a program can in principle receive a signal between any two instructions. For example, you can send a program the interactive attention ("interrupt") signal while it is running in the foreground by pressing the appropriate key sequence (typically, Delete or Control-C). The program can be doing just about anything when the signal is delivered to it. Unless it has taken explicit action to handle the delivery of this signal, the program will terminate when the signal is delivered.

Not all signals are truly asynchronous. If your program performs an erroneous arithmetic operation such as dividing by zero, it will cause generation of an arithmetic exception signal. Clearly, this can only occur after certain instructions in a program. In fact, signals are the software equivalent of hardware exceptions, or interrupts, which can occur both synchronously and asynchronously with respect to an executing program.

A process can choose what it wishes to do when it receives a signal. (There are exceptions, as we shall see below.) If the process takes no action, then there is a default behavior defined for each signal. In most cases, the default is for the signal to terminate the process. Thus, typically when you type the interrupt character at the terminal it ends the executing program. The possible actions a process can request of the system are:

- Ignore the signal.

- Execute a signal-handling function of the process's choosing when the signal is delivered. If this action is chosen and the signal is delivered, then whatever the process is doing is interrupted and the signal-handling function is executed. It is invoked as if it had been passed a single int argument, the number of the signal that was caught. If it returns, the process resumes execution where it was interrupted. This is illustrated in Figure 5.1.

- Restore the default action of the signal.

In UNIX systems, dating back at least to 6th Edition UNIX, programs have specified signal actions by using the *signal()* function. We explain the action of *signal()* below, but be warned: *signal()* is *not* supported in POSIX! A strictly conforming POSIX.1 application must not use the *signal()* function. To understand why, we must explain *signal()*'s semantics. First, here is a prototype of *signal()*, taken from the C standard:

```
#include <signal.h>
void (*signal(int sig, void (*func)()(int)))(int);
```

This rather daunting prototype says that *signal()* takes two parameters. The first, sig, is an integer that specifies the signal number for which an action is being established. The second argument, func, is a pointer to a function that is of type void and that takes a single int argument. The return type of *signal()* is a pointer to the same kind of function—that is, *signal()* returns a pointer to a function of type void that takes a single int argument.

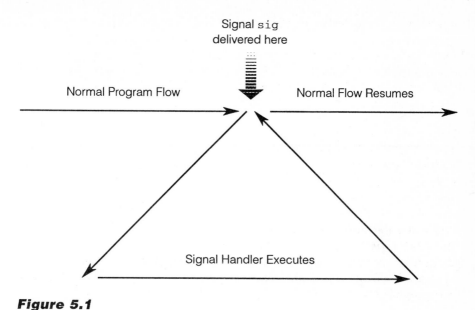

Figure 5.1

Program Flow When a Signal Is Caught

The function argument to *signal()* is the name of the signal handler—the function that you want to be invoked when the signal is delivered. The return value is a pointer to the function that was the previous signal handler for that signal. All of this can be made clearer by an example; Figure 5.2 shows a program that uses *signal()*. Remember that this is *not* POSIX.1 conforming code.

This code is designed to annoy anyone who tries to run it. It first establishes that the signal-handling function for SIGINT, the interactive attention signal, will be the *catcher()* function:

```
signal(SIGINT, catcher);
```

Then it prints the character value of the variable ch "forever". At first this is a. What happens if you're sitting at a terminal, watching a's pour onto the screen, and you try to interrupt the program? If you type an interrupt, it causes a SIGINT to be generated and delivered to the program. This will interrupt whatever is happening and invoke *catcher()*. The result will be that, instead of typing a's, the program now types b's. If you try to interrupt again, the character will change back to a. Fortunately, the UNIX system allows you to deliver another signal interactively—the quit signal, SIGQUIT, usually generated by typing Control-\. This program does not catch SIGQUIT, so generating a SIGQUIT for this program will cause it to terminate.

```
#include <signal.h>
volatile char        ch = 'a';        /* See Section 5.1.1 */

main(void)
{
    extern void catcher(int);

    signal(SIGINT, catcher);
    while(1)
        printf("%c", ch);
}

void catcher(int sig)
{
    signal(SIGINT, catcher); /* Why is this here? See 5.2 */
    ch = (ch == 'a') ? 'b' : a;
}
```

Figure 5.2

Sample Nonconforming Program Using *signal()*

The symbol SIGINT in the code is the number that identifies the interactive attention signal. Every signal is identified by an integer, which in turn has a name defined in the header <signal.h>. This header also defines the symbols SIG_DFL and SIG_IGN. These are symbols whose types are void(*)( )—in words, pointer to a function returning void—and whose values cannot be the addresses of any function defined by a program. The call

```
signal(sig, SIG_DFL);
```

establishes that the signal-handling action for signal sig should be restored to the default. The call

```
signal(sig, SIG_IGN);
```

establishes that delivery of signal sig should be ignored.

Signal-handling is useful in many different contexts. A simple example, and one of the most common, is cleaning up temporary files and exiting "gracefully" when a program is interrupted. Suppose your program creates some temporary files and, before normal termination, removes them. If the program is terminated by an uncaught signal, then it will not have a chance to do this cleanup. However, you can catch SIGINT and SIGQUIT and arrange that upon delivery of either signal the cleanup is done before termination:

```
void graceful_exit(int signo)
{
    cleanup();              /* Unlink temp files, etc. */
    exit(2);
}

/* ... */
signal(SIGINT, graceful_exit);
signal(SIGQUIT, graceful_exit);
```

Remember, this code simply illustrates the use of old-style signals. It is not POSIX conforming.

5.1.1   The C Keyword `volatile`

You may have noticed that in Figure 5.2 the variable ch is declared with the type qualifier `volatile`. This is a reserved word added to the C language by the ANSI C committee. If a variable is declared with the `volatile` qualifier, then the compiler is warned that the variable can be modified by asynchronous events. This should prevent the compiler from aliasing the variable in ways that could lead to erroneous results.

To see how these erroneous results could occur, consider the program in Figure 5.2, without the keyword `volatile`. A C compiler trying to do optimization could determine that the variable ch is never modified inside the `while` loop and arrange for faster access to ch by keeping a copy of it— an *alias*—inside a register and only referring to the register in this loop. However, the code generated for function *catcher()* might refer to ch through its memory location. Thus, when a SIGINT is delivered, the value of ch stored in memory might be changed, but the alias will not be, and the main program will continue to print the original value, a. Declaring ch as `volatile` tells the compiler that every reference to ch should be to the actual value stored in memory.

The use of global variables in signal handlers to tell a process whether a signal has been delivered is fairly common. (An example occurs in the discussion of *alarm()* in Section 5.8, below.) Such variables should always be declared as `volatile`. However, this can lead to portability problems, as this keyword is not recognized by common usage C compilers. You can solve this problem by using code that tests whether or not the compiler is a standard C compiler. Such a compiler is guaranteed to have the symbol _ _STDC_ _ predefined and equal to 1. One way to make use of _ _STDC_ _ is like this:

```
#if _ _STDC_ _ == 1
    volatile char ch = 'a';
#else
    char ch = 'a';
#endif /* _ _STDC_ _ == 1 */
```

Another possibility is to hide the problem inside a private header file. You can have the following code in a header that you include in all your applications that use signals or that need volatile variables for other reasons:

```
#if __STDC__ == 1
#define VOLATILE volatile
#else
#define VOLATILE
#endif /* __STDC__ == 1 */
```

In your application programs, use the qualifier VOLATILE. This will do what is required on standard C compilers and will do nothing on common usage C compilers.

5.2   The Unreliability of UNIX Signals

Look again at the code in Figure 5.2. Notice the call to *signal()* in the body of *catcher()*. The reason for this call is also the reason that *signal()* has been replaced in POSIX. The semantics of UNIX System V.3 *signal()* include the following proviso: when a signal is caught by a signal handler established by *signal()*, before the signal-handling function is invoked the action associated with the signal is reset to the default.* Thus, for *catcher()* to remain as the signal-handling function for SIGINT, it must call *signal()*.

The fact that when a signal is caught its action is reset causes a serious problem. Suppose that, in the above program, an impatient user repeatedly typed interrupts. It could happen that one is caught and, in the time between the invocation of the *catcher()* function and the call to *signal()*, another SIGINT is delivered. What happens? The program terminates, because in that short interval the action for SIGINT has been reset to the default. Now, in this case program termination is no tragedy. But the point is that signal-handling using the *signal()* function is unreliable. There is no way to guarantee that a particular signal will always be caught. In other circumstances, the consequences could be much more serious.

The ANSI C standard includes the *signal()* function, but with slightly different semantics. This standard specifies that, when a signal is caught, either the action is reset to the default or an implementation-defined blocking of the signal is performed. However, a portable program cannot depend on this to assure reliable signal-handling. Another alternative would be to change the semantics of *signal()* to not reset the signal handler. (In fact, this was done

---

* There are exceptions. The actions for the signals SIGILL and SIGTRAP are not reset in System V.3.

in the 4.3BSD version of UNIX.) However, this breaks many existing programs that rely on the current semantics. Consequently, POSIX.1 has replaced *signal()* with an entirely new mechanism.

5.3 Signal Data Structures in POSIX.1

POSIX.1 signal-handling relies on two data structures: the *signal set* and the *sigaction structure*. A signal set is an object of type `sigset_t`; this type is defined in `<signal.h>`. An object of type `sigset_t` represents some subset of the set of all possible signals. An important feature of this type is that it is always an integral or structure type. Thus, you can take the address of a `sigset_t` object.

Every POSIX.1 system supports at least the set of signals shown in Figure 5.3. The default action for all the signals listed in Figure 5.3 is termination of the process.

Signal	Description
SIGABRT	Abnormal termination; see *abort().*
SIGALRM	Timeout; see *alarm().*
SIGFPE	Erroneous arithmetic operation (e.g., divide by zero).
SIGHUP	Hangup on controlling terminal.
SIGILL	Invalid hardware instruction.
SIGINT	Interactive attention signal (interrupt).
SIGKILL	Termination. **Cannot be caught or ignored.**
SIGPIPE	Write on a pipe that is not open for reading by any process.
SIGQUIT	Interactive termination signal (quit).
SIGSEGV	Invalid memory reference.
SIGTERM	Termination signal.
SIGUSR1	Application-defined signal 1.
SIGUSR2	Application-defined signal 2.

Figure 5.3

Signals Defined for All POSIX Systems

Signal	Description	Default Action
SIGCHLD	Child process stopped or terminated.	Ignored.
SIGCONT	Continue.	Continue if stopped.
SIGSTOP	Stop. **Cannot be caught or ignored.**	Stop the process.
SIGTSTP	Interactive stop.	Stop the process.
SIGTTIN	Read from controlling terminal by background process.	Stop the process.
SIGTTOU	Write to controlling terminal by background process.	Stop the process.

Figure 5.4

Signals Supported by POSIX Job Control Systems

It is not possible to catch or ignore the SIGKILL signal. Thus, there is always a sure way to terminate a runaway process.

Implementations that support job control must also support at least the set of signals shown in Figure 5.4. If a POSIX.1 implementation does not support job control, then the symbols naming these signals must still be defined in <signal.h>. Note that the signal named SIGCHLD is not the same as the System V.3 SIGCLD signal. Although SIGCHLD behaves much like SIGCLD, it need not be supported on systems that do not support job control. On such systems, when a child process terminates, a signal need not be generated for the parent.

It is not possible to catch or ignore the SIGSTOP signal.

All the signals listed in Figures 5.3 and 5.4 must have distinct values, which must be positive integers. A POSIX.1 implementation is free to support other signals if it so wishes.

One feature of POSIX's handling of signals is that a POSIX.1 process can choose to block certain signals from delivery. At any given moment, a POSIX.1 process has a *signal mask*, which is a set of signals that are currently blocked. Each process starts out with a signal mask inherited from its parent. A process also has a set of pending signals, which includes those signals (if any) that have been generated but are currently blocked from delivery. (See Chapter 2, Figure 2.1.) If a signal is generated but is blocked from delivery, it is added to the process's set of pending signals.* If a signal is blocked from

---

* If the action for the signal has been set to SIG_IGN, then this is not necessarily true. A POSIX.1 implementation is free to discard blocked signals if the current action is to ignore them. In general, there is no reason to block a signal that you are ignoring, and a portable POSIX.1 application should refrain from doing so.

delivery and more than one instance of that signal is generated for a process, it is implementation-defined whether one, or several, instances of the signal are left pending.

When a POSIX process describes to the system the action it wants to take upon receipt of a signal, it specifies more than just a function name. The action is described using a sigaction structure, which has at least the following members:

```
struct sigaction {
    void    (*sa_handler)(); /* Signal handling function */
    sigset_t sa_mask;        /* Extra mask during handling */
    int      sa_flags;       /* Only used for SIGCHLD */
    /* Possibly other members */
};
```

The sa_handler member is a pointer to the signal-handling function. It corresponds to the second argument to *signal()*. The sa_mask is a set of signals to be blocked during execution of the signal-handling function. This set is in addition to the process's current signal mask. More precisely, when a signal whose action is prescribed by a sigaction structure is caught, a new signal mask is constructed for the process before the signal handler is invoked. This mask consists of the union of the current signal mask, the set of signals in sa_mask, and the signal being caught. Figure 5.5 illustrates the change in

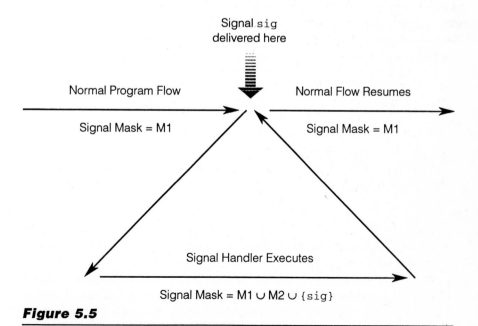

Figure 5.5

Signal Mask Manipulation When a Signal Is Caught

the signal mask if the process's signal mask is M1 before the signal is delivered and the value of sa_mask is M2.

Thus, when a signal is caught it is blocked from further delivery while the signal handler runs. This solves the UNIX system *signal()* reliability problem. If the signal handler returns normally, the previous process signal mask is restored.

The sa_flags member of the sigaction structure contains flag bits that can be used to modify the behavior of the signal to which the sigaction structure applies. The sa_flags member is discussed in Section 5.6.

5.4   Establishing Signal Actions in POSIX.1

The POSIX.1 counterpart to the *signal()* function is the *sigaction()* function. Before we can describe how *sigaction()* works, we need to discuss the functions that POSIX.1 provides to manipulate objects of type sigset_t. There are five such functions, collectively known as the *sigsetops*. Their prototypes are:

```
#include <signal.h>
int sigemptyset(sigset_t *set);
int sigfillset(sigset_t *set);
int sigaddset(sigset_t *set, int signo);
int sigdelset(sigset_t *set, int signo);
int sigismember(const sigset_t *set, int signo);
```

Note that these functions take pointers to signal sets, not signal sets themselves, as arguments. The *sigemptyset()* function creates sets that are "empty". More precisely, suppose we have declared a signal set as follows:

```
sigset_t sigmask;
```

Then the call

```
sigemptyset(&sigmask);
```

ensures that sigmask does not contain any of the signals defined in the POSIX standard. No guarantees are made about other implementation-defined signals. Similarly, *sigfillset()* creates "full" sets. The call

```
sigfillset(&sigmask);
```

ensures that sigmask contains all of the signals defined in the POSIX.1 standard (but says nothing about any other, implementation-defined, signals). The *sigaddset()* and *sigdelset()* functions add signals to and delete signals from sigset_t objects. All four of these functions return zero on success and –1 on error. The *sigismember()* function is somewhat different. It does not modify the sigset_t pointed to by its argument. Rather, it tests whether the named signal is or is not a member of the set. The *sigismember()* function returns 1 if the signal is in the set, zero if it is not, and –1 if an error occurs.

We can use the sigsetops to construct signal masks in the sa_mask member of a sigaction structure, for use with *sigaction()*. A prototype for *sigaction()* is:

```
#include <signal.h>
int sigaction(int sig, struct sigaction *act,
                       struct sigaction *oact);
```

The sig argument is the signal for which an action is being established. The act argument is the address of a sigaction structure that describes the actions to be taken for sig. The oact argument is the address of a sigaction structure that will be filled with the previous action for sig. If oact is NULL, then it is ignored. Similarly, if act is NULL, then the current action for the signal is reported in *oact and is not changed. Figure 5.6 shows the program from Figure 5.2, rewritten to be a strictly conforming POSIX.1 application. In this program, we do not block any additional signals when *catcher()* runs; thus, the call to *sigemptyset()*. However, SIGINT will automatically be blocked while *catcher()* runs.

```
#define _POSIX_SOURCE
#include <unistd.h>            /* For definition of NULL */
#include <signal.h>
volatile char   ch = 'a';

main(void)
{
    extern void catcher(int);
    struct sigaction sigact;

    sigact.sa_handler = catcher;
    sigemptyset(&sigact.sa_mask);
    sigact.sa_flags = 0;
    sigaction(SIGINT, &sigact, NULL);
    while(1)
        printf("%c", ch);
}

void catcher(int sig)
{
    ch = (ch == 'a') ? 'b' : 'a';
}
```

Figure 5.6

POSIX.1 Version of the Program in Figure 5.2

5.5   Blocking Signals

A process can manipulate its signal mask with the *sigprocmask()* function. A prototype for this function is:

```
#include <signal.h>
int sigprocmask(int how, sigset_t *set, sigset_t *oset);
```

The set argument points to a signal set that describes the changes to be made to the process's signal mask. If this argument is NULL, then the mask is not changed. The oset argument points to a signal set that is set to the previous value of the process's signal mask. If it is NULL, it is ignored. The how argument describes the nature of the change being requested. It can have one of the following three values:

SIG_BLOCK   The process signal mask becomes the union of the current mask and the set pointed to by set. Thus, set specifies a set of signals to block.

SIG_UNBLOCK   The process signal mask becomes the intersection of the current mask and the complement of the set pointed to by set. Another way to put this is that the mask becomes the set difference of the current mask and the set pointed to by set. Thus, set specifies a set of signals to unblock.

SIG_SETMASK   The mask becomes the set pointed to by set.

If the set argument is NULL, then the how argument is ignored.

A process cannot block SIGKILL or SIGSTOP. If it tries to do so, no error will occur, but these signals will not be added to the signal mask; the request is just ignored. If changing the signal mask causes one or more pending blocked signals to become unblocked, then at least one such signal will be delivered to the process before *sigprocmask()* returns. If several such pending signals are unblocked, then the order in which they are delivered is implementation-dependent. Whether only one such signal, or more than one, is delivered before the return of *sigprocmask()* is also implementation-dependent.

A process can find out whether or not there are blocked signals pending for it with the *sigpending()* function. A prototype for *sigpending()* is:

```
#include <signal.h>
int sigpending(sigset_t *set);
```

After a call to *sigpending()* the signal set pointed to by the set argument contains the blocked pending signals for the caller. Incidentally, this function is an invention of the POSIX.1 committee. The other POSIX.1 signal-handling functions are based on similar functions in 4.2BSD.

5.5.1 Actions for Blocked Signals

Suppose that a signal is blocked and pending for a process, and while it is pending the process calls *sigaction()* to change the action to be taken for it. If the signal is then unblocked and delivered, what action is taken? There are two logical possibilities: the action in force at the time the signal was made pending and the action in force at the time it was delivered. The answer is the second choice; the POSIX.1 standard states that "the determination of which action is taken in response to a signal is made at the time the signal is delivered, allowing for any changes since the time of generation." However, there are two exceptions to this rule.

We have already encountered one exception: if a signal is blocked from delivery and the action for the signal is to be ignored, then the implementation is free to discard the signal or to leave it pending. (The action of the implementation is *unspecified*, so it need not even be documented.) Thus, if you choose to ignore a signal, then block it, then choose to catch it, and then unblock it, and in the interim the signal was generated for my process, on some implementations the signal may be delivered and on others it may not.

The second exception also has to do with ignored signals. Suppose that the action for a signal is something other than SIG_IGN, but the signal is blocked from delivery. Suppose that an instance of a signal is pending, and you change the signal action to be SIG_IGN. Then all pending instances of the signal are immediately discarded.

5.6 Special Considerations for Job Control Signals

On systems that support job control, delivery of signals can cause processes to be stopped and restarted. For readers who have not used job control systems, we give a brief overview of job control facilities from the user's point of view. Recall (from Chapter 2, Section 2.1) that a job is a command pipeline and corresponds to a process group.

If a user is running a job in the foreground on a job control system, he or she can stop the job with an appropriate keystroke sequence. (Control-Z is typical.) A stopped job behaves like a blocked process. It is, in fact, blocked and waiting for an event, which is a request that it be continued. When the job stops the shell continues, allowing the user to type commands. These can include commands to continue the job, either in the foreground or in the background. If a job is running in the background, it can be moved to the foreground. A background job that requires input from the keyboard will stop. Users can control whether background jobs that have output to the screen should stop or should write, mingling their output with that from foreground jobs.

From the point of view of executing processes, job control is implemented as a collection of signals. Typing Control-Z causes the SIGTSTP signal to be sent to the foreground process group. A user command to continue a job simply sends a SIGCONT signal to the job's process group. If a background process tries to read from the controlling terminal, the system generates a SIGTTIN signal for its process group, causing the process to stop. If a background process tries to write to the controlling terminal and a certain flag (TOSTOP; see Chapter 7) is set, the system generates a SIGTTOU signal for the process's group, causing it to stop.

Sometimes processes need to be informed if one of their children has stopped. The shell is a good example. If a shell is waiting for a command to complete but the command stops instead, the shell should continue as if the command had finished. (The shell usually first issues a message indicating that the command has stopped.) How does the shell know? It receives a signal, SIGCHLD.

Most processes do not need to be signaled when a child stops or terminates. If a process wants to wait for a child, it can use the *wait()* or *waitpid()* functions. (These functions are discussed in Chapter 6.) Thus, the default action for SIGCHLD is to be ignored. Sometimes a process would like a SIGCHLD to be delivered to it if a child process terminates, but not if a child stops. It can request this behavior by setting the SA_NOCLDSTOP flag in the sa_flags member of a sigaction structure. Here is an example:

```
#include <signal.h>
struct sigaction s;
void chld_catcher(int sig);
/* ... */
s.sa_handler = chld_catcher;
sigemptyset(&s.sa_mask);
s.sa_flags = SA_NOCLDSTOP;
sigaction(SIGCHLD, &s, NULL);
```

After the execution of this code, termination of a child process will cause generation of a SIGCHLD signal, which will be caught by *chld_catcher()*, but stopping of a child process will not generate a signal. The SA_NOCLDSTOP flag is the only flag defined by POSIX.1 for sa_mask.

The SIGCHLD signal is the only POSIX.1 signal whose default action is to be ignored. Suppose that a SIGCHLD signal, or an implementation-defined signal with the same default action, is pending. This could happen, for example, if the process changed the action for such a signal to be caught and then blocked it. Here is a code fragment that could accomplish this:

```
#include <signal.h>
struct sigaction s;
sigset_t sigmask;
void chld_catcher(int sig)
```

```
{ /* Do nothing */
}

catch_chld()
{
    s.sa_handler = chld_catcher;
    sigemptyset(&s.sa_mask);
    s.sa_flags = 0;
    sigaction(SIGCHLD, &s, NULL);
}

/* ... */
catch_chld();
sigemptyset(&sig_mask);
sigaddset(&sig_mask, SIGCHLD);
sigprocmask(SIG_SETMASK, &sigmask);
/* ... */
```

Now suppose that a SIGCHLD is generated for this process. It will be blocked. Suppose then that the process executes the following code:

```
s.sa_handler = SIG_DFL;
sigaction(SIGCHLD, &s, NULL);
```

In other words, the action for the signal is changed to the default. Then the pending signal will be discarded.

Suppose that a process sets the action for SIGCHLD to be SIG_IGN. Will this have any effect? After all, being ignored is the default for this signal anyway. In fact, doing this will have unspecified consequences. This is due to the special behavior of the System V signal SIGCLD. We discuss this behavior in connection with the *wait()* function, in Chapter 6, Section 6.3.1. But as the behavior is unspecified, a strictly conforming POSIX.1 application should not do this.

5.7   Sending Signals

A process can send a signal to another process or group of processes if it has permission to do so. The POSIX function for sending signals is *kill()*. This function inherits its misleading name from the corresponding UNIX system function, whose behavior is very similar. A prototype for *kill()* is:

```
#include <sys/types.h>
#include <signal.h>
int kill(pid_t pid, int sig);
```

The *kill()* function is so named because, by default, sending most signals to a process causes the process to terminate. The sig argument is the number of the signal being sent. The `pid` argument describes the process or processes for which the signal should be generated, according to the following rules:

- If `pid` is positive, then the `sig` signal is generated for the process whose process ID is `pid`.

- If `pid` is zero, then the `sig` signal is generated for all processes with the same process group ID as the caller and for which the caller has permission to send a signal. An implementation-defined set of system processes is excluded.

- If `pid` is –1, then the behavior of *kill()* is unspecified. This allows systems that have historically used a `pid` of –1 for system administrative reasons to continue to do so.

- If `pid` is negative and is not –1, then the absolute value of `pid` is treated as a process group ID, and `sig` is sent to all processes with that process group ID for which the caller has permission to send a signal.

For example, the call

```
kill(getppid(), SIGUSR1);
```

causes a `SIGUSR1` signal to be generated for the parent process of the caller. Similarly, the call

```
kill(-getpgrp(), SIGKILL);
```

causes a `SIGKILL` signal to be generated for every process in the caller's process group, including the caller.

To use *kill()* to send a signal to a process, either the caller must have appropriate permissions or the caller's real or effective user ID must be equal to the real or effective user ID of the process being sent the signal. On POSIX.1 systems where `_POSIX_SAVED_IDS` is defined, the target process's saved set-user-ID is checked in place of its effective user ID. (Thus, if your process had some effective user ID earlier, *fork()*ed a child, and then called *setuid()* to change its effective user ID, it can still send a signal to the child.) If a signal is being sent to a process group and the sender has permission to send signals to some but not all of the processes in that process group, then the signal is generated for those processes only, and no error is reported.

If the value of `sig` is zero, then *kill()* performs error checking but does not actually send a signal. This is useful for finding out if a process or process group with a given ID exists. If the process or process group specified by `pid` does not exist, then `errno` is set to `ESRCH` and *kill()* returns –1. If the process or process group exists but the caller does not have permission to send the signal to any of the processes, then `errno` is set to `EPERM` and *kill()* returns –1. Implementations are free to impose extended security controls further limiting the sending of signals. This can include denying the existence of processes that actually exist.

Suppose that your process calls *fork()* to create a child and the child process then calls an *exec()* function to overlay itself with a new executable image. If the file containing the new image has the S_ISUID bit set, then the new image may execute with a different effective user ID. Can your process still send the child signals with *kill()*?* Such behavior is permitted, but not required, by the standard. A portable application must assume that this behavior may not be permitted. Thus, when sending signals to one of your child processes with *kill()*, you should be prepared for the possibility of an EPERM error.

5.8   Scheduling and Waiting for Signals

Signals are useful for process synchronization. Sometimes a process wishes to wait until it receives a signal, in order to know that some cooperating process has opened a FIFO, written a file, changed a terminal parameter, or otherwise completed a task for which the current process must wait. UNIX provided the *pause()* function for this purpose, and *pause()* is in POSIX.1 as well. Its prototype is:

```
#include <unistd.h>
int pause(void);
```

The *pause()* function suspends the caller until the caller receives a signal— any signal—that either is caught or terminates the process. If the signal is caught and the signal-catching function returns, then *pause()* returns –1 with errno set to EINTR. If the signal is not caught, the caller is terminated and *pause()* does not return.

A useful extension to *pause()* is provided by the *sigsuspend()* function. This function has the following prototype:

```
#include <signal.h>
int sigsuspend(sigset_t *sigmask);
```

The effect of *sigsuspend()* is to suspend the process until a signal is received, but with a particular signal mask in place. The mask is that pointed to by the sigmask argument. Again, the process is blocked until receipt of either a catchable or a terminating signal. If a process is blocked in *sigsuspend()* and a signal is delivered that is to be caught, and the signal-catching function returns, then *sigsuspend()* returns –1 with errno set to EINTR, and the previous

---

*   It might seem that the child and the parent would still have the same real user ID. However, this is not necessarily true. Perhaps the child's new effective user ID gives it the appropriate privileges to change its real user ID as well, and it has done so.

signal mask is restored. If a signal is delivered whose effect is to terminate the process, then, of course, *sigsuspend()* does not return. The call

```
sigsuspend(&mask);
```

is almost equivalent to the following sequence:

```
sigprocmask(SIG_SETMASK, &mask, &save_mask);
pause();
sigprocmask(SIG_SETMASK, &save_mask, NULL);
```

The difference is that the call to *sigsuspend()* is atomic with respect to the delivery of signals. That is, no signal can be delivered between the time the process signal mask is changed to mask and the time the process pauses to wait for a signal. This difference can be crucial in avoiding race conditions. To see why, consider the following example.

Suppose that your process must synchronize with another one. The way you have arranged the synchronization is that you will *pause()*, and when the other process sends you a SIGUSR1 you'll continue. You set up a signal-handling function to catch SIGUSR1 and do nothing. Because your process and the other one run asynchronously, it's possible that the SIGUSR1 will be delivered before you *pause()*. To prevent this, you first arrange to block this signal:

```
sigset_t mask, save_mask;
sigemptyset(&mask);
sigaddset(&mask, SIGUSR1);
sigprocmask(SIG_BLOCK, &mask);     /* Block SIGUSR1 */
     /* ...code prior to synchronization... */
```

Then, just before the *pause()*, you unblock SIGUSR1:

```
sigprocmask(SIG_SETMASK, NULL, &mask); /* Get current mask */
sigdelset(&mask, SIGUSR1);
sigprocmask(SIG_SETMASK, &mask, &save_mask);
     /* Race condition here!!! */
pause();
sigprocmask(SIG_SETMASK, &save_mask, NULL); /* Restore mask */
```

Unfortunately, if SIGUSR1 is delivered just before the *pause()*, your process will lose the signal, and perhaps *pause()* forever. It is precisely this problem that *sigsuspend()* is designed to prevent. You simply replace the above code with:

```
sigprocmask(SIG_SETMASK, NULL, &mask); /* Get current mask */
sigdelset(&mask, SIGUSR1);
sigsuspend(&mask);
```

Now a SIGUSR1 can only be delivered while the process is waiting. If the signal has been generated before the *sigsuspend()* call and is pending, it will be delivered immediately.

A process can arrange for generation of a SIGALRM signal to itself after a specified number of seconds with the *alarm()* function. The prototype for *alarm()* is:

```
#include <unistd.h>
unsigned int alarm(unsigned int seconds);
```

The POSIX.1 version of *alarm()* is identical to its UNIX system counterpart. In particular, the return value of *alarm()* is the number of seconds left on any previously scheduled alarm, and an argument of 0 seconds has the effect of cancelling any outstanding alarms. Only one alarm is remembered for each process, so you cannot stack alarms. Also, there is no guarantee that the alarm will actually go off after the scheduled interval. A heavy load on the processor, for example, could delay it.

You can use *alarm()* to prevent any function that can block, such as *read()* or *fcntl()*, from indefinitely suspending execution of your program. The following fragment shows how you can use *alarm()* to wait for an input character, but not indefinitely:

```
#define    DELAY 30        /* Wait for 30 seconds */
volatile  int rang = 0; /* incremented if the alarm goes off */
struct sigaction s;
int ch;

void alarm_catcher(int sig)
{
    if ( sig == SIGALRM )
        rang++;
}
/* ... */
s.sa_handler = alarm_catcher;
sigemptyset(&s.sa_mask);
s.sa_flags = 0;
sigaction(SIGALRM, &s, NULL);
alarm(DELAY);
ch = getchar();
alarm(0);  /* Cancel alarm if input character arrived. */
if (rang)
{
    /* Alarm went off ... */
}
else
{
    /* Process input character ... */
}
```

If you want to *pause()*, but not indefinitely, you should use *sleep()*. The *sleep()* function suspends its caller for a specified interval, or until a signal is delivered. A prototype for *sleep()* is:

```
#include <unistd.h>
unsigned int sleep(unsigned int seconds);
```

The `seconds` argument specifies the amount of time the process should be suspended. Historically, some versions of the UNIX system have implemented *alarm()* in terms of *sleep()* or vice versa. This leads to some undesirable interactions between these two functions. To preserve compatibility with such systems, POSIX specifies the following restrictions:

- If a process is blocked in *sleep()*, a `SIGALRM` is generated for the process, and the process has arranged to block or ignore `SIGALRM`, it is unspecified whether the signal causes *sleep()* to return.

- If a process is blocked in *sleep()*, a `SIGALRM` is generated for the process for some reason other than a prior call to *alarm()* (for instance, from a call to *kill()* by another process), and the `SIGALRM` signal is not being blocked or ignored by the sleeping process, then the signal causes the *sleep()* to return. However, it is unspecified whether the signal has any other effect. In particular, if the process is catching `SIGALRM`, it is unspecified whether a signal-handling function is executed or whether the `SIGALRM`, if uncaught, terminates the process.

- If a process is blocked in *sleep()*, the sleep is interrupted by a caught signal, and the signal-catching function for that signal calls *alarm()*, changes the action associated with `SIGALRM`, adds `SIGALRM` to the process signal mask, or removes `SIGALRM` from the mask, the results are unspecified.

For these reasons, it is a good idea for portable application programs to avoid any possible interactions between *alarm()* and *sleep()*. If possible, do not use both in the same program.

Note that, because the arguments to *alarm()* and *sleep()* are of type `unsigned int`, the longest amount of time for which a portable program can sleep or schedule an alarm is 65,535 seconds. (The ANSI C standard requires that `UINT_MAX` be at least 65,535.) This is a bit more than 18 hours. The *sleep()* function returns the amount of unslept time left. This will be zero unless it was interrupted by a caught signal.

5.9   Signals and Reentrancy

If a signal is delivered to your process while one of your functions is executing, you know what will happen: either you haven't arranged anything for the signal (in which case the default action occurs), you've arranged to ignore the signal (in which case nothing occurs), or you've arranged to catch the signal (in which case the current function is interrupted, the signal handler runs, and then the current function resumes). But what happens if the signal arrives while some system interface is executing?

We have already seen the answer in many cases, and it's the same for just about every POSIX.1 function: if the function is one that can be interrupted by a signal, then it returns an error value (either –1 or NULL) and sets errno to EINTR. We've also seen two exceptions to this rule: *read()* and *write()* are permitted (but not required) to have alternate behavior if they have transferred some portion of the data.

Suppose you want to use some POSIX.1 interface inside a signal-handling function. For example, to clean up temporary files before *exit()*, you might want to call *unlink()*. But what if you were in the middle of an *unlink()* call when the signal was delivered? Can one instance of *unlink()* be interrupted by a function that invokes another instance of *unlink()*?

A function is said to be *reentrant with respect to signals* if it can be invoked without restriction from a signal-catching function. (In general, a function is said to be reentrant if more than one instance of it can safely be active at once. Such a function must avoid altering static or global variables.) The POSIX.1 standard specifies a list of POSIX interfaces that are reentrant, or "safe", with respect to signals. This list is reproduced in Appendix E. Any POSIX.1 function not on this list should not be invoked in a signal-handling function.

You should also be concerned with the reentrancy of your own signal-handling functions. There are a number of ways in which a signal-handling function could be interrupted by a signal that then invokes the same function. Here is one example:

```
struct sigaction s;

void handler(int sig)
{
    if ( sig == SIGUSR1 )
        kill(getpid(), SIGUSR2);
}
/* ... */
s.sa_handler = handler;
s.sa_flags = 0;
sigemptyset(&s.sa_mask);
sigaction(SIGUSR1, &sa, (struct sigaction *)NULL);
sigaction(SIGUSR2, &sa, (struct sigaction *)NULL);
```

What happens if a SIGUSR1 is delivered to this process? It will be caught by *handler()*, which will immediately generate a SIGUSR2 for the same process. This will be caught by *handler()* as well—before the first instance of *handler()* has exited. In this case, the signal-handling function is reentrant. But suppose this is the signal catcher:

```
void handler(int sig)
{
    static char buffer[80];
    char *p;

    if ( sig == SIGUSR1 || sig == SIGUSR2 )
    {
        strcpy(buffer, "Terminal:");
        strcat(buffer, ttyname(0));
        strcat(buffer, "\nUser:");
        strcat(buffer, getlogin());
        strcat(buffer, "\nSignal:");
        strcat(buffer, (sig == SIGUSR1)? "USR1": "USR2");
    }
    printf("%s\n", buffer);
}
```

This function prints the terminal, user name, and signal when a SIGUSR1 or SIGUSR2 is delivered. But it uses a static buffer, which makes it non-reentrant. Moreover, *strcat()* and *strcpy()* are not safe with respect to signals. If a SIGUSR1 is caught by *handler()* and while it is executing a SIGUSR2 is delivered, the buffer will be printed twice. The second time (which will be for the SIGUSR1) the buffer will still contain the contents of the SIGUSR2 message. (Trace what happens if, for example, the SIGUSR2 is delivered just after the first *strcat()* call.)

Another way that a signal handler can be reentered is if it unblocks the signal that it caught. In this case, another signal of the same type can cause the handler to be invoked. Here is how this could happen:

```
void handler(int signo)
{
    sigset_t mask;
    sigemptyset(&mask);
    sigaddset(signo, &mask);
    sigprocmask(SIG_UNBLOCK, &mask, (sigset_t *)NULL);
    /* ...signo can now be delivered again... */
}
```

A POSIX-portable program might need to do this to emulate the behavior of the obsolescent *signal()* function (but without the race condition).

5.10 Signals and Non-Local Gotos

The C standard provides two functions, *setjmp()* and *longjmp()*, which programs can use to perform non-local gotos. (A goto is *non-local* if it branches

outside of its function. This is not possible with the C goto statement.) They
have these prototypes:

```
#include <setjmp.h>
int setjmp(jmp_buf env);
void longjmp(jmp_buf env, int val);
```

The call

```
setjmp(env);
```

saves a portion of the process environment in env, an object of type jmp_buf.
This type is defined in <setjmp.h>, a header required by the C standard.
The call

```
longjmp(env,val);
```

resumes execution from the point of the corresponding *setjmp()*. (In this case,
corresponding means the call to *setjmp()* that stored an environment in the buf
variable passed to *longjmp()*.) The function from which *setjmp()* was called must
not have returned before the corresponding *longjmp()* is called. Values of
global variables are as they were at the time of the call to *longjmp()*. Values of
local variables that are still in scope and have changed between the call to
setjmp() and *longjmp()* are indeterminate. The idea is that *setjmp()* saves information in the env argument, which keeps enough status for the program
to resume execution at the point where the contents of the jmp_buf were
saved. This presumably includes the value of important hardware registers
such as a stack pointer or a frame pointer.

A call to *setjmp()* always returns zero. A call to *longjmp()* does not appear to return. Instead, the program continues as if the call to the corresponding *setjmp()* had just returned, but with a nonzero value. The value is
the val argument to *longjmp()*, except that if that value is zero it is treated as
if it were 1. Note that the use of *setjmp()* and *longjmp()* is comparable to the
use of gotos. Using these interfaces excessively can make your programs
difficult to understand, debug, and modify.

A common use of *setjmp()* and *longjmp()* is to jump out of a signal handler to a known state. Note that *longjmp()* is not on the list of functions required by POSIX.1 to be reentrant with respect to signals. However, the *X/Open
Portability Guide* does make this requirement, and in fact calling *longjmp()*
from a signal handler is a common practice. Here is a fragment of code that
does that:

```
jmp_buf buf;

main(void)
{
    struct sigaction sa;
    extern void catcher(int);
```

```
    sa.sa_handler = catcher;
    sa.sa_flags = 0;
    sigemptyset(&sa.sa_mask);
    sigaction(SOME_SIGNAL, &sa, (struct sigaction *)NULL);
    if ( setjmp(buf) != 0 )
    {   /* Really returned from longjmp() */
        cleanup_for_restart();
    }
    /* whatever... */
}
void catcher(int sig)
{
    if ( sig == SOME_SIGNAL )
        longjmp(buf, 1);
    /* whatever... */
}
```

The idea in this code is that if SOME_SIGNAL is caught, the program should restart, after doing appropriate cleanup. (The appropriate cleanup may be quite extensive, as the signal can be delivered in the middle of almost any function. If you use this technique, you should restore the state of files, streams, and I/O buffers as well as variables.) To restart, the program does a *longjmp()* back to *main()*. However, this example illustrates a problem. When the process starts, it has a signal mask, which is inherited from its parent. Typically, this signal mask is empty. When the process is in its signal handler, it has another signal mask that at least includes the caught signal. If it leaves its signal handler via *longjmp()*, what is the process signal mask after the *longjmp()*?

The C standard does not address this issue. It isn't an issue in ANSI C, because the notion of a signal mask does not exist in that context. Because a POSIX program must be able to control its signal mask, the POSIX.1 standard provides two more non-local goto functions, *sigsetjmp()* and *siglongjmp()*. Their prototypes are:

```
#include <setjmp.h>
int sigsetjmp(sigjmp_buf env, int savemask);
int siglongjmp(sigjmp_buf env, int val);
```

The type sigjmp_buf is defined in <setjmp.h>. The semantics of these functions are as follows:

- In a call to *sigsetjmp()*, the signal mask is saved if the value of the savemask argument is nonzero and is not saved if savemask is zero.

- A call to *sigsetjmp()* always returns zero.

- A call to *siglongjmp()* restores the signal mask if and only if its env buffer was set in a call to *sigsetjmp()* that saved the mask.

- A call to *siglongjmp()* does not appear to return. Instead, execution resumes at the corresponding *sigsetjmp()*, which appears to have returned val. However, if *siglongjmp()* is called with a val argument of zero, this value is ignored and the apparent return value from *sigsetjmp()* is 1.

Here is the previous fragment, rewritten to use *sigsetjmp()* and *siglongjmp()*:

```
sigjmp_buf env;
#define  SAVE_MASK     1
#define  NOSAVE_MASK   0

main(void)
{
    struct sigaction sa;
    extern void catcher();

    sa.sa_handler = catcher;
    sa.sa_flags = 0;
    sigemptyset(&sa.sa_mask);
    sigaction(SOME_SIGNAL, &sa, (struct sigaction *)NULL);
    if ( sigsetjmp(env, SAVE_MASK) != 0 )
    {
        cleanup_for_restart();
    }
    /* whatever... */
}

void catcher(int sig)
{
    if ( sig == SOME_SIGNAL )
        siglongjmp(env, 1);
    /* whatever... */
}
```

This fragment has more reliable behavior. Each time the process catches SOME_SIGNAL, it restores its signal mask to the value in effect at the time the original *sigsetjmp()* call was made.

Exercises for Chapter 5

1. What is the output of the following program? Explain.

```
#define _POSIX_SOURCE
#include <sys/types.h>
#include <sys/wait.h>
#include <signal.h>
sigset_t mask;
pid_t child1,            /* Proc ID of first child */
```

```
        child2,            /* Proc ID of second child */
    int stat1,             /* Exit/signal status of child 1 */
        stat2,             /* Exit/signal status of child 2 */
    struct sigaction s;    /* For catching signals */

    void catcher()         /* Does nothing */
    {
    }

    main()
    {
        if ( (child1 = fork()) == 0 )
        {
            /* first child process */
            pause();
            exit(3);
        }
        sigemptyset(&mask);
        s.sa_handler = catcher;
        s.sa_mask = mask;
        sigaction(SIGUSR1, &s, NULL);
        if ( (child2 = fork()) == 0 )
        {
            /* second child process */
            pause();
            exit(5);
        }
        /* parent process code */
        sleep(1); /* see Exercise 2 */
        kill(child1, SIGUSR1);
        kill(child2, SIGUSR1);
        waitpid(child1, &stat1, 0);
        waitpid(child2, &stat2, 0);
        if (WIFEXITED(stat1))
            printf("Child1 exited with status %d\n",
                WEXITSTATUS(stat1));
        else if (WIFSIGNALED(stat1))
            printf("Child1 terminated by signal %d\n",
                WTERMSIG(stat1));
        if (WIFEXITED(stat2))
            printf("Child2 exited with status %d\n",
                WEXITSTATUS(stat1));
        else if (WIFSIGNALED(stat2))
            printf("Child2 terminated by signal %d\n",
                WTERMSIG(stat2));
    }
```

2. There is a race condition in Exercise 1: if the parent process sends the SIGUSR1 to child2 before child2 does the *pause()*, the child will *pause()*

SIGNALS

131

"forever". (Why?) Get rid of the race condition. (Hint: block the delivery of SIGUSR1, but not while waiting for a signal.)

3. The following program is not written in a portable POSIX way. Rewrite it as a strictly conforming POSIX application. What is its output? Will it always be the same?

```
#include <signal.h>
int pid1,
    pid2,
    pid,
    status;

void catcher()
{
}

main()
{
    char    *which_kid;
    int n;

    signal(SIGALRM, catcher);
    if ( (pid1 = fork()) == 0 )
    {
        signal(SIGALRM, SIG_DFL);
        alarm(5);
        pause();
        exit(2);
    }
    if ( (pid2 = fork()) == 0 )
    {
        alarm(2);
        pause();
        exit(4);
    }
    for(n = 0; n < 2; n++)
    {
        pid = wait(&status);
        which_kid = (pid == pid1) ? "Child1" : ((pid == pid2)
            ? "Child2" : "unknown child");
        if (status & 0377)
            printf("%s terminated by signal %d/n",
                            which_kid, status & 077);
        else
            printf("%s exited with status %d/n",
                            which_kid, (status >>8) & 0377);
    }
}
```

4. What is the output of the following program? Is it determinate? Explain.

```
#define _POSIX_SOURCE
#include <signal.h>
#include <sys/types.h>

struct sigaction s;
sigset_t mask;
pid_t pid;

void catcher(int signo)
{
    sigset_t mask;
    printf("Caught signal %d\n", signo);
    if (signo == SIGTERM)
    {
        sigemptyset(&mask);
        sigaddset(&mask, SIGUSR2);
        sigprocmask(SIG_UNBLOCK, &mask, NULL);
    }
}

main()
{
    if ( (pid = fork()) == 0 )
    {
    /* child process */
    sigfillset(&mask);
    sigprocmask(SIG_SETMASK, &mask, NULL);
    s.sa_handler = catcher;
    s.sa_mask = mask;
    sigaction(SIGTERM, &s, NULL);
    sigdelset(&mask, SIGUSR1);
    s.sa_mask = mask;
    sigaction(SIGUSR1, &s, NULL);
    sigaction(SIGUSR2, &s, NULL);
    sigfillset(&mask);
    sigdelset(&mask, SIGTERM);
    sigsuspend(&mask);
    _exit(0);
    }
    sleep(3);          /* Ignore race condition; assume child */
                       /* is suspended when we awaken */
    kill(pid, SIGUSR1);
    kill(pid, SIGUSR2);
    kill(pid, SIGTERM);
}
```

5. What happens when this code fragment is executed?

```
sigemptyset(&s.sa_mask);
s.sa_handler = SIG_IGN;
sigaction(SIGUSR1, &s, NULL);
kill(getpid(), SIGUSR1);
s.sa_handler = SIG_DFL;
sigaction(SIGUSR1, &s, NULL);
```

6. What happens when this code fragment is executed?

```
sigfillset(&mask);
sigprocmask(SIG_SETMASK, &mask, NULL);
kill(getpid(), SIGUSR1);
s.sa_handler = SIG_IGN;
sigemptyset(&s.sa_mask);
sigaction(SIGUSR1, &s, NULL);
s.sa_handler = SIG_DFL;
sigaction(SIGUSR1, &s, NULL);
sigprocmask(SIG_UNBLOCK, &mask, NULL);
```

7. Move the *kill()* call in Exercise 6 down below the first call to *sigaction()*. What happens now?

8. Suppose an implementation supports job control. What will this program print? Can you say anything about the value printed in the last line?

```
#define _POSIX_SOURCE
#include <signal.h>
#include <sys/types.h>

struct sigaction s;
pid_t pid;
int status,
    stopped;
unsigned x;

void STOP_catch()
{
    printf("Caught a SIGCHLD.\n");
}
void cont_catch()
{
    /* stopped */
    printf("Caught a SIGCONT.\n");
}

main()
{
```

```
    s.sa_handler = STOP_catch;
    sigemptyset(&s.sa_mask);
    s.sa_flags = 0;
    sigaction(SIGCHLD, &s, NULL);
    if ( (pid = fork()) == 0 )
    {
        s.sa_handler = cont_catch;
        sigaction(SIGCONT, &s, NULL);
        stopped = 0;
        x = 0;
        while (!stopped)
            x++;
        exit(x);
    }
    sleep(1);
    kill(pid, SIGSTOP);
    printf("About to continue\n");
    kill(pid, SIGCONT);
    while (wait(&status) != pid)
        ;
    printf("Exit status is %u\n", WEXITSTATUS(status));
}
```

9. Consider the following code:

```
struct sigaction OS;

waste_one(int signo)
{
    extern void restore();
    struct sigaction S;

    s.sa_handler = restore();
    sigfillset(&s.sa_mask);

    sigaction(signo, &S, &OS);
}

void restore(int signo)
{
    sigaction(signo, &OS, NULL);
}
```

Suppose a process calls waste_one(SIGUSR1) and then SIGUSR1 is delivered. What happens? What if SIGUSR1 is delivered twice? Suppose a process calls:

```
waste_one(SIGUSR1); waste_one(SIGUSR2);
```

and then the signals SIGUSR1, SIGUSR2, SIGUSR1, SIGUSR2 are delivered in that order. What happens?

Process Creation and Synchronization

Sometimes it is necessary for an application to use several cooperating processes executing concurrently. POSIX provides the facilities for a process to create other processes, to execute programs, to wait until they have finished, and to determine their exit status. For the most part, these facilities are nearly identical to their UNIX system counterparts. However, there are some important POSIX.1 innovations as well.

6.1 Process Creation

The only way for a POSIX.1 process to create another process is through the use of the *fork()* function. A prototype for *fork()* is:

```
#include <sys/types.h>
#include <unistd.h>
pid_t fork(void);
```

This differs from the UNIX system *fork()*, in which the return type is int. There are a few other differences, all minor and involving the difference between the attributes of a UNIX system process and the attributes of a POSIX.1 process. Nevertheless, we discuss *fork()* rather thoroughly, both because it may be unfamiliar to many programmers and because it is closely connected to the *waitpid()* function, which is new in POSIX.1.

When a process calls *fork()*, before the call returns an almost exact duplicate of the calling process is created. Then *fork()* returns in both processes. The order in which this occurs is unspecified: the original caller of *fork()*—the parent process—may return first, or the newly created process—the child process—may return first, or (on a system with more than one processor)

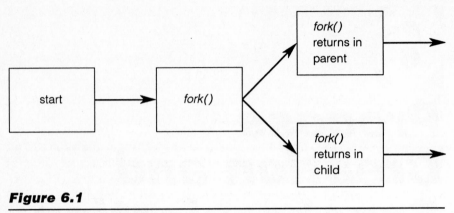

Figure 6.1

Flow of Control after *fork()*

they may return simultaneously. Each process continues executing from the return of *fork()*. Figure 6.1 illustrates the flow of control after *fork()*.

The return value of *fork()* allows you to know which process you have returned to. In the parent process the return value is the process ID of the child process; this is guaranteed never to be zero. In the child process the return value is zero. If *fork()* encounters an error, such as not having enough memory or enough process table slots, it returns –1 and does not create a child process. Here is an example of the use of *fork()*:

```
pid_t   child_pid;        /* Return value from fork() */
/* ... */
if ( (child_pid = fork()) == -1 )
{
    fprintf(stderr, "Cannot fork(); errno = %d\n", errno);
    exit(1);
}
else if ( child_pid == 0 )
{   /* Code for child process goes here */
    printf("Child: PID = %d, child_pid = %d\n", (int) getpid(),
        (int) child_pid);
    /* ... */
}
else
{   /* Code for parent process goes here */
    printf("Parent: PID = %d, child_pid = %d\n", (int) getpid(),
        (int) child_pid);
    /* ... */
}
```

If this fragment of code is executed, the two `printf` lines produce output something like:

```
Parent:  PID = 2183, child_pid = 2186
Child:   PID = 2186, child_pid = 0
```

The order in which these lines appear is indeterminate; in fact, they might be intermingled.

Just after a *fork()*, the contents of the address spaces of the parent and child processes—that is, their executable instructions and the values of all their variables—are identical, except for the memory cells that hold the *fork()* return value. However, the values of some system attributes of these processes will differ. Figure 6.2 summarizes the changes that occur for a POSIX.1 child process's system attributes after a *fork()*. (The figure also gives the behavior of process attributes after execution of one of the *exec()* family of functions, which we discuss in Section 6.2.) This list differs from the corresponding list for UNIX systems in that not all of the attributes listed here are defined in all UNIX systems. Conversely, many UNIX systems define additional process attributes about which POSIX.1 says nothing.

As Figure 6.2 indicates, the time on the child process's alarm clock is cleared to zero. Thus, a `SIGALRM` scheduled to be generated for the parent will not be generated for the child. Similarly, because the child process's pending signal set is empty, any signals that are already pending for the parent will not be pending for the child. The process times of the child process (as returned by *times()*; see Chapter 2, Section 2.5) are all set to zero.

If the parent process has any open file descriptors, the child gets duplicates of these file descriptors. The parent and child descriptors share a common open file description. Therefore, they share a file offset. Look at the program shown in Figure 6.3. This program creates a file open for both reading and writing, writes the string `abcdef` to it, resets the file offset to the start of the file, and then forks. The parent and child each read 3 bytes from the open file. What do they read? One of them will read `abc` and one will read `def`. It is indeterminate which will read what; however, as the file descriptors of parent and child share a file offset, a *read()* by one advances the file offset of the other.

The presence of the *wait()* call guarantees that the child will write its output first. (If you are unfamiliar with *wait()*, see Section 6.3, below.) Therefore, the output of this program will be either

```
Child: abc
Parent: def
```

or

```
Child: def
Parent: abc
```

Process Attribute	Under *fork()*	Under *exec()*
Process ID	Changed	Unchanged
Process group ID	Unchanged	Unchanged
Parent process ID	Changed	Unchanged
Session membership	Unchanged	Unchanged
Real UID	Unchanged	Unchanged
Effective UID	Unchanged	May change
Real GID	Unchanged	Unchanged
Effective GID	Unchanged	May change
Saved set-user-ID	Unchanged	May change
Saved set-group-ID	Unchanged	May change
Supplementary group IDs	Unchanged	Unchanged
Time left on alarm clock	Cleared to zero	Unchanged
Process signal mask	Unchanged	Unchanged
Pending signals	Cleared to empty	Unchanged
Signal actions	Unchanged	Caught reset to SIG_DFL
Process times	Cleared to zero	Unchanged
Open file descriptors	Duplicated	Closed if FD_CLOEXEC set
Open directory streams	Duplicated or copied	Unchanged
File locks	Not inherited	Unchanged if file still open
Current working directory	Unchanged	Unchanged
Root directory	Unchanged	Unchanged
File mode creation mask	Unchanged	Unchanged
Login user name	Unchanged	Unchanged
Controlling terminal	Unchanged	Unchanged

Figure 6.2

Effects of *fork()* and *exec()* on POSIX.1 Process Attributes

```
#define _POSIX_SOURCE
#include <unistd.h>
#include <sys/types.h>
#include <sys/stat.h>
#include <fcntl.h>

char string[] = "abcdef";

main()
{
    pid_t pid;
    int fd;
    char    *filename = "tempfile";
    char    buf[3];
    int status;

    if ( (fd = fopen(filename, O_RDWR | O_CREAT, S_IRWXU)) < 0 )
        exit(1);
    if ( write(fd, string, strlen(string)) < strlen(string) )
        exit(1);
    (void) lseek(fd, (off_t) 0, SEEK_SET);
    if ( (pid = fork()) < 0 )
        exit(1);
    else if ( pid == 0 )
    {   /* CHILD PROCESS CODE */
        read(fd, buf, 3);
        printf("Child: %3.3s\n", buf);
        exit(0);
    }
    else
    {   /* PARENT PROCESS CODE */
        read(fd, buf, 3);
        (void) wait(&status);
        printf("Parent: %3.3s\n", buf);
        exit(0);
    }
}
```

Figure 6.3

Example of Duplicated File Descriptors

If the call to *wait()* in the parent is omitted, then not only is the output indeterminate, but also the order in which the output occurs is indeterminate as well. Even intermingled output, like:

```
ChiParent: abc
ld: def
```

is possible.

Now, suppose we change the program slightly. Figure 6.4 shows a modified version. In this program, the file is created and closed, and the parent and child then each reopen it for reading. Thus, each file descriptor is associated with its own open file description and, consequently, with its own file offset. The output of this program is determinate (assuming no error occurs in the *fork()*). It will be:

```
Child: abc
Parent: abc
```

The behavior of open directory streams after a *fork()* may be similar to that of files, or it may differ. The POSIX.1 standard allows, but does not require, both processes to share stream positioning. Because a portable program cannot rely on this behavior, you should either open directory streams after a *fork()* or only have one process use the stream after the *fork()*.

6.1.1 Handling *fork()* Failure

It is possible for *fork()* to fail for transient reasons. You may wish to write your programs in such a way that they can recover from such failures and retry the *fork()* a number of times. Unfortunately, it is not easy to determine what the cause of a *fork()* failure is. The POSIX.1 standard specifies a number of possible causes. One is that the system lacks the necessary resources to create another process (e.g., the system process table is full or there is not enough memory to create another process). In this case errno is set to EAGAIN. Another cause is that creating the process would cause the system to exceed the limit CHILD_MAX on the number of processes owned by a single user ID. Unfortunately, POSIX specifies that errno be set to EAGAIN for this error as well. Finally, if the system detects that creating the process "requires more space than the system is able to supply"[3] it sets errno to ENOMEM. In practice, not all UNIX systems can give this error, and when the error does occur it indicates a lack of disk swapping or paging space, not a shortage of virtual memory.

In general, EAGAIN is intended to indicate a transient error, for which it makes sense to try again, perhaps after waiting a suitable amount of time. If a *fork()* fails because of a lack of system resources, you may want to retry it a number of times before giving up, as the termination of other processes could free those resources. On the other hand, if *fork()* fails because your user

```
#define _POSIX_SOURCE
#include <unistd.h>
#include <sys/types.h>
#include <sys/stat.h>
#include <fcntl.h>

char string[] = "abcdef";

main(void)
{
    pid_t pid;
    int   fd;
    char *filename = "tempfile";
    char buf[3];
    int   status;

    if ( (fd = fopen(filename, O_WRONLY | O_CREAT, S_IRWXU)) < 0 )
        exit(1);
    if ( write(fd, string, strlen(string)) < strlen(string) )
        exit(1);
    close(fd);
    if ( (pid = fork()) < 0 )
        exit(1);
    else if ( pid == 0 )
    {   /* CHILD PROCESS CODE */
        if ( (fd = fopen(filename, O_RDONLY)) < 0 )
            exit(1);
        read(fd, buf, 3);
        printf("Child: %3.3s\n", buf);
        exit(0);
    }
    else
    {   /* PARENT PROCESS CODE */
        if ( (fd = fopen(filename, O_RDONLY)) < 0 )
            exit(1);
        read(fd, buf, 3);
        wait(&status);
        printf("Parent: %3.3s\n", buf);
        exit(0);
    }
}
```

Figure 6.4

Processes with Unshared File Descriptors

ID has too many processes, waiting and retrying the *fork()* may fail indefinitely. Because the same value of errno is used for both of these circumstances, you can't easily distinguish them.

One possible strategy is to specify a number of retries, sleeping between each one. Figure 6.5 shows two possible implementations of the routine *refork()*, which takes as an argument a retry count and tries to *fork()* that many times. The first version sleeps 1 second between tries. The second version sleeps an increasing number of seconds between retries. The amount slept grows exponentially. This strategy is known as *exponential back-off*. In the example, we use sleeping intervals from the Fibonacci series

$$1, 1, 2, 3, 5, 8, 13, 21, \ldots$$

in which each term is the sum of the two preceding terms. The terms of this series grow exponentially, but more slowly than powers of two.

If you want to replace system behavior with a preferred behavior of your own, writing routines like *refork()* is a common technique. You can build

```
#define _POSIX_SOURCE
#include <unistd.h>
#include <sys/types.h>
extern int errno;

/*********************** Version 1 *************************
**
**   Sleeps 1 second between retries
*/
pid_t refork(int retries)
{
    pid_t pid;

    do {
        errno = 0;
        if ( (pid = fork()) >= 0 )
            return(pid);
        (void) sleep(1);
        retries--;
    } while ( errno == EAGAIN && retries > 0 );
    return (-1);
}
```

Figure 6.5 *(continued on facing page)*

Two Ways to Retry Failed *fork()*s

up a private library of such routines. However, you have to use them carefully. Note, for example, that a call to *refork()* could return –1 with `errno` set to `EINTR` if a signal is caught during one of the calls to *sleep()*. The POSIX.1 standard does not specify `EINTR` as a possible error value from *fork()*. Thus, you should not check for an error return from *refork()* the same way that you would check for an error from *fork()*.

6.2 Program Execution

The most common use of *fork()* is to create another process that will run a program different from the parent. To do this, the child process has to overlay its code and data with that of another program. The *exec()* family of

```
/*********************** Version 2 ************************
**
** Sleeps delay seconds between retries, where delay is
** calculated according to the Fibonacci series and takes
** on the values 1, 2, 3, 5, 8, 13, ...
*/
pid_t refork(int retries)
{
    pid_t pid;
    int delay_0, delay_1, delay;

    delay_0 = 0;
    delay_1 = 1;
    do {
        errno = 0;
        if ( (pid = fork()) >= 0 )
            return(pid);
        delay = delay_0 + delay_1;
        delay_0 = delay_1;
        delay_1 = delay;
        (void) sleep(delay);
        retries--;
    } while ( errno == EAGAIN && retries > 0 );
    return (-1);
}
```

Figure 6.5 *(continued from facing page)*

Two Ways to Retry Failed *fork()*s

functions does this. POSIX.1 supports the same six versions of *exec()* that UNIX systems do: *execl()*, *execv()*, *execle()*, *execve()*, *execlp()*, and *execvp()*. Their prototypes are:

```
#include <unistd.h>
int execl(char *path, char *arg0, ...);
int execle(char *path, char *arg0, ...);
    /* last arg is char **envp */
int execlp(char *file, char *arg0, ...);
int execv(char *path, char **argv);
int execve(char *path, char **argv, char **envp);
int execvp(char *file, char **argv);
```

In this case, the prototype format does not provide all the information we would like. For *execl()* and *execlp()*, the last argument must be (char *)0, to indicate the end of the argument list. For *execle()* the second-to-last argument must be (char *)0.

The semantics of these functions are largely unchanged from the UNIX system. A successful *exec()* creates a new process image, but not a new process. This is an important fact: the program changes, but the process ID remains the same. The path argument in *execl()*, *execle()*, *execv()*, and *execve()* names the pathname of the *process image file*—the file in which the new process image can be found. The file argument in *execlp()* and *execvp()* gives a filename that is concatenated with a prefix taken from the PATH environment variable to find the new process image file. You should be aware of the following semantic differences from UNIX systems:

- Although you can pass a process environment to the new process image with *execle()* and *execve()* using the envp argument, you cannot portably use an envp argument in *main()* to read the environment. You must access the environment through the *getenv()* function (which is the preferred method) or through the external variable char **environ. In conformance with the C standard, *main()* must be invoked with either zero or two arguments, as

      int main(void)

  or as

      int main(int argc, char **argv)

- Some UNIX implementations of the *exec()* functions use the following convention: if *execl()*, *execv()*, *execle()*, or *execve()* is invoked with a path variable naming a file that is not an executable image, it fails with errno set to ENOEXEC. If, however, *execlp()* or *execvp()* is invoked with a file variable naming such a file, the file is assumed to be a shell script, and the program /bin/sh is *exec()*ed instead, with file as its argument. This is not a portable POSIX.1 construct. The POSIX.1 standard permits, but does not require, such an implementation, and a portable program cannot rely on it. In fact, the POSIX.1 standard doesn't recognize the existence of the shell or of any command line utilities. It is strictly an operating system interface. A system can conform to POSIX.1 without providing /bin/sh or anything like it.*

- The constant ARG_MAX describes the amount of space available for the process's argument list and environment variables together. If the form of *exec()* being called is not *execle()* or *execve()*, then the environment of the new process image is inherited from the caller through the environ variable. Whether null bytes, null pointers, or alignment bytes are counted in the total amount of space used is implementation-defined. This makes it virtually impossible for a portable program to use ARG_MAX. However, as the minimum value of ARG_MAX is 4,096, it is rare that a program will approach the limit. If you need to worry about the limit, assume that null bytes and null pointers are counted, and count on at least 4-byte alignment for each pointer.

Refer briefly to Figure 6.2 for a list of the process attributes that change when a successful *exec()* occurs. If the S_ISUID bit in the mode of the process image file is set, the effective user ID of the process becomes the owner ID of the file. Similarly, if the file's S_ISGID bit is set, the effective group ID of the process becomes the group ID of the file. If the POSIX implementation supports saved set-user- and set-group-IDs, then after an *exec()* the new effective user and group IDs are saved as the process's saved set-user- and set-group-IDs, respectively.

If the caller of *exec()* was ignoring a signal (i.e., if it had set the action for that signal to SIG_IGN), then the signal remains ignored in the new process image. If the action for a signal was the default, it remains the default in the new process image. However, if the signal was being caught, it is reset to the default action in the new process image. After all, if the old program had requested that signal SIGINT be caught by function *foo()*, that can hardly be honored in a program that doesn't have a function *foo()*.

In general, an open file descriptor in a process that calls *exec()* remains open in the new process image. (This is how UNIX system commands inherit the standard input, output, and error files from the shell.) However, a program can arrange for a file descriptor to be closed upon successful completion of an *exec()*. You can do this with *fcntl()*. The call

```
fcntl(fd, F_SETFD, FD_CLOEXEC);
```

sets the file descriptor's FD_CLOEXEC flag. File descriptors with this flag set are closed in the new process image file. As we noted in Chapter 3, the

---

* A different POSIX committee, the IEEE 1003.2 committee, is developing a standard for the shell and utilities. However, the 1003.1 and 1003.2 standards are, in principle, independent of one another.

`FD_CLOEXEC` flag is associated with a file descriptor, not with the underlying file description. Thus, the sequence

```
fd2 = dup(fd1);
fcntl(fd1, F_SETFD, FD_CLOEXEC);
```

creates two file descriptors associated with the same open file description, but only one of them—`fd2`—remains open across an *exec()*.

On most UNIX systems there's a simpler way to invoke another program: the *system()* function. If, for example, your program needs to run a program named `prog2` and save its output in a file named `stdout`, you can write:

```
system("prog2 > stdout");
```

The *system()* function is not part of the POSIX.1 standard, for the reason given earlier: it relies on a program, the shell, that may not be present. In fact, *system()* on UNIX systems works by calling one of the *exec()* functions with `/bin/sh` as its first argument. The standard that specifies the behavior of the shell and associated utilities is POSIX.2, which at this writing is still in draft form. POSIX.2 also specifies a number of C functions, among them *system()*. If we assume that the program `/bin/sh` is present, then we can use *fork()* and *exec()* to implement *system()*. Figure 6.6 shows one way to do this. In fact, the implementation in the figure is only a sketch; moreover, it has a defect that we correct in the next section.

6.3　Synchronizing with Termination of a Child Process

The typical uses of *fork()* and *exec()* are found in the shell: a new process is created, a command is set running in that process, and—if the command line did not end with an ampersand—the shell waits until the command completes before resuming. It does this with *wait()*. On systems with job control, the shell must wait in such a way that if the foreground process stops instead of terminating, the shell will run. The 4.3BSD UNIX system implemented a variation of *wait()*, called *wait3()*, that allows a process to do this. POSIX.1 uses the function *waitpid()*, which is loosely based on *wait3()* but has somewhat different syntax and semantics. Prototypes for *wait()* and *waitpid()* are:

```
#include <sys/types.h>
#include <sys/wait.h>
pid_t wait(int *stat_loc);
pid_t waitpid(pid_t pid, int *stat_loc, int options);
```

When a process calls *wait()*, it is suspended until information is available about one of its terminated child processes. This could be immediately, if a child process has already terminated and has not yet been waited for.

```
#define _POSIX_SOURCE
#include <unistd.h>
#include <errno.h>
#include <sys/types.h>
#include <sys/wait.h>

extern int errno;

int system(char *cmd)
{
    pid_t pid,
          rpid;
    int    status;

    if ( (pid = fork()) == -1 )
        return(-1);
    else if ( pid == 0 )
    {   /* CHILD PROCESS */
        execl("/bin/sh", "sh", "-c", cmd, (char *)0);
        exit(-1);                /* Only happens if execl() fails */
    }
    else
    {   /* PARENT PROCESS */
        errno = 0;
        while ( (rpid = wait(&status)) != pid &&
            ((rpid != -1) || (errno == EINTR)) )
                ;
        if ( rpid == -1 )
        {
            errno = ENOEXEC;
            return(-1);
        }
        return(status);
    }
}
```

Figure 6.6

A Possible Implementation of the *system()* Function

Figure 6.7 illustrates the flow of control when a process *fork()*s a child and then *wait()*s for it.

A call to *wait()* will also return immediately, with return value –1, if the caller has no unwaited-for children. The *wait()* function really needs to return two values to its caller: the process ID of the child for which it is returning

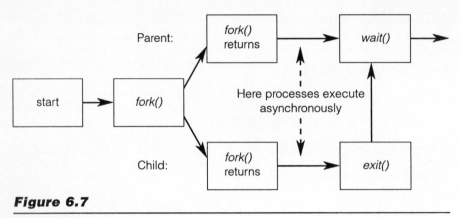

Figure 6.7

Flow of Control Using *fork()* and *wait()*

status information and the status information itself. Thus, it takes as an argument the address of an `int`. The return status information is stored at that address. If the value of `stat_loc` is `(int *)NULL`, then no status information is stored, but *wait()* still waits until a child terminates and then returns its PID.

Consider the following statement taken from Figure 6.5:

```
while ( (rpid = wait(&status)) != pid &&
  ((rpid != -1) || (errno == EINTR)) )
    ;
```

The purpose of this statement is to block the calling process until the child with process ID `pid` terminates and reports its status. If `rpid`, the return value from *wait()*, is not equal to `pid` and is not equal to –1, then the status being reported is that of another child process. If we are only concerned with the status of process `pid`, we stay in the `while` loop until this status is reported. This has the unfortunate consequence that we cannot later *wait()* for, and get the exit status of, the first child process that reported.

If *wait()* returns a value of –1, we have to determine why. POSIX.1 specifies two reasons that will cause *wait()* to return –1. One is that *wait()* is interrupted by a caught signal. That is, while your process is blocked in *wait()* a signal is delivered to it that it has arranged to catch. In that case, the signal handler will be executed and, if it returns, the *wait()* call will then return –1 with `errno` set to `EINTR`. If this occurs, the proper thing to do is to continue to *wait()*, which the above loop does.

The other reason that a call to *wait()* can return –1 is if the process has no unwaited-for children. In the code in Figure 6.5 that could "never" happen, because we only get to the *wait()* call if we have successfully called *fork()*. But a POSIX.1 implementation can specify additional reasons for a call to *wait()* to fail (and in addition, things that can "never" happen sometimes do happen). Therefore, the code checks for a value of –1 for `rpid` after the `while` loop exits.

The *waitpid()* function generalizes *wait()*. Thus, *wait()* is superfluous. (It is retained in the standard both because it's very convenient and because it is heavily used in existing software.) The call

```
pid = wait(&status);
```

is equivalent to the call

```
pid = waitpid(-1, &status, 0);
```

The pid argument to *waitpid()* describes what the caller wants to wait for. It has the following semantics, which are modified by the options argument in a manner to be described below:

- If pid equals –1, *waitpid()* will wait for **any child process.**

- If pid equals zero, *waitpid()* will wait for any child process in the same process group as the caller.

- If pid is positive, *waitpid()* will wait for the child process whose process ID is pid. If other children terminate, they do not cause *waitpid()* to return and their statuses will be available for later calls to *wait()* or *waitpid()*. The only possible return values from such a call are –1 (if an error occurs), zero (as described below), and pid.

- If pid is negative and not –1, *waitpid()* will wait for any child process whose process group ID is equal to the absolute value of pid.

The options argument provides *waitpid()* with two kinds of optional behavior. Ordinarily, if no child process has a status to report, *waitpid()* blocks the caller until a child status is available. If the WNOHANG flag is set in options, then a call to *waitpid()* returns immediately. If no children are ready, the return value is zero. (A user process is guaranteed never to have a process ID of zero.) On systems with job control, *waitpid()* can also report the status of child processes that have stopped, not terminated. It will do so if the WUNTRACED flag is set in options. The strange name of this flag comes from 4.3BSD. In that system, *wait3()* can report on child processes that are being traced by the *ptrace()* system call and have stopped. Setting WUNTRACED means that you want the status of children that have stopped for reasons other than being traced. POSIX.1 does not support *ptrace()*, but has kept the name of the flag. Leaving this flag clear means that you only want the status of terminated children.

6.3.1   Interpreting Child Status

A significant new feature of POSIX.1 is the way that the parent process decodes child status. In System V.3, the child status is encoded in 16 bits of an int. If the child exited due to a signal, the signal number is encoded in the lower 7 bits. If it exited normally, the exit value is encoded in the second-lowest 8 bits. (The exit value is the lower 8 bits of the argument to a call to *exit()* or *_exit()* or of a value returned from *main()*.) The status word structure of System V.3 is shown in Figure 6.8. Therefore, the following fragment of code has become a programming cliché:

```
wait(&status);
if (status & 0377)
    printf("Child exited due to signal %d\n", status & 0177);
else
    printf("Child exit status is %d\n", (status >> 8) & 0377);
```

The bit masks and shifts pick out either the signal number or the exit value. However, this structure imposes an unfortunate limit. Because there are only 7 bits for the signal, the number of signals is limited to 127. This may not seem like a severe limitation. Does any implementation really need more than 127 different signals? Well, the signal number used to be passed back in 6 bits (in earlier versions of the UNIX system), allowing only 63 signals, and 63 signals were not enough.

The BSD version of *wait()* solves the problem by defining the parameter to be a pointer to an object of type `union wait`. This union contains bit fields that can be referenced by name. Implementations needing more signals could enlarge the size of the bit fields. The only problem with this approach is that it's incompatible with lots of programs that pass a pointer to an `int` as the argument to *wait()*.

POSIX, as usual, solves the problem by replacing a concrete construction with an abstraction. The following six macros are defined in the `<sys/wait.h>` header; assume that the argument `status`, of type `int`, was pointed to by a call to *wait()* or *waitpid()* that has returned without an error, e.g., `wait(&status)`:

- `WIFEXITED(status)`. This macro evaluates to a nonzero value if and only if `status` indicates that the child process terminated normally.

- `WEXITSTATUS(status)`. If `WIFEXITED(status)` is true, then this macro evaluates to the lower 8 bits of the value passed to *exit()* or *_exit()* or returned from *main()* by the terminated process.

Eight exit code bits   Seven signal number bits

Bit D is set if the signal caused "actions," e.g., a core dump

Figure 6.8

System V.3 Process Exit Status Word

- WIFSIGNALED(status). This macro evaluates to a nonzero value if and only if status indicates that the process terminated due to the receipt of a signal that was not caught.

- WTERMSIG(status). If WIFSIGNALED(status) is true, then this macro evaluates to the number of the signal that terminated the child process.

- WIFSTOPPED(status). This macro evaluates to a nonzero value if and only if status indicates that the process is currently stopped.

- WSTOPSIG(status). If WIFSTOPPED(status) is true, then this macro evaluates to the number of the signal that caused the child process to stop.

Thus, the POSIX programming cliché that replaces the System V.3 code is:

```
wait(&status);
if ( WIFSIGNALLED(status) )
    printf("Child exited due to signal %d\n",
        WTERMSIG(status));
else
    printf("Child exit status is %d\n", WEXITSTATUS(status));
```

In this case, the program need not test WIFSTOPPED, as *wait()* will not return for a stopped child.

6.3.2   Advantages of *waitpid()* over *wait()*

The *waitpid()* function has a major advantage over *wait()*: it allows you to wait for a specific child process. If other children terminate in the interim, you will not lose their statuses. Recall the following loop from Figure 6.6, the implementation of *system()*:

```
while ( (rpid = wait(&status)) != pid &&
    ((rpid != -1) || (errno == EINTR)) )
        ;
```

The effect of this code is to wait for children until the one with process ID pid terminates or until no children are left. As we have seen, if a previously *fork()*ed child terminates in the interim, it is waited for and its status is discarded. You can't *wait()* for it later. If we replace this code with

```
while ( (rpid = waitpid(pid, &status, 0)) == -1 &&
    (errno == EINTR) )
        ;
```

and another child terminates in the interim, that child will not cause *waitpid()* to return and the parent will not lose track of the other child's exit status.

Since POSIX.1 made the *waitpid()* function available, the specification of *system()* in POSIX.2 was changed to require this behavior: a call to *system()* cannot cause the caller to lose the status of any child processes in existence at the time of the call. For an implementation of *system()* that conforms to the requirements of POSIX.2, see Chapter 11, Figure 11.7.

6.3.3   Interactions between *wait()* and SIGCHLD

In Chapter 5, Section 5.6, we indicated that setting the action for SIGCHLD to SIG_IGN has unspecified consequences, even though the default for SIGCHLD is to be ignored. The reason has to do with so-called zombie processes. A process is a zombie if it has exited or been terminated but its status has not yet been reported to its parent. Such a process need not occupy any memory, but it still takes up a slot in the system's process table, where its process ID and exit status are kept. This slot cannot be freed, because if the process's parent eventually decides to *wait()* for it the status must be available. On the other hand, if the parent process doesn't want to *wait()* for its children the process table slot is wasted. Eventually the system may run out of process table slots, with unfortunate consequences.

If a parent exits without waiting for its children, the children are inherited; that is, they get a new parent process ID, which is that of an implementation-defined system process. (In the UNIX system, it's usually process ID 1.) This process can *wait()* for any inherited children and thus free process table slots. But suppose the parent is going to run a long time, is going to produce many child processes, and does not want to *wait()* for them. System V.3 makes the following provision: if a process sets the action for SIGCLD (remember, that's not a POSIX.1 signal) to SIG_IGN, then the behavior of *wait()* changes. When a child of such a process terminates, its process table slot is freed. If the parent chooses to *wait()* for a child, the parent will block until all its children terminate, but then *wait()* will return –1 with errno = ECHILD.

Why should we worry about this non-POSIX behavior? Well, it's quite feasible for a POSIX.1 system to implement both SIGCLD and SIGCHLD, perhaps as the same signal. The POSIX.1 standard was carefully written to allow this. That's why the standard declares that, when the action for SIGCHLD is set to SIG_IGN, the behavior is unspecified.

6.4   Process Termination

Processes can terminate in two ways—normally or abnormally. If a process calls *exit()* or *_exit()* or simply returns from its *main()* function, it terminates normally. If it calls *abort()* or is terminated by an uncaught signal, it terminates abnormally. The *abort()* function is included by POSIX.1 from the C standard. Its prototype is:

```
#include <stdlib.h>
void abort(void);
```

Calling *abort()* is almost equivalent to sending yourself a SIGABRT signal:

```
kill(getpid(), SIGABRT);
```

However, the equivalence is not exact. The reason has to do with a somewhat cryptic provision in the C standard, which states that "the abort function causes normal program termination to occur, unless the signal SIGABRT is being caught and the signal handler does not return".[4] In other words, if you provide a signal handler for SIGABRT that does *not* return, then the signal handler will be executed. If you provide a signal handler for SIGABRT that *does* return, the signal handler will be executed but the program will terminate abnormally in any case; the return will not actually return control to your program. If you do not catch SIGABRT, then the program terminates abnormally. An example of a signal handler that does not return could include one that calls *longjmp()* or *siglongjmp()* to transfer control outside of its own scope, as well as a signal handler that exits.

Here's a more mysterious situation: suppose you have installed a signal handler for the SIGABRT signal, but you have also arranged to block this signal. If you call *abort()*, does the signal handler get executed? The original standard was ambiguous on this point; the revised standard specifies that, for the purposes of determining whether or not *abort()* causes process termination, "a signal that is blocked shall not be considered caught".[5] The best alternative in this case is to avoid the issue entirely. If you want to call *abort()*, you should unblock SIGABRT and not catch it. Any actions that you need to perform when the signal is delivered can be performed before the *abort()* call.

POSIX.1 supports the ANSI C standard *exit()* function, but also provides *_exit()*. The reason for providing *_exit()* is really a technicality: ANSI C provides semantics for *exit()* that, in the words of the 1003.1 Rationale, "are beyond the scope of POSIX.1".[6] For example, functions registered by the ANSI C *atexit()* function, which is not supported by POSIX.1, will be invoked when a program calls *exit()*. They need not be invoked by a call to *_exit()*. Here is a prototype for *_exit()*:

```
#include <unistd.h>
void _exit(int status);
```

The *exit()* function does appear in the list of C standard functions that are included as part of the POSIX.1 standard. There is no reason to avoid *exit()*.

The following steps are taken when a POSIX.1 process terminates normally:

- All open file descriptors and directory streams are closed.

- If the parent process is blocked in a call to *wait()* or *waitpid()*, it is notified and passed the low-order 8 bits of the status argument. If the parent process is not in a call to *wait()* or *waitpid()*, then the status argument is saved for subsequent return.

- Any children of the terminating process are assigned a new parent process ID.

- If the implementation supports the SIGCHLD signal, then a SIGCHLD is generated for the parent process.

- If the process is a controlling process (a session leader with a controlling terminal), then a SIGHUP signal is generated for every process in the foreground process group of the controlling terminal.

- If the process is a controlling process, the controlling terminal is disassociated from the session.

- If the implementation supports job control, if the termination of this process will cause a process group to become orphaned,* and if any process in that process group is stopped, then a SIGHUP followed by a SIGCONT is generated for each process in that process group. This prevents stopped processes from being stopped forever.

If a process terminates abnormally because of a call to *abort()*, the same actions are taken, except that instead of passing a status word to a *wait()*ing parent, the status of a process killed by an uncaught SIGABRT is passed.

---

* A process group becomes orphaned if the parent of every process in the group either is also in the group or is not in the same session. Another way to put it is that a process group is *not* orphaned if at least one process in the group has a parent that is in the same session but in a different process group. On a UNIX system that supports job control, if you run a job in the background and then kill the shell, the process group of the job becomes orphaned.

Exercises for Chapter 6 _____

1. Explain what the following program does:

```
#define _POSIX_SOURCE
#include <unistd.h>
#include <sys/types.h>
#include <sys/wait.h>

int count = 0;

main()
{
    pid_t   pid,
            top_level;
    int     status;

    top_level = getpid();
    while ( (pid = fork()) == 0 )
        count++;
    if ( pid == -1 )
        exit(count);
    else if ( getpid() != top_level )
    {
        (void) wait(&status);
        exit(WEXITSTATUS(status));
    }
    else
    {
        wait(&status);
        printf("%d\n", WEXITSTATUS(status));
        exit(0);
    }
}
```

2. Suppose there is a process image file in the current directory named prog1. Write a function that executes prog1, waits for its exit status, and returns that value.

3. Modify your answer to Exercise 2 so that the standard output of prog1 is directed to a file called prog1.out.

4. Suppose that there are two process image files in the current directory, named prog1 and prog2. Write a function that executes prog1 and prog2 concurrently, with the standard ouptut of prog1 piped as the standard input of prog2. Your function should return the exit status of prog2.

5. Modify your solution to Exercise 4 so that it will work if prog1 and prog2 are not necessarily in the current directory, but can be found somewhere in a directory named in your process's PATH environment variable.

6. Explain how to create a sequence of NPROC processes (where NPROC is some defined constant) and then wait for them to terminate, and report their exit statuses on the standard output, in the reverse order of their creation.

7. Explain how to arrange for your program to execute program prog so that, when prog begins executing, it ignores SIGINT and SIGQUIT and blocks SIGCHLD and SIGHUP.

7

Controlling Terminal Devices

The method POSIX.1 uses to provide program control of terminal attributes is a curious mix of old and new. The data structures are virtually unchanged from the UNIX system, but the functions that use those data structures are entirely a POSIX.1 invention. They stem from a dissatisfaction with UNIX's *ioctl()* function, which the POSIX.1 committee felt was doing too many things in too many different ways. In particular, *ioctl()* uses a variable number of arguments, and the third argument, when present, can have different types and sizes.

Another serious defect of *ioctl()* arises when it is used in a multivendor distributed environment. The meaning of an *ioctl()* call depends on the value of its second argument. There's no reason to expect different vendors to have implemented the same commands with the same numerical values. There are *ioctl()* calls that change the terminal attributes and *ioctl()* calls that simply return the current values of these attributes to the caller, and in a networked environment these are not easily distinguished. In addition, since the introduction of *ioctl()* in 7th Edition UNIX, it has evolved differently in the AT&T and BSD environments. It has been replaced in POSIX.1 by a collection of functions.

7.1   Controlling Terminals

Controlling terminals are allocated to a session, in an implementation-defined manner. The fact that there is no POSIX-portable way for a process to acquire a controlling terminal is inconvenient for application programs. But as long as your program takes no explicit action to give up its controlling terminal (e.g., a call to *setsid()*) you can generally assume that it has one.

157

A POSIX.1 process can have several terminal files open simultaneously, but at most one is a controlling terminal. The controlling terminal is special to the process in a number of ways, including the following:

- Certain special characters typed at the controlling terminal can generate SIGINT or SIGQUIT signals for the foreground process group.

- On systems that support job control, background processes cannot read from the controlling terminal (and may be inhibited from writing to it as well).

- Most functions that control terminal attributes cannot be used by a member of a background process group to change the attributes of the controlling terminal.

Note that terminal attributes apply to the underlying port, not just to the open file descriptor. Thus, if a process changes terminal attributes and does not restore them, they are changed for any other processes currently using the same terminal and also may remain changed for subsequent programs that use the port.

Most of the functions that manipulate terminal characteristics refer to the terminal device via a file descriptor. Before using such a function on standard input, output, or error files, you should ensure that these files are indeed associated with terminals. The function *isatty()* can be used to determine whether a file descriptor is associated with a terminal device. Its prototype is:

```
#include <unistd.h>
int isatty(int fildes);
```

The call

```
isatty(fildes);
```

returns 1 if fildes is a valid open file descriptor and is associated with a terminal, and returns zero otherwise.

7.2   Input Processing

POSIX supports type-ahead in the same manner as UNIX: input that arrives when there is not an outstanding *read()* for the device file is stored in an input queue. The queue can have a size limit, MAX_INPUT, and if more than MAX_INPUT bytes are placed on the queue the behavior is implementation-defined. (Historically, many UNIX systems have discarded the entire contents of the queue when the limit overflows.) There is little a portable program can do to protect itself against such an overflow, other than to provide good user instructions.

7.2.1 Special Characters

Certain characters are treated specially when input from the controlling terminal. Precisely which characters are so treated, and under what circumstances, is under the control of the program. Figure 7.1 lists the categories of special characters recognized by a POSIX system. They are described further in this section. Each of these characters only has its special effect when enabled by a flag bit in a data structure associated with the terminal.

The special characters CR and NL have constant values. It is implementation-dependent whether the values of the special characters STOP and START can be modified. The other special characters can be set to any character value that the program chooses.

In thinking about terminal I/O, it is important that you distinguish between *characters* and *bytes*. To make matters confusing, the C standard specifies that an object of type char is a byte, not a character. (Thus, char is a misnomer.) The term *character* in POSIX.1 corresponds to the term *multibyte character* in the C standard. Such characters may be single bytes (as in the ASCII character encoding) or multiple bytes (as in encodings for some Asian

Character	Enabled by	Left in Input Queue	Description
CR	ICANON	Y	\r. May be translated to NL.
EOF	ICANON	N	Line delimiter.
EOL	ICANON	Y	Line delimiter.
ERASE	ICANON	N	Erases previous input character.
INTR	ISIG	N	Generates a SIGINT.
KILL	ICANON	N	Erases input up to previous line delimiter.
NL	ICANON	Y	Line delimiter \n.
QUIT	ISIG	N	Generates a SIGQUIT.
SUSP	ISIG	N	Generates a SIGTSTP on job control systems.
STOP	IXON/IXOFF	N	Suspends output.
START	IXON/IXOFF	N	Resumes output.

Figure 7.1

POSIX Terminal Special Characters

languages). A character displayed on a terminal can occupy more than one space. The terminal special characters need not be single bytes.

7.2.2   Canonical and Noncanonical Modes

POSIX.1 maintains the UNIX system's distinction between canonical and noncanonical mode input processing. If you've used a UNIX system, you know the difference: in canonical mode, input is processed in units of lines, allowing you to erase characters or "kill" whole lines before the input is passed to the reading program. In noncanonical mode, input is not processed in units of lines and may be passed to the reading program in units as small as a single character if so desired. UNIX system users can control the mode and other attributes using the stty utility. As you may not have much experience controlling terminal characteristics "from the other side of the screen", we briefly review the distinction in terms of terminal attributes controllable by a program. If you're familiar with the differences between canonical and noncanonical modes in UNIX from the program's point of view, you can quickly skim the rest of this section.

In both canonical and noncanonical mode, the basic rule for when a *read()* returns is the same: if the file was opened with O_NONBLOCK clear, the *read()* request blocks the caller until data is available to be read or until a signal is received. If the O_NONBLOCK flag is set, the *read()* either returns as much data as is available, up to the requested number of bytes, or—if no data is available—returns –1 with errno set to EAGAIN. The difference between the two modes lies in the definition of when "data is available" to be read.

7.2.2.1   Canonical Mode   When a terminal file is in canonical mode, data is not available until a line delimiter character is entered. At that point the *read()* will return as many bytes as were requested, up to the number available in the line. Under no circumstances will it return more than one line, regardless of how much is requested or how much data is available. If the *read()* requested fewer bytes than are available, only the requested number are returned. The remainder of the input line is left in the queue. In that case, the next *read()* will return immediately, with some or all of what remains of the line. There are three line delimiter characters: NL (which is always the character \n), EOF, and EOL. The values of EOF and EOL are under program control. (Traditionally, they default to Control-D and \0, respectively.) If the EOF character is used to terminate a line, it is discarded from the input queue when read and thus is not returned by *read()*. The NL and EOL characters are left in the input queue.

For example, suppose that the user types the following sequence of characters as standard input:

```
1234567890\n12345<EOF>12345<EOL>
```

(The symbols <EOF> and <EOL> stand for the EOF and EOL characters, respectively.) This constitutes three lines of input. Suppose that a program issues the following requests:

```
read(0, buf1, 5);
read(0, buf2, 50);
read(0, buf3, 50);
read(0, buf4, 50);
```

What input goes into each buffer? Well, the first *read()* returns the 5 requested bytes: 12345 is stored in buf1. The second *read()* will read 6 bytes, up to the end of the first line: 67890\n is stored in buf2. The third *read()* will read the entire second line. It gets 5 bytes: 12345. The EOF character is not read. The fourth *read()* will read the entire third line: it gets the 6 bytes 12345<EOL>. Note that, even though the EOF character is not put into the input queue and other input follows it, it acts as a line delimiter. If O_NONBLOCK is not set, the results of each of these *read()*s are independent of the timing of the *read()* calls and the input.

If an ERASE character is entered in canonical mode, it has the effect of removing the previous character from the input queue, up to but not including the previous line delimiter. You cannot erase backwards past a line delimiter. Entering a KILL character has the effect of removing all the characters up to the previous line delimiter from the input queue. The values of ERASE and KILL are under program control. These characters are never placed in the input queue; if one of them is entered when there is no input in the current line, then it is ignored.

7.2.2.2 Noncanonical Mode

When a terminal file is in noncanonical mode, the availability of data does not depend on line delimiters; rather, it is governed by two parameters that are stored in a data structure associated with the terminal. The parameters are MIN and TIME. The data structure is called struct termio in UNIX System V.3. The corresponding (but not necessarily identical) structure is called struct termios in POSIX.1. See Section 7.3 for a description of this structure.

In noncanonical mode, data is made available after a certain number of bytes have been entered or after a timeout has occurred. No ERASE or KILL processing is done. The MIN parameter gives the minimum number of bytes that must be entered before a *read()* will return. The TIME parameter gives the amount of delay, in 1/10-second increments, before a *read()* times out and returns. There are four different cases to be considered:

- MIN > 0 and TIME > 0. In this case, TIME acts as an inter-byte timer that is not set until the first byte is entered and is reset after each byte. If MIN characters are received before the timer expires, the data becomes available and a *read()* will return. It will return the smaller of MIN and the number of bytes actually read. Note that because the timer does not start until the first byte is received, a *read()* can block indefinitely. Moreover, a *read()* will always return at least 1 byte, unless interrupted by a signal.

- MIN > 0 and TIME = 0. In this case, TIME is ignored. Data is not made available to a *read()* request until MIN bytes have been received. Again, in this case *read()*s can block indefinitely.

- MIN = 0 and TIME > 0. In this case, TIME is a timer activated as soon as the process calls *read()*. Data is made available as soon as a single byte is entered. It is not possible for a *read()* to block indefinitely in this case. After TIME/10 seconds, if no data has been entered, a *read()* will return zero.

- MIN = 0 and TIME = 0. In this case, a *read()* always returns immediately. If data has already been entered, it is available, and (up to the number of bytes requested) is returned. If no data is available, *read()* returns zero.

Note that once data is available, it remains available until it has been read. For example, suppose that a program enters noncanonical mode and sets the value of MIN to 10 and the value of TIME to 0. Suppose that it then calls

```
read(0, buf, 6);
```

If no data has been entered, the *read()* will block until at least MIN = 10 characters have been typed. Suppose that the user now types

```
1234567890
```

As soon as the zero (the tenth character) is typed, and before any line delimiter is entered, the *read()* will return. It will have read the 6 bytes requested: 123456. The remaining 4 bytes are still available. Suppose that the program now calls

```
read(0, buf, 50);
```

This *read()* will return immediately, having read the 4 available bytes 7890.

7.3   The termios Data Structure

The basic data structure for manipulating terminal attributes is struct termios, defined in the header <termios.h>. This name is deliberately chosen to be nearly identical to System V.3's struct termio, which is defined in a header named <termio.h>. However, <termio.h> is not a POSIX.1 header. Do not use it!

The `termios` structure contains at least the following members:

```
struct termios {
    tcflag_t  c_iflag;          /* Input modes */
    tcflag_t  c_oflag;          /* Output modes */
    tcflag_t  c_cflag;          /* Control modes */
    tcflag_t  c_lflag;          /* Local modes */
    cc_t      c_cc[NCCS];       /* Control characters */
    /* Possibly other members */
};
```

The types `tcflag_t` and `cc_t` are defined in `<termios.h>` and are unsigned integral types. Traditionally, `cc_t` has been `unsigned char`, but as we have seen it need not be just 1 byte long. The constant `NCCS` is also defined in `<termios.h>`. So are all the flags and bit masks that we describe in this section. Except for the types, this structure looks like the corresponding UNIX structure. Each of the objects of type `tcflag_t` is built out of bit masks. However, the contents of these four structure members are not necessarily the same as those of their UNIX counterparts.

The bit masks in `c_iflag` control the system's handling of input parity, CR–NL translation, flow control, character stripping, and response to a "break" condition. (A break is a continuous sequence of zero-valued bits that lasts for longer than the time required to transmit a single byte. Most terminals have a key that, if pressed, causes a break to be transmitted.) It's rare that an application program needs to change any of the settings of these flags. Nevertheless, for that rare occasion, here are the flags in `c_iflag`, with their meanings:

IGNCR   If this is set, a received CR character (`\r`) is ignored (not placed into the input queue).

ICRNL   If this is set and IGNCR is not set, then a received CR character is translated into an NL character (and thus becomes a line delimiter).

INLCR   If this is set, a received NL character (`\n`) is translated into a CR character (and thus is not a line delimiter, unless EOF or EOL is equal to CR).

INPCK   If this is set, input parity checking is enabled. The type of parity is determined by flags in the `c_cflag`. If INPCK is not set, no input parity checking is performed.

IGNPAR   If this is set, bytes with parity errors are ignored, as are bytes with framing errors (extra or missing bits) other than break conditions.

PARMRK   If this is set and IGNPAR is not set, then a byte with a framing or parity error is placed in the input queue as the 3-byte sequence `\377`, `\0`, X, where X is the erroneous byte. (The notation `\xxx` specifies the character value given by the octal digits xxx. Thus, \377 represents an unsigned char with value 255.) If the PARMRK and IGNPAR flags are both clear, then a parity error is placed in the input queue as a single null byte (\0).

ISTRIP   If this is set, then valid input bytes are stripped to 7 bits before being placed in the input queue. (Because some hardware has 9-bit or 10-bit bytes, this can cause more than 1 bit of input to be stripped.) If ISTRIP is not set, an input character of \377 is potentially ambiguous and is therefore placed in the input queue as the 2-byte sequence \377, \377. This flag is of questionable value on systems that can expect other than ASCII input. (For example, characters in the ISO 8859 character set for certain European languages make use of the eighth bit.) You should not set this flag if there is a possibility that your program will run in environments where 8 or more bits per byte are significant.

IGNBRK   If this is set, then a break condition is ignored. If IGNBRK is clear and BRKINT is also clear, a break condition is put into the queue as a single null byte (if PARMRK is clear) or as the 3-byte sequence \377, \0, \0 (if PARMRK is set).

BRKINT   If this is set and IGNBRK is clear, a break causes the input and output queues to be flushed. In addition, if the terminal on which the break occurs is the controlling terminal of a foreground process group, a SIGINT signal is generated for that process group.

IXON   If this is set, start/stop output control is enabled: a received STOP character suspends output, and a received START character restarts output. In this case, STOP and START characters are not placed in the input queue. If IXON is not set, then STOP and START characters are placed in the input queue.

IXOFF   If this is set, start/stop input control is enabled. This means that the system shall send one or more STOP characters to cause the terminal to stop transmitting data, to avoid exceeding the MAX_INPUT limit on the size of the input queue. The system will also send one or more START characters to cause the terminal to restart transmission. Of course, the terminal may or may not recognize these characters.

The c_oflag member of struct termios has only a single bit mask, and its meaning is implementation-defined:

OPOST   If this is set, implementation-defined output processing is performed to make the output appear in a way appropriate for the given terminal. If OPOST is clear, output bytes are transmitted unchanged.

There is never any reason for a portable application program to change the value of the OPOST flag. The UNIX output processing flags that specify translation of CR, tab and line-feed delays, etc., are not defined in POSIX, because a portable program cannot make effective use of them.

The c_cflag member contains masks that refer to the terminal hardware: the number of bits in a character, whether the line is connected to a modem, and whether parity generation and detection are enabled and, if so, whether parity is even or odd. The bit masks are:

CLOCAL   If set, the modem status lines are ignored (the terminal is assumed to be connected to the system locally). This means that an *open()* call to the terminal device file will return immediately, whether or not the *open()* is made with O_NONBLOCK clear. If CLOCAL is clear, the modem lines are monitored.

CREAD   If set, receiving of characters is enabled. Otherwise, characters will not be received.

CSTOPB   If set, two stop bits are sent after each character. Otherwise, only one is sent. (Most ASCII hardware expects two stop bits per character when receiving at 110 baud, but only one when receiving at 300 baud or higher.)

CSIZE   This mask is *not* a single bit, but a mask that can have any of four values: CS5, CS6, CS7, or CS8. These stand for 5, 6, 7, and 8 bits per byte, respectively.

PARENB   If set, parity generation and detection are enabled.

PARODD   If set, and if PARENB is set, odd parity is generated and expected. If PARODD is clear and PARENB is set, even parity is generated and expected.

HUPCL   If set, when the last process that has the terminal file open closes the file (perhaps by terminating), the modem lines will be lowered, causing a disconnect.

You can see that the most essential requirement for these flags is that they accurately reflect the state of the hardware to which they are attached. Therefore, there is rarely a reason for a portable application program to modify any of these values.

The last flag in struct termios is c_lflag. Finally, we encounter some flag bits that are commonly the concern of application programs. In particular, programs that wish to manipulate a full screen (such as screen editors) must, directly or indirectly, control the flags in c_lflag. The bit masks are:

ICANON   If set, the terminal is in canonical input mode. (See Section 7.2.2.) Otherwise, the terminal is in noncanonical input mode.

ECHO   If set, echoing of characters is enabled. Otherwise, characters are
            not echoed back to the terminal.

ECHOE   If set, and if ICANON is also set, then an ERASE character will, if
            possible, cause the terminal to erase the previous character from the
            display. (This is most commonly done by causing an ERASE to echo
            as backspace-space-backspace.)

ECHOK   If set, and if ICANON is also set, then a KILL character will either
            cause the terminal to erase the current line from the display or will
            echo a \n character.

ECHONL   If set, and if ICANON is also set, a received \n character will be
            echoed even if ECHO is not set.

ISIG   If set, then the input characters INTR, QUIT, and (on job control
            systems) SUSP take on their special meaning. They generate signals
            when entered and are not placed in the input queue. If ISIG is clear,
            then these characters have no special meaning to the system and are
            placed in the input queue.

NOFLSH   If set, then the input and output queues are not flushed when a
            signal is generated due to receipt of an INTR, QUIT, or SUSP
            character. If NOFLSH is clear, then generation of such a signal causes
            the input and output queues to be flushed.

IEXTEN   If set, implementation-defined special characters and special func-
            tions are enabled. Whether these functions are controlled by ICANON
            or ISIG is also implementation-defined. If IEXTEN is clear, then no
            special characters and functions other than those listed in Figure 7.1
            shall be recognized.

TOSTOP   If set on a system that supports job control, then a SIGTTOU signal
            is generated for the process group of any background process that
            attempts to *write()* to its controlling terminal. However, if the writ-
            ing process has arranged to block or ignore SIGTTOU, then the
            signal is not generated and the output is sent. If TOSTOP is not set,
            then data transmitted by a *write()* to the controlling terminal from
            a background process is put on the output stream. See Section 7.4.

Note that, in contrast to the UNIX system, the baud rate is not explicitly
encoded in any of these flags. (In UNIX System V.3 the CBAUD bit mask
specifies bits in the c_cflag that encode the baud rate for both input and
output.) In fact, two baud rates—for input and output—are implicitly stored
somewhere in the termios structure, but they can only be manipulated
abstractly, not by bit masking.

7.4   Controlling Terminal Attributes

The values in the termios structure associated with an open terminal device file can be determined and set using a number of functions that are new to POSIX. The two basic functions are *tcgetattr()* and *tcsetattr()*. They have the following prototypes:

```
#include <termios.h>
int tcgetattr(int fd, struct termios *tp);
int tcsetattr(int fd, int actions, const struct termios *tp);
```

If you pass *tcgetattr()* the file descriptor of an open terminal file and the address of a termios structure, it fills in the structure with the terminal's attributes. For example, if standard input is a terminal and term is the name of a termios structure, the call

```
tcgetattr(0, &term);
```

puts the attributes of the terminal into term.

The *tcsetattr()* function sets the attributes of the terminal associated with the named file descriptor to those in the specified termios structure. The actions argument to *tcsetattr()* determines when the change will take place. The possible values of actions and their semantics are:

TCSANOW   Set the terminal attributes immediately.

TCSADRAIN   Set the terminal attributes after all output that has already
               been written to fd has been transmitted.

TCSAFLUSH   Set the terminal attributes after all output that has already
               been written to fd has been transmitted. Discard all input that
               has not been read before setting the attributes.

The constants TCSANOW, TCSADRAIN, and TCSAFLUSH are defined in the <termios.h> header. A process that is not in the foreground process group cannot call *tcsetattr()* for its controlling terminal.

The values of the special characters are stored in the c_cc array. To locate a particular special character, use its corresponding subscript. Figure 7.2 shows the constants that you use for these subscripts; they are defined in <termios.h>. Some of these subscripts are meaningful in both canonical and noncanonical mode. Others are only meaningful in one of these modes.

For historical reasons, it is permitted for the value of VMIN to equal VEOF and for VTIME to equal VEOL. This is because UNIX systems have traditionally overloaded these cells in the c_cc array. However, this has consequences.

Suppose that you want to put the terminal into noncanonical mode, with a MIN value of 32 and a TIME value of 100. Here's how you could do it:

```
struct termios term;
/* ... */
errno = 0;
if ( tcgetattr(0, &term) < 0 )
    fprintf(stderr, "Can't get tty attributes; error %d\n",
        errno);
else
{
    term.c_lflag &= ~ICANON;        /* Turn off ICANON bit */
    term.c_cc[VMIN] = 32;           /* 32-byte minimum */
    term.c_cc[VTIME] = 100;         /* 10 seconds */
    if ( tcsetattr(0, TCSANOW, &term) < 0 )
        fprintf(stderr, "Can't set tty attributes: error %d\n",
            errno);
}
```

However, eventually, you'll want to restore canonical mode. Suppose that you simply turn canonical mode back on:

```
term.c_lflag |= ICANON;          /* Restore canonical mode */
tcsetattr(0, TCSANOW, &term);    /* This can cause a problem */
```

This can have unfortunate consequences, as the values of EOF and EOL may have been altered by setting MIN and TIME. As a general rule, a program that changes terminal attributes should restore them to the values they had when the program began executing. (Obviously, this does not apply to all programs; for instance, it is the *purpose* of a program like the UNIX system's stty utility to change terminal attributes.) The best way to do this is to save the attributes in a structure:

```
struct termios term, saveterm;
/* ... */
tcgetattr(0, &term);
saveterm = term;    /* Remember original terminal attributes */
/* ...modify term... */
tcsetattr(0, TCSANOW, &term);
/* ...Before program exit... */
tcsetattr(0, TCSAFLUSH, &saveterm);
```

You should also catch interrupt, hangup, and quit signals, and—if you want such signals to terminate execution—restore the original terminal attributes in the signal-handling functions for these signals. Figure 7.3 illustrates this flow of control.

Subscript	Meaning	Canonical	Noncanonical
VEOF	Location of EOF character	X	
VEOL	Location of EOL character	X	
VERASE	Location of ERASE character	X	
VKILL	Location of KILL character	X	
VINTR	Location of INTR character	X	X
VQUIT	Location of QUIT character	X	X
VSUSP	Location of SUSP character	X	X
VSTOP	Location of STOP character	X	X
VSTART	Location of START character	X	X
VMIN	Location of MIN parameter		X
VTIME	Location of TIME parameter		X

Figure 7.2

Subscripts for Special Characters in c_cc

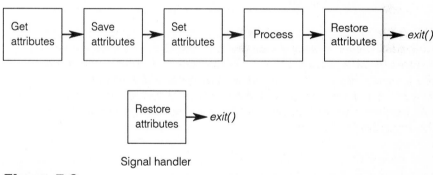

Signal handler

Figure 7.3

Saving and Restoring Terminal Attributes: Part 1

There are four functions whose purpose is to extract and modify the baud rates encoded in the termios structure. Their prototypes are:

```
speed_t cfgetispeed(struct termios *tp);
int cfsetispeed(struct termios *tp, speed_t speed);
speed_t cfgetospeed(struct termios *tp);
int cfsetospeed(struct termios *tp, speed_t speed);
```

B0	Hang up		
B50	50 baud	B600	600 baud
B75	75 baud	B1200	1200 baud
B110	110 baud	B2400	2400 baud
B134	134 baud	B4800	4800 baud
B150	150 baud	B9600	9600 baud
B200	200 baud	B19200	19200 baud
B300	300 baud	B38400	38400 baud

Figure 7.4

Baud Rate Constants Defined in `<termios.h>`

The type `speed_t` is an unsigned integral type, defined in `<termios.h>`, that can represent the value of any of the constants shown in Figure 7.4, which are also defined in `<termios.h>`. These constants are the possible return values of *cfgetispeed()* and *cfgetospeed()*, which return the input and output baud rates, respectively, that are stored in the `termios` structure pointed to by the first argument.

The *cfsetispeed()* and *cfsetospeed()* functions change the baud rate stored in the corresponding `termios` structure. Note that they do not actually set the baud rate. You must call *tcsetattr()* to do that. Similarly, to learn the baud rate of a terminal you must first call *tcsetattr()* and then call *cfgetispeed()* or *cfgetospeed()* to extract the rate from the `termios` structure that is returned.

Setting an output baud rate of B0 causes the modem control lines to be dropped. This will hang up a connection on a modem. Setting an input baud rate of B0 causes the input baud rate to be set equal to the output baud rate. (A subsequent change to the output rate will change both rates.) None of the rates shown in Figure 7.4 is guaranteed to be supported by the hardware. In addition, not all hardware supports different baud rates for input and output. If you attempt to set a rate that is not supported, or to set different input and output rates when that is not supported, it is implementation-defined whether or not the *cfset[io]speed()* function returns an error. In any case, the attempt will be ignored.

7.4.1   Errors in Setting Terminal Attributes

Suppose that you request a number of changes in terminal attributes in a single call to *tcsetattr()*. For example, you might wish to clear ICANON, set VMIN and VTIME, and change the input and output baud rates to 1200 baud.

Suppose that it is possible for the system to carry out some, but not all, of these actions. (The hardware might not support 1200 baud, for instance.) What does *tcsetattr()* do, and what does it return?

The answers to these questions proved somewhat vexing to the POSIX.1 committee. Some members felt that ideally the call should either succeed in its entirety and return success or change nothing and return failure. But this has problems. For an application to know what it can and cannot change, it would have to change one field at a time. Moreover, as a single call to *tcsetattr()* can cause a sequence of discrete actions on the hardware, some of these might have to be undone when an error is discovered. Such an implementation would be difficult. Other alternatives were for the call to do whatever it could and report an error, to do whatever it could and report success, or to stop making changes after encountering the first failure and report an error. Each of these has advantages and disadvantages.

In the end, the committee chose the following semantics: "The *tcsetattr()* function shall return success if it was able to perform any of the requested actions, even if some of the requested actions could not be performed." This choice has the advantage of being easily implementable and is no more difficult for the application to deal with than any other choice. It has the disadvantage of making *tcsetattr()* the only POSIX.1 function in which an error can return zero. In my opinion, this is a serious deficiency. In any case, it means that a careful application should use *tcsetattr()* as follows:

- Save the original attributes with a call to *tcgetattr()*.

- Change the attributes as desired with a call to *tcsetattr()*.

- If *tcsetattr()* returns an error, deal with it appropriately. This occurs if no part of the request could be honored. If the terminal whose characteristics you are changing is standard input, standard output, or standard error, then dealing with this problem by asking the user how to proceed is a mistake, and you should probably just abort with a suitable error indication.

- If *tcsetattr()* returns success, then call *tcgetattr()* again. This gets the new actual attributes of the terminal.

- Compare the new attributes to those you requested. If they agree, then the call to *tcsetattr()* really succeeded. Otherwise, some fields could not be changed. Again, deal with this error appropriately.

- If *tcsetattr()* really succeeded, continue processing. Remember to restore the original attributes on exit or if interrupted by a signal.

Admittedly, this is a pain in the neck. However, it is the only reliable way to use *tcsetattr()* to change more than one terminal attribute at a time. Figure 7.5 illustrates the flow of control for this discipline.

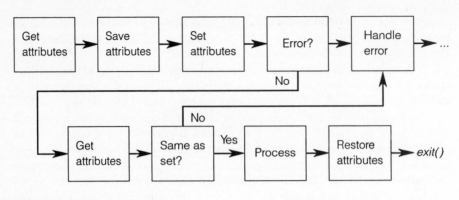

Figure 7.5

Saving and Restoring Terminal Attributes: Part 2

7.5   Line Control

A number of functions that have nothing to do with terminal attributes but
were included in UNIX's *ioctl()* function have their own functions in POSIX.
These include sending a break, waiting for output to drain, flushing the
input or output queues, and flow control. Prototypes for the relevant functions are:

```
#include <termios.h>
int tcsendbreak(int fd, int duration);
int tcdrain(int fd);
int tcflow(int fd, int action);
int tcflush(int fd, int queue_selector);
```

None of these functions can be called by a process in a background process
group if fd refers to the controlling terminal.

   If the file descriptor fd is associated with an asynchronous communications line, then calling *tcsendbreak()* causes the transmission of a break
condition—a continuous sequence of zero-bits. If the duration argument to
tcsendbreak() is zero, the transmission lasts for at least one-quarter of a second.
Other values of duration cause the break to last for an implementation-
defined period. If the file descriptor is not associated with an asynchronous
communications line, the behavior of *tcsendbreak()* is implementation-defined.

   The *tcdrain()* function simply blocks its calling process until all the
output written to the device referred to by the fd argument has been transmitted. This may include output written by other processes.

   The *tcflow()* function controls the flow of output, and attempts to control the flow of input, for the device referred to by fd. The possible values of

the `action` argument are given by constants defined in `<termios.h>`. The constants, and their associated semantics, are:

`TCOOFF` This causes the system to suspend output from the device.

`TCOON` This causes the system to restart suspended output from the device.

`TCIOFF` This causes the system to transmit a `STOP` character, with the intention of stopping the terminal from sending any data.

`TCION` This causes the system to transmit a `START` character, with the intention of telling the terminal to restart the transmission of data.

Not every terminal recognizes `START` and `STOP` characters.

The *tcflush()* function allows a process to flush (discard) input received but not yet read, or output written but not yet transmitted, from or to a particular device. Again, the effect of the function call is not just on the open file referred to by the file descriptor, but on all input and/or output associated with the device. The possible values of the `queue_selector` argument are constants defined in `<termios.h>` that tell the function which queue to flush. The possibilities are:

`TCIFLUSH` Flush all data received but not yet read—the input queue.

`TCOFLUSH` Flush all data written but not yet transmitted—the output queue.

`TCIOFLUSH` Flush both the input queue and the output queue.

7.6 Terminal Access and Job Control

Recall that when a system supports job control, every user process is in either a foreground or a background process group. Access to the terminal from background processes is restricted. The behavior depends on how the process is handling job control signals. The following discussion only applies to job control systems and only to the controlling terminal.

If a background process attempts to read from its controlling terminal and the process has not arranged to block or ignore the `SIGTTIN` signal, then a `SIGTTIN` is generated for the process. The default action of `SIGTTIN` is to stop the receiving process. Thus, a background process attempting to get keyboard input ordinarily stops. If the process has arranged to ignore or block `SIGTTIN`, then the signal is not generated, and the *read()* returns –1 and sets `errno` to `EIO`. In this case, no signal is sent. If the process has arranged to catch `SIGTTIN`, then the signal is generated and caught, interrupting the *read()*.

If a background process attempts to write to its controlling terminal, the situation is a bit more complex. The behavior depends on the value of the TOSTOP flag in the c_lflag member of the terminal's termios structure. If TOSTOP is not set, the process is allowed to write to the terminal. If TOSTOP is set but the process has arranged to block or ignore the SIGTTOU signal, it is also allowed to write to the terminal. If TOSTOP is set and the background process has not arranged to block or ignore the SIGTTOU signal, then an attempt by the process to write to the controlling terminal causes a SIGTTOU to be generated for the process group.

To further complicate matters, there is an exception to these rules for both *read()* and *write()*. If the background process is a member of an orphaned process group, then no signal is generated. (See Chapter 2, Section 2.1.3, for the definition of an orphaned process group.) Instead, the *read()* or *write()* returns –1, with errno set to EIO.

A POSIX process can determine the process group ID of the foreground process group and, if it has permission, can change it. This is how the shell can move a process from the background to the foreground and vice versa. The functions that can do this are *tcgetpgrp()* and *tcsetpgrp()*, which have the following prototypes:

```
#include <unistd.h>
#include <sys/types.h>
pid_t tcgetpgrp(int fd);
int tcsetpgrp(int fd, pid_t pgrp_id);
```

A call to *tcgetpgrp()* with an fd argument that is the file descriptor of the process's controlling terminal returns the process group ID of the terminal's foreground process group. This function can be called by a background process. If a process wants to change the foreground process group, it can call *tcsetpgrp()* with fd equal to a file descriptor for the device and pgrp_id equal to the desired process group ID. For a call to *tcsetpgrp()* to succeed, fd must refer to the caller's controlling terminal, and pgrp_id must be the process group ID of a process group in the same session as the calling process.

CONTROLLING TERMINAL DEVICES 175

Exercises for Chapter 7 _____

1. Explain what the following program does:

```
#define _POSIX_SOURCE
#include <unistd.h>
#include <termios.h>

#define BIGLINE 1024

main()
{
    struct termios  term,
                    termsave;
    int ch;
    char    line[BIGLINE];
    char    *p;
    if ( ! isatty(0) )
        exit(1);
    if ( tcgetattr(0, &term) < 0 )
        exit(2);
    termsave = term;
    term.c_lflag &= ~(ECHO | ECHOK | ECHOE | ECHONL);
    if ( tcsetattr(0, TCSANOW, &term) < 0 )
        exit(3);
    p = line;
    while ( (ch = getchar()) != EOF )
    {
        if (p < line + BIGLINE)
            *p++ = ch;
        if ( p == '\n' )
        {
            while (--p >= line)
                    putchar(*p);
            putchar('\n');
            p = line;
        }
    }
    (void) tcsetattr(0, TCSANOW, &termsave);
    exit(0);
}
```

2. Modify the program in Exercise 1 so that, if it is interrupted by a SIGINT, SIGHUP, or SIGQUIT signal, the original terminal attributes are restored and the program then exits.

3. Write function *get_one_char()*, which reads standard input and returns one byte. The function should block if no byte is available, and should return a byte as soon as it has been typed (i.e., without waiting for the user to type a newline).

4. Modify the function written in Exercise 3 so that, when called, it flushes any pending input before reading.

5. Explain how to set the attributes of your process's controlling terminal so that, if a break is received:

   (a) it is ignored.

   (b) it causes a SIGINT to be generated for your process.

   (c) it is received as a recognizable sequence of characters. In this case, is there any other sequence of input characters that will be read as the same sequence? Why or why not?

6. Careful use of *tcsetattr()* requires that you be able to compare two termios structures and determine if their portable contents are the same. (Remember that an implementation is free to add members to this structure, but a portable application cannot refer to them in any way.) Write such a function.

8

ANSI C Standard Functions

The efforts to standardize the C language (undertaken by ANSI) and the POSIX interface (undertaken by the IEEE) proceeded in parallel. The POSIX 1003.1 committee decided to refer to the ANSI C standard for many of the C-specific details of their own standard. The IEEE committee finished first; 1003.1 was adopted in August 1988. This is somewhat unfortunate, because the POSIX.1 standard depends on the C standard, and not the other way around. Therefore, the adopted POSIX 1003.1-1988 standard refers to the then-most-current draft of the C standard and contains phrases like "Until the C Standard is ratified...". The C standard was revised in December 1988, and some of the changes affected POSIX.1. The revised C standard was ratified in December 1989.

The relationship between these two standards is somewhat complex. Remember that a POSIX.1-conforming system need not support ANSI C. Rather, it has to support some headers and interfaces from the C standard library. These are listed in Figures 8.1 and 8.2, below. Most of them are supported in all C environments today. In addition, each POSIX.1 implementation must document whether it provides common usage C support or standard C support. If it provides common usage C support, then it must support the same headers and interfaces, but not necessarily with the semantics documented in the C standard. Any differences must be documented by the implementation. Even if a POSIX.1 implementation provides standard C support, it still need not provide a full ANSI C library. It must support the interfaces shown in Figure 8.2, with the semantics given in the C standard. In either case, a POSIX.1 system need not support the ANSI C library functions that are not listed there. Thus, the C standard library is *not* a subset of POSIX.1. Examples of functions in the C standard library that are omitted from POSIX.1 include the functions that deal with wide characters

177

and multibyte characters, such as *mbtowc()*, and the *signal()* function, which we discussed in Chapter 5.

Of course, to conform to both the POSIX.1 standard and the C standard, an implementation must support all the functions specified in both standards. It is likely that there will be many such implementations.

To achieve maximum portability, you should assume that your POSIX application programs will run on standard C systems and will also run on common usage C systems. It's generally possible to write code that works in both environments; after all, the C standard is supposed to codify existing practice. However, it would be good if your code could take advantage of some of the improvements that the C standard has made to the language. Chief among them is the use of prototypes.

8.1   Prototypes and Headers

The use of prototypes provides at least two advantages for the programmer. The first is that it allows the compiler to do extensive type checking, of the sort that the UNIX `lint` utility performs. In addition, prototypes allow the compiler to generate code for automatic type conversions. These conversions occur for arguments in function calls.

Here's an example: suppose that you have two functions, whose prototypes are:

```
void func1(long arg1);
void func2(short arg2);
```

Suppose now that you call both of these functions with arguments that are of type `int`:

```
func1(6);
func2(6);
```

On a common C system, one of these calls is almost* certain to be passed the wrong value, because the `int` constant 6 is either too long for `arg2` or too short for `arg1`. But because of the prototype declarations, a standard C compiler will convert the actual argument to the type of the parameter before passing it. Common C compilers perform some default conversions on arguments—for example, a `char` argument is always converted to an `int` or to an `unsigned int` before being passed—but these promotions do not depend on the type expected by the called function. If no prototype is present, a standard C compiler will do the same. But in the presence of a prototype, standard C treats the passing of an argument as an assignment to an

---

*   "Almost," because it's conceivable that an implementation of C could make `short`s, `int`s, and `long`s all the same size. On such an implementation, this code would work. But it is *not* portable.

anonymous variable of the correct type. To quote from the C standard (Section 3.3.2.2):

> If the expression that denotes the called function has a type that does not include a prototype, the integral promotions are performed on each argument and arguments that have type float are promoted to double. These are called the *default argument promotions....* If the function is defined with a type that includes a prototype, and the types of the arguments after promotion are not compatible with the types of the parameters . . . the behavior is undefined.

> If the expression that denotes the called function has a type that includes a prototype, the arguments are implicitly converted, as if by assignment, to the types of the corresponding parameters. The ellipsis notation causes argument type conversion to stop after the last declared parameter. The default argument promotions are performed on trailing arguments.[7]

To use prototypes and still make your code portable to non-ANSI systems, you need to use conditional compilation. The C standard requires that, on conforming systems, the symbol _ _STDC_ _ be defined and equal to 1. (There are two underscores before the STDC and two after.) Thus, you can write code like this:

```
#if (_ _STDC_ _ == 1)
int getline(char *buf, int maxlen)
#else
int getline(buf, maxlen)
char *buf;
int maxlen;
#endif
{
    /* body of function getline() */
}
```

This is kind of ugly, but it works, and it provides you with compile-time type checking that traditional C compilers cannot do. Note that many references give this compile-time test as

```
#ifdef _ _STDC_ _
```

This is wrong. The symbol _ _STDC_ _ is defined but has a value other than 1 on some systems that do not support the full C standard. Some authors prefer to use the test

```
#if _ _STDC_ _
```

(which is true if _ _STDC_ _ is defined and not zero) on the grounds that later revisions of the C standard will specify that the symbol _ _STDC_ _ have the value 2, or 3, and so forth.

We mentioned that some parts of the draft C standard changed after the adoption of the POSIX.1 standard and necessitated revisions to the latter standard. The removal of the CLK_TCK symbol from ANSI C is an example. However, one part of the C standard that remained stable consists of the specifications of the library functions. There are more than 140 such functions or macros specified as part of ANSI C. POSIX.1 includes 110 of these, whose descriptions it simply adopts from ANSI C. (The POSIX standard states: "Any implementation claiming conformance to POSIX.1 with the C Language Binding shall comply with the requirements outlined in this chapter, the requirements stipulated in the rest of this part of ISO/IEC 9945, and the requirements in the indicated sections of the C Standard".) Of these 110 functions, nine have additional semantics for POSIX.1. We have already seen three of these—*rename()*, *getenv()*, and *abort()*. In this chapter we discuss the others, which deal principally with internationalization and with time. We also discuss the interaction of low-level I/O with the stream-oriented I/O functions of the C library. A complete description of all the standard C library functions supported by POSIX.1 is beyond the scope of this book. In Appendix B we give prototypes of all of these functions, with their associated headers and a brief description of their semantics and returned values. The C standard requires that every standard C library function have a prototype in a specified header.

8.1.1   Headers in ANSI C and POSIX

The C standard states that symbols can be defined in more than one header, that the headers defined in that standard can be included in a program any

Headers Whose Contents Are Specified by:

POSIX.1 and ANSI C	POSIX.1 Only	ANSI C Only
<errno.h>	<dirent.h>	<assert.h>
<limits.h>	<fcntl.h>	<ctype.h>
<setjmp.h>	<grp.h>	<float.h>
<signal.h>	<pwd.h>	<flow.h>
	<sys/stat.h>	<locale.h>
	<sys/times.h>	<math.h>
	<sys/types.h>	<stdarg.h>
	<sys/utsname.h>	<stddef.h>
	<sys/wait.h>	<stdio.h>
	<tar.h>	<stdlib.h>
	<termios.h>	<string.h>
	<unistd.h>	<time.h>
	<utime.h>	

Figure 8.1

Standards Defining the Contents of Headers

number of times, and that they can be included in any order. POSIX.1 guarantees the first two statements, but says nothing about the order in which headers may be included. In fact, the specifications of many POSIX.1 functions include multiple headers, and you should include those headers in the order given. For example, the description of *stat()* gives the headers `<sys/types.h>` and `<sys/stat.h>`. These should be included in that order; types such as `uid_t` and `mode_t` are defined in `<sys/types.h>` and are used in the `stat` structure defined in `<sys/stat.h>`. Figure 8.1 shows the headers whose contents are specified by both POSIX.1 and ANSI C, only by POSIX.1, and only by ANSI C, respectively. Although ANSI C requires the headers `<float.h>`, `<stdarg.h>`, and `<stddef.h>`, no POSIX.1 function refers to any of these headers.

Figure 8.2 lists the ANSI C library functions required to be supported by every POSIX.1 system, arranged by the headers in which they must be declared.

<assert.h>	*assert()*
<ctype.h>	*isalnum(), isalpha(), iscntrl(), isdigit(), isgraph(), islower(), isprint(), ispunct(), isspace(), isupper(), isxdigit(), tolower(), toupper()*
<locale.h>	*setlocale()*
<math.h>	*acos(), asin(), atan(), atan2(), ceil(), cos(), cosh(), exp(), fabs(), floor(), fmod(), frexp(), ldexp(), log(), log10(), modf(), pow(), sin(), sinh(), sqrt(), tan(), tanh()*
<setjmp.h>	*setjmp(), longjmp()*
<stdio.h>	*clearerr(), fclose(), feof(), ferror(), fflush(), fgetc(), fgets(), fopen(), fprintf(), fputc(), fputs(), fread(), freopen(), fscanf(), fseek(), ftell(), fwrite(), getc(), getchar(), gets(), perror(), printf(), putc(), putchar(), puts(), remove(), rename(), rewind(), scanf(), sscanf(), setbuf(), sprintf(), tmpfile(), tmpnam(), ungetc()*
<stdlib.h>	*abort(), abs(), atof(), atoi(), atol(), bsearch(), calloc(), exit(), free(), getenv(), malloc(), qsort(), rand(), realloc(), srand()*
<string.h>	*strcat(), strchr(), strcmp(), strcpy(), strcspn(), strlen(), strncat(), strncmp(), strncpy(), strpbrk(), strrchr(), strspn(), strstr(), strtok()*
<time.h>	*asctime(), ctime(), gmtime(), localtime(), mktime(), strftime(), time()*

Figure 8.2

ANSI C Library Functions Supported by All POSIX.1 Systems

8.2   Stream I/O

C has had a standard I/O library for a long time, substantially predating the effort to standardize the language itself. The purpose of the standard I/O library is to provide a set of portable, efficient routines—functions and macros—for reading and writing files. The types and data structures used to support these routines are defined in the header <stdio.h>. Probably most C programs currently written use the standard I/O library, particularly the functions *fopen()*, *getc()*, and *putc()*. We assume that you are familiar with these functions. In Figure 8.3, we show a program that is equivalent to the programs of Figures 4.4 and 4.5. It will probably have performance intermediate between those two.

The program in Figure 8.3 is a strictly conforming POSIX.1 application. It will also execute in many non-POSIX environments—in fact, in almost any environment that supports C. This will be true of any program that only requires the functions shown in Figure 8.2.

Of the POSIX.1 interfaces listed in Figure 8.2, 35 are defined in <stdio.h>. Taken together, these constitute a complete I/O package that is seemingly unrelated to the low-level I/O based on *open()*, *close()*, *read()*, and *write()*. In fact, on a POSIX.1 system they are closely related, and any POSIX program that uses both kinds of I/O must take the interactions into account. To see why, consider the program in Figure 8.4.

What happens if this program is executed? Before you continue reading, take a few moments to try to determine what the effect of executing this program will be on a UNIX system. Then, if you have a system handy, type it in and compile and run it, and compare your answer with the actual results.

On most UNIX systems, the file myfile will be created with contents bbaacccccc. What happens is this: the *open()* call creates myfile and creates an open file description for it, with associated file descriptor fd. The *fopen()*

```
#define _POSIX_SOURCE
#include <stdio.h>

main()
{
    int c;

    while ( (c = getchar()) != EOF )
        putchar(c);
}
```

Figure 8.3

A Simple Copy Program

call creates another open file description for the same file, with an anonymous file descriptor (which is in some way associated with the FILE structure pointed to by fout). These two open file descriptions have separate file
pointers, both of which start out at zero. The first *write()* writes four characters to the file. Then the *fprintf()* writes 2 bytes, not to the file but to a buffer in
the calling program's address space. Then the second *write()* writes six characters to the file. At this point, the file contents are aaaacccccc. When *fclose()* is
called, it forces the buffer to be flushed; it does this by calling *write()*. The
write() is done with the anonymous file descriptor and with the second open
file description; consequently, the bytes are written at position 0 in the file,
and they overwrite the aa.

```
#define _POSIX_SOURCE
#include <stdio.h>
#include <fcntl.h>
#include <sys/types.h>
#include <sys/stat.h>

#define MODE (S_IRUSR | S_IWUSR | S_IRGRP | S_IROTH)
char    *fname = "myfile";

main()
{
    int fd;
    FILE    *fout;

    if ( (fd = open(fname, O_WRONLY | O_CREAT, (mode_t)MODE)) < 0 )
        exit(1);
    if ( (fout = fopen(fname, "w")) == (FILE *) NULL )
    {
        close(fd);
        exit(1);
    }
    write(fd, "aaaa", 4);
    fprintf(fout, "%s", "bb");
    write(fd, "cccccc", 6);
    fclose(fout);
    close(fd);
    exit(0);
}
```

Figure 8.4

A Program That Mixes Low- and High-Level I/O

What happens if you execute this program on a POSIX.1 system? The results are unpredictable. If you want to mix high-level and low-level I/O on the same files, the POSIX.1 standard describes the conditions under which the output is predictable. We give these rules in Section 8.2.1, below. If you violate these rules (as the program in Figure 8.3 does) on a POSIX.1 system, there are no guarantees about what the output will be. Before giving the rules, we need to discuss the relationship between low- and high-level I/O a bit more.

The routines of <stdio.h> were designed to be implementable under just about any operating system. Because different operating systems refer to open files in different ways, these functions make use of the abstract type FILE, which is associated with a *stream*—a sequence of bytes. This type can be implemented on many systems that are unrelated to UNIX systems; on some of these systems, the notion of a file descriptor is not meaningful. A FILE object can be associated with a file descriptor, or a file control block, or whatever data structure the host system uses to control open files. Moreover, to deal with historical problems in the implementation of text files, ANSI C describes two different types of streams: *text streams* and *binary streams*.

This distinction need not concern us, because on POSIX.1 systems text streams and binary streams are required to be identical. Moreover, in POSIX an object of type FILE is always associated with an underlying file descriptor. Thus, when a process calls *fopen()* and successfully opens a stream, the effect is as if a call to *open()* has also been made and a file descriptor allocated. (In practice, on UNIX systems *fopen()* calls *open()*.) Sometimes it is useful for a POSIX program to use both kinds of I/O. POSIX provides two functions that relate streams and file descriptors. These are *fileno()* and *fdopen()*, both of which are also supported in System V and BSD. Their prototypes are:

```
#include <stdio.h>
int fileno(FILE *stream);
FILE *fdopen(int fildes, char *type);
```

The *fdopen()* function associates a stream with a file descriptor. More precisely, if fildes is a file descriptor that refers to an open file, then *fdopen()* returns a FILE pointer whose underlying file descriptor is fildes. The type argument describes the access mode of the stream. It must be allowed by the access mode associated with the file descriptor. Thus, if the file descriptor fildes describes a file open only for reading, do not use "w" as the value for type. Valid values and their associated meanings are given in Figure 8.5. Implementations may define other valid values for type, but a portable program should not use them.

You may notice that the values given in Figure 8.5 are among the valid values for the type argument to *fopen()*. However, the C standard states that if you *fopen()* a file with type equal to "w" or "w+", the file is truncated. If you *fdopen()* a file with one of these types, the file is *not* truncated.

type
Value	Meaning
`"r"`	Open for reading
`"w"`	Open for writing
`"a"`	Open for appending (writing at end-of-file)
`"r+"`	Open for update (reading and writing)
`"w+"`	Open for update
`"a+"`	Open for update at end-of-file

Figure 8.5

Valid Values for the `type` Argument to *fdopen()*

The *fileno()* function works the other way: given an open stream, it returns the file descriptor underlying the stream. The C standard names three standard streams, which are defined in `<stdio.h>`. These are `stdin`, `stdout`, and `stderr`. Of course, on a POSIX system these are associated with file descriptors 0, 1, and 2, respectively. In fact, POSIX requires that the header `<unistd.h>` define three constants:

```
#define    STDIN_FILENO    0
#define    STDOUT_FILENO   1
#define    STDERR_FILENO   2
```

It is good POSIX programming practice to use the symbolic constants rather than the numeric values.

When a process invokes a low-level I/O function, the effect of the I/O is reflected in the state of the open file description by the time the function returns. In other words, low-level I/O always communicates with the system. This involves overhead that can make low-level I/O inefficient. High-level I/O uses buffers in the process's address space. In fact, on many systems the *getc()* and *putc()* functions are actually implemented as macros that don't even have the overhead of a function call most of the time that they're called. Using these interfaces can be much more efficient. However, there's a price for this efficiency: it's not clear from the program text when I/O really occurs—that is, when data is really transferred between the process and the system. For example, if your process does a *write()* to a file, and another process then does a *read()* from that file, the data read will reflect the data written. (This will be true even if the data has not yet been written to disk. If it is still in a system buffer, the *read()* will read from that buffer.) But if your process does a *putc()* to a file, and another process then does a *getc()* from the file, the data read may or may not reflect the data written. Another difference involves the *exec()* family of functions. An open file remains open across *exec()*s, unless its FD_CLOEXEC flag is set. A stream is considered inaccessible across an *exec()*, regardless of whether or not it actually remains open (which is unspecified).

The POSIX.1 standard specifies an association between some of the functions in the standard I/O library and *underlying* POSIX.1 functions. There is no requirement that the <stdio.h> function actually be implemented using its underlying function(s). This association is purely a notational convenience. For example, POSIX.1 does not explicitly specify the values of errno set by the standard I/O functions. Rather, it simply states: "If any of the functions [in the standard I/O library] return an error indication, the value of errno shall be set to indicate the error condition. If that error condition is one that this part of ISO/IEC 9945 specifies to be detected by one of the corresponding underlying functions, the value of errno shall be the same as the value specified for the underlying function".[8] For example, the underlying function for *fopen()* is *open()*. If a process attempts to *fopen()* a file that does not exist, then errno shall be set to ENOENT, because that is what *open()* would do in the same circumstance. Another relationship between standard I/O functions and their underlying functions is that a standard I/O function is considered to affect the file offset if it has an underlying function that affects the file offset.

The association of stream functions and underlying functions is as follows:

- *fopen()* has the underlying function *open()*.

- *fclose()* has the underlying functions *write()* and *close()*.

- *freopen()* has the underlying functions *open()*, *write()*, and *close()*.

- *fflush()* has the underlying functions *read()*, *write()*, and *lseek()*.

- *fgetc()*, *fgets()*, *fread()*, *getc()*, *getchar()*, *gets()*, *scanf()*, and *fscanf()* have the underlying functions *read()* and *lseek()*.

- *fputc()*, *fputs()*, *fwrite()*, *putc()*, *putchar()*, *puts()*, and *printf()* have the underlying functions *write()* and *lseek()*.

- *fseek()*, *ftell()*, and *rewind()* have the underlying functions *lseek()* and *write()*.

There is another relationship between functions in <stdio.h> and their underlying functions. We have seen that certain POSIX.1 functions, when called, have side effects such as updating the modification or access times of files. Calling some functions from the standard I/O library may have the same side effects. We say *may*, and not *does*, because whether or not the effect occurs can depend on whether or not the function call actually performs any I/O. In particular, if an underlying POSIX.1 function updates any of the file's time fields (st_atime, st_ctime, or st_mtime), then the stream function may do the same.

8.2.1 File Handles

A *handle* for an open file description is either a file descriptor or a stream associated with the open file description. As we have seen, a single open file description can have many handles. Handles can be created by *open()*, *creat()*, *dup()*, *dup2()*, *fcntl()*, *fopen()*, *fdopen()*, *freopen()*, *fileno()*, *fork()*, and possibly other functions. I/O operations on any handle can affect the open file description's offset. To mix low-level and high-level I/O on a given open file description, we need to know how they interact. The POSIX.1 standard specifies a complicated set of circumstances under which using multiple handles is safe. However, the easiest thing to do to follow these two rules:

If you have been using a handle that is a stream and wish to use another handle for the same file, call *fflush()* or *fclose()* on the stream first.

If you wish to switch handles and using the old handle may have affected the file offset, then *fseek()* (if the new handle is a stream) or *lseek()* (if the new handle is a file descriptor) to the correct location.

Occasionally, this will lead to a superfluous function call, but it will prevent the sort of garbled output that is produced by the program in Figure 8.4. Figure 8.6 shows a version of the same program, with the appropriate calls added. The output of this program is a file whose contents are aaaabbcccccc, precisely the characters written in the order in which the I/O calls are made.

8.2.2 Which Kind of I/O Should You Use?

In general, it's not a good idea to mix high-level and low-level I/O to the same file in the same process. But there's no reason that you can't use both in the same process, on different files. Each has advantages and disadvantages. We discuss some of them here.

High-level I/O has an advantage that may or may not be important for your application: it is portable to many non-POSIX environments. If you are writing a program that does not need operating system interfaces other than I/O—for example, a program that requires no external interfaces other than those listed in Figure 8.2—you can write a program that should be portable to all POSIX.1 environments and all ANSI C environments. But such a program must restrict itself to high-level I/O.

```
#define _POSIX_SOURCE
#include <stdio.h>
#include <fcntl.h>
#include <sys/types.h>
#include <sys/stat.h>

#define MODE (S_IRUSR | S_IWUSR | S_IRGRP | S_IROTH)
char    *fname = "myfile";

main()
{
    int fd;
    FILE    *fout;

    if ( (fd = open(fname, O_WRONLY | O_CREAT, (mode_t)MODE)) < 0 )
        exit(1);
    if ( (fout = fopen(fname, "w")) == (FILE *) NULL )
    {
        close(fd);
        exit(1);
    }
    write(fd, "aaaa", 4);
    fseek(fout, 0L, SEEK_END);          /* Go to end of file */
    fprintf(fout, "%s", "bb");
    fflush(fout);
    lseek(fd, (off_t)0, SEEK_END);      /* To end of file again */
    write(fd, "cccccc", 6);
    fclose(fout);
    close(fd);
    exit(0);
}
```

Figure 8.6
_____

A Program That Safely Mixes Low- and High-Level I/O

Another advantage of high-level I/O is its conceptual simplicity. You can read and write one byte at a time efficiently. Compare the following fragments, slightly modified from Figures 8.3 and 4.2, respectively:

```
while ( (c = getchar()) != EOF )
    putchar(c);
```

and

```
while ( read(STDIN_FILENO, &c, 1) == 1 )
    write(STDOUT_FILENO, &c, 1);
```

Both of these loops copy standard input to standard output. The first is both simpler and much more efficient than the second, because the system is free to write a few larger buffers to the file instead of being constrained to execute a system call for each character.

Figure 8.7 shows an extended example of a program that uses the standard I/O library. This program removes C-style comments from its input file, replacing each comment with a single space. The standard C library is particularly useful in this case because we need a one-character look-ahead to detect the start and end of comments. When we encounter a / character outside of a comment, we need to know if the next character is an *, and when we encounter an * inside a comment, we need to know if the next character is a /. In each case, if the look-ahead character is not the second character of a character delimiter, we must push it back on the input stream because it might be the first character of a comment delimiter. For instance, consider the following C statement:

```
pi_over_2 = pi //** Terrible place for a comment! **/ 2;
```

Although this is truly awful style, it is legal C, and our de-commenting program must recognize the second / as the start of a comment. It must also recognize the second * in **/ as part of the end of the comment. For these purposes, the <stdio.h> function *ungetc()* is very useful. When we encounter the first /, we look ahead one character. As the next character is not an *, we have to consider the possibility—as in the above example—that it is the beginning of a comment. The easiest way to do that is to push it back on the input stream.

As high-level I/O is so convenient and efficient, you might wonder why you would ever want to use low-level I/O. But there are some things that you can only do with file descriptors. For example, you cannot directly control the mode of a file created with *fopen()*. On a POSIX.1 system it is always created with mode (S_IRUSR | S_IWUSR | S_IRGRP | S_IWGRP | S_IROTH | S_IWOTH), modified by the calling process's umask. You cannot create a pipe or FIFO with *fopen()*, nor can you open a stream in nonblocking mode, nor can you reliably inherit an open stream in a child process. You cannot control a terminal file with *tcsetattr()* without referring to its file descriptor. If you put a terminal into raw mode, reading it using high-level I/O is inviting disaster, because you don't directly control the number of bytes requested. In other words, high-level I/O is perfectly suitable when you don't want to do anything unusual. But low-level I/O gives you much more control when you need it. It allows you to manipulate those features of a file, such as its mode and status flags, that are not meaningful in an arbitrary C environment.

In Figure 8.8, we show a version of the program from Figure 8.7 rewritten to use low-level I/O. This program has a simple additional feature: the output file is guaranteed to have the same mode as the input file. (In this respect the program behaves like the UNIX cp utility.) The code is a bit more

```
/*
** This program is invoked with two arguments.  The first is
** the name of the input file, and the second is the name of the
** file that will be created.
*/

#define _POSIX_SOURCE
#include <stdio.h>
#include <stdlib.h>

#define  TRUE   1
#define  FALSE  0

FILE    *fin,       /* Input stream */
        *fout;      /* Output stream */

char    *infile,    /* Name of input file */
        *outfile;   /* Name of output file */

main(int argc, char *argv[])
{
    int c;
    int in_comment = FALSE;

    if ( argc != 3 )
    {
        fprintf(stderr, "usage: uncomment source dest\n");
        exit(1);
    }
    if ( (fin = fopen((infile = *argv[1]), "r")) == (FILE *)NULL )
    {
        fprintf(stderr, "%s: cannot open\n", infile);
        exit(1);
    }
    if ((fout = fopen((outfile = *argv[2]), "w")) == (FILE *)NULL)
    {
        fprintf(stderr, "%s: cannot create\n", outfile);
        exit(1);
    }
```

Figure 8.7 *(continued on facing page)*

Sample Program to Remove C-Style Comments from an Input File

```
/* Read characters one at a time until end of file */
while ( (c = getc(fin)) != EOF )
{
    if ( ! in_comment )
    {
        if ( c == '/' )           /* Is it start of a comment? */
        {
            c = getc(fin);
            if ( c == '*' )       /* Yes */
                in_comment = TRUE;
            else
            {                     /* No */
                putc('/', fout);
                if ( c != EOF )
                    ungetc(c, fin);
            }
        }
        else
            putc(c, fout);
    }
    else if ( c == '*' )          /* Is it end of a comment? */
    {
        c = getc(fin);
        if ( c == '/' )           /* Yes */
        {
            in_comment = FALSE;
            putc(' ', fout);      /* Replace w/ a space */
        }
        else                      /* No */
            ungetc(c, fin);
    }
} /* while */
fclose(fin);
fclose(fout);
exit(0);
}
```

Figure 8.7 *(continued from facing page)*

Sample Program to Remove C-Style Comments from an Input File

complex than in the previous example. Because there is no equivalent to *ungetc()*, we have to manage the one-character look-ahead ourselves.

One feature of standard I/O that is extremely useful is its ability to do formatted input and output: the *printf()/scanf()* family of functions. Some of these functions predate the standard I/O library; *printf()* is as old as C. There

```
/*
** This program is invoked with two arguments.  The first is
** the name of the input file, and the second is the name of the
** file that will be created.
*/

#define _POSIX_SOURCE
#include <stdio.h>
#include <stdlib.h>
#include <sys/types.h>
#include <sys/stat.h>
#include <fcntl.h>

#define TRUE    1
#define FALSE   0
#define NONE   -1

int     *fdin,          /* Input file descriptor */
        *fdout;         /* Output file descriptor */

char    *infile,        /* Name of input file */
        *outfile;       /* Name of output file */

extern int errno;

main(int argc, char *argv[])
{
    char        c;
    int         peek_c = NONE;
    int         in_comment = FALSE;
    struct      stat st;
    ssize_t     nbytes;

    if ( argc != 3 )
    {
        fprintf(stderr, "usage: uncomment source dest\n");
        exit(1);
    }
    if ( (fdin = open((infile = *argv[1]), O_RDONLY)) < 0 )
    {
        fprintf(stderr, "%s: cannot open\n", infile);
        exit(1);
    }
    if ( fstat(fdin, &st) < 0 )
    {
        fprintf(stderr, "Can't stat %s: errno = %d\n", infile, errno);
        exit(1);
    }
```

Figure 8.8 *(continued on facing page)*

Another Program to Remove C-Style Comments from an Input File

```
        (void) umask((mode_t)0);
        if ( (fdout = open((outfile = *argv[2]), O_WRONLY | O_CREAT,
            st.st_mode)) < 0 )
        {
            fprintf(stderr, "%s: cannot create\n", outfile);
            exit(1);
        }
        /* Read characters one at a time until end of file */
        while ( peek_c != NONE || read(fdin, &c, 1) == 1 )
        {
            if ( peek_c != NONE)
            {
                c = peek_c;
                peek_c = NONE;
            }
            if ( ! in_comment )
            {
                if ( c == '/' )   /* Is it start of a comment? */
                {
                    nbytes = read(fdin, &c, 1);
                    if ( nbytes == 1 && c == '*' ) /* Yes */
                        in_comment = TRUE;
                    else                            /* No */
                    {
                        write(fdout, "/", 1);
                        if ( nbytes == 1 )
                            peek_c = c;
                    }
                }
                else
                    write(fdout, &c, 1);
            }
            else if ( c == '*' )  /* Is it end of a comment? */
            {
                nbytes = read(fdin, &c, 1);
                if ( nbytes == 1 && c == '/' )     /* Yes */
                {
                    in_comment = FALSE;
                    write(fdout, " ", 1);   /* Replace w/ space */
                }
                else                            /* No */
                    peek_c = c;
            }
        }  /* while */
    close(fdin);
    close(fdout);
    exit(0);
}
```

Figure 8.8 *(continued from facing page)*

Another Program to Remove C-Style Comments from an Input File

is no realistic substitute for these functions in low-level I/O. (You could write your own version of *printf()*, but why bother?) However, if you want to avoid streams you can use *sprintf()* to do formatting in your program's address space and then use *write()* to write to files.

The use of formatted I/O does present a portability problem on POSIX.1 systems. Suppose you want to write a decimal version of a process ID, user ID, link count, file serial number, or other value whose type is defined by a typedef. In principle, we know that these are arithmetic types, but we know little more. (The type pid_t must be signed, and uid_t must be unsigned. But what about ino_t?) So if you want to *printf()* a process ID, what conversion specification do you use? The safest thing to do in this case is to cast the process ID as a long and use %l. But when you're dealing with an arithmetic type and you don't know whether or not it's signed, it's not clear how to proceed. If, for example, ino_t is defined as unsigned long on some system and a particular value of an ino_t variable is greater than LONG_MAX but less than ULONG_MAX, using %l will give you the wrong value:

```
printf("File serial number = %l\n", (long) st.st_ino);
```

will print a negative value under these circumstances. On the other hand, suppose that on another system ino_t is defined as plain long and negative values are used for error indications. Or, less likely but legal, the system uses positive and negative serial numbers, with some meaning attached to a negative file serial number. In that case, using a cast to unsigned long and a conversion specifier of %ul could give the wrong result:

```
printf("File serial number = %ul\n",
    (unsigned long) st.st_ino);
```

will never print a negative value.

There is no general solution to the problem of *printf()* with variables of defined type. (You could cast the value to unsigned long and print it in hex, which is unambiguous but probably not what is wanted.) Fortunately, this is rarely a serious problem. In the above example negative file serial numbers are unlikely to be used. In most cases a suitable cast will work on the vast majority of systems.

8.3   Internationalization

Both C and the UNIX system are heavily imbued with assumptions about the ASCII character set and U.S. formats for times, real numbers, etc. Many of these assumptions are not valid outside the United States. For example, the printable ASCII characters are encoded using only the low seven bits in each byte; many European character sets need all eight. The number that Americans write as 1,234,567.89 is written as 1.234.567,89 in many other countries; the U.S. mm/dd/yy format for dates is hardly used anywhere else in the world—

the dd/mm/yy format is much more common. Internationalization deals with writing programs that do not make assumptions about character sets and formatting conventions that vary from one place to another.

The C standard makes provisions for internationalization in two different ways. This support is provided, not through any change to the language itself, but in the library. The standard provides a way to provide *locale-dependent* data—information regarding monetary formats, nonmonetary numeric formats, date/time formats, and character collating sequences—to an executing program. And it makes provision for character sets in which characters do not fit into a single byte.

Only part of this support is included in the POSIX.1 standard. POSIX includes the function *setlocale()* from the header `<locale.h>`. But POSIX does not include other objects from this header. Moreover, none of the functions to manipulate *wide characters* or *multibyte characters* are required by POSIX.1, although they may be supported. These are two forms of extended character support provided by ANSI C.*

8.3.1 Locale Categories

The *setlocale()* function allows you to control five categories of information about your process's locale. A prototype for *setlocale()* is:

```
#include <locale.h>
char *setlocale(int category, const char *locale);
```

The possible values of the `locale` argument are `NULL`, `" "`, `"C"`, or some other string whose meaning is implementation-defined. The lack of standardized format strings for different locales makes it difficult for a portable program to use *setlocale()*, but as we shall see certain defaults are possible. The possible values of the `category` argument are the constants `LC_CTYPE`, `LC_COLLATE`, `LC_TIME`, `LC_NUMERIC`, `LC_MONETARY`, and `LC_ALL`, which are defined in `<locale.h>`. Additional implementation-defined categories may be defined there, but they cannot be used by a portable program. The meaning of the categories is as follows:

- The `LC_CTYPE` category affects the behavior of the character-handling functions declared in `<ctype.h>`, such as *ispunct()*.

- The `LC_COLLATE` category affects the behavior of two ANSI C functions that are not part of the POSIX.1 standard: *strcoll()* and *strxfrm()*.

---

* A wide character is an object of type `wchar_t`, an arithmetic type defined in `<stddef.h>`. A multibyte character is a character stored in a sequence of (one or more) bytes (objects of type `char`). The C standard does not specify any character set encodings of these types, but it does provide functions to manipulate such objects if they are provided by the implementation.

Thus, a Strictly Conforming POSIX.1 Application should not be affected by the setting of the LC_COLLATE **category.**

- The LC_TIME category affects the *strftime()* function, an ANSI C function that is part of the POSIX.1 standard. The *strftime()* function formats time and date information into strings, much as *sprintf()* formats strings. Special substrings recognized by *strftime()* include conversion specifications such as %A, which is replaced by the locale's full weekday name. This might be "Wednesday", "mercredi", or "Woensdag", for example, depending on the LC_TIME category. We discuss *strftime()* in Section 8.4.

- The LC_NUMERIC category affects the decimal point for the formatted input/output functions (the *printf()*/*scanf()* family) and the string conversion functions (e.g., *atof()*). It also affects nonmonetary numeric formatting locale information used by the C standard but not by POSIX.

- The LC_MONETARY category affects monetary formatting information stored in the lconv structure, which is defined in the C standard but not explicitly referenced by POSIX.

- The LC_ALL category affects all of the above. So does the LANG environment variable.

A call to *setlocale()* sets the specified category to the named locale and returns the previous locale for that category. If the value of locale is NULL, then the category's locale is not changed. This call can be used to query the environment for the current locale. The fragment

```
char    *curr_locale;
curr_locale = setlocale(category, NULL);
```

returns a pointer to a string that describes the current value of the locale for category. The format of this string is unspecified, but it can be used as a locale argument in a later call to *setlocale()* to restore the category's locale.

If the locale argument is an empty string (" "), then the C standard specifies that the category is set to an implementation-defined value. In this case POSIX extends the semantics of *setlocale()* as follows: if an environment variable named LC_ALL is defined and not null, then the value of this variable is used for locale. If LC_ALL is not defined but an environment variable with the same name as the requested category (e.g., LC_TIME) is defined and not null, then its value is used for locale. If neither of these environment variables is defined but the environment variable LANG is defined and not null, then its value is used. If none of these is defined, the results are implementation-defined. If the value of an environment variable is used for locale but the value is not supported, then *setlocale()* returns a NULL pointer and does not change the category's locale.

8.3.2 Using Locales

To explain the meaning of the "C" locale, we have to stray slightly from the POSIX.1 domain. The header <locale.h> defines the data structure struct lconv. It includes these members:

```
struct lconv {
        char    *decimal_point;
        char    *thousands_sep;
        char    *grouping;
        char    *int_curr_symbol;
        char    *currency_symbol;
        char    *mon_decimal_point;
        char    *mon_thousands_sep;
        char    *mon_grouping;
        char    *positive_sign;
        char    *negative_sign;
        char    frac_digits;
        char    p_cs_precedes;
        char    p_sep_by_space;
        char    n_cs_precedes;
        char    n_sep_by_space;
        char    p_sign_posn;
        char    n_sign_posn;
};
```

This structure contains information that allows a program to format numeric and monetary quantities according to local convention. Note that all but the first three members affect only monetary quantities. Note also that *the* decimal_point *field is specified as a string, not a* char!

POSIX.1 does not explicitly refer to the lconv structure. The reason that POSIX programs are affected by this structure is that the C standard specifies the contents of this structure for a particular locale, the "C" locale. In the "C" locale:

- The string decimal_point has the value ".".

- All other strings in the structure have the value "".

- All char members of the structure have the value CHAR_MAX.

Both the C and POSIX.1 standards specify that, when a process begins execution, the equivalent of the call

```
setlocale(LC_ALL, "C");
```

is performed. Thus, all POSIX.1 C programs start with a known locale.

Given all this, how can a strictly conforming POSIX.1 application best take advantage of *setlocale()*? The most portable way to set locale categories is to rely on the environment variables, carefully documenting this in both the program code and the user instructions. If you want your program to work in international environments, make sure that your user instructions document which environment variables the user must set. Then, in your program, test for those variables. For example, suppose you want the user to set the LC_ALL environment variable. Your code should have something like this:

```
char    *lc_env;
if ( (lc_env = getenv("LC_ALL")) == (char *)NULL )
{
    printf("Warning: environment variable LC_ALL not set.\n\
Will use system default.\n");
    if ( (lc_env = getenv("LANG")) != (char *)NULL )
        printf("Using value of LANG variable: %s\n", lc_env);
}
if ( setlocale(LC_ALL, "") == (char *)NULL )
    printf("Cannot set LC_ALL locale; check environment\n");
```

Whether or not you should continue if *setlocale()* fails depends on the extent to which your program depends on locales.

Incidentally, the name of the "C" locale has come under some criticism, as the contents of the locale have nothing to do with the C language per se. The 1003.1 committee has created the "POSIX" locale. It is identical to the "C" locale except that implementations are free to extend it.

8.4   Time Functions

The C standard specifies a number of functions that are concerned with determining and formatting time values. Seven of these functions are included in POSIX.1. They are *asctime()*, *ctime()*, *gmtime()*, *localtime()*, *mktime()*, *strftime()*, and *time()*. Five of these functions have additional semantics imposed by POSIX.1.

The ANSI C *time()* function is derived from the corresponding function from the UNIX system. We discussed this function in Chapter 2, but we review its semantics here. It has the prototype:

```
#include <time.h>
time_t time(time_t *tloc);
```

The current time is returned, and if the value of tloc is not NULL the current time is also stored there. Although the C standard leaves the format of the time unspecified, POSIX.1 requires that it be the number of seconds since January 1, 1970, 0:00 UTC.

The remaining time functions make use of the `tm` structure. This data structure has the following members:

```
struct tm {
    int tm_sec;     /* In the range [0,59] */
    int tm_min;     /* In the range [0,59] */
    int tm_hour;    /* In the range [0,23] */
    int tm_mday;    /* In the range [1,31] */
    int tm_mon;     /* In the range [0,11] */
    int tm_year;    /* Years since 1900 */
    int tm_wday;    /* In the range [0,6]. 0 = Sunday */
    int tm_yday;    /* In the range [0,365]. January 1st = 0 */
    int tm_isdst;   /* Flag for Daylight Savings Time */
}
```

The contents of a `tm` structure are referred to as a "broken-down time". The `tm_isdst` member is interpreted as follows: if it is positive, Daylight Savings Time is in effect; if zero, Daylight Savings Time is not in effect; if negative, then no information about Daylight Savings Time is available.

8.4.1 Time Zones and Daylight Savings Time

The time functions in POSIX.1 are capable of translating from the system time to external time representations without any need for the programmer to worry about time zones or Daylight Savings Time (DST, also known as *summer time*). Thus, an application programmer will rarely have to use the information in this section. However, we provide it for the sake of completeness and because a library implementor will need it.

The C standard leaves as implementation-defined the method by which the system determines the current time zone and whether or not DST is in effect. POSIX.1 is more specific: the information is contained in the `TZ` environment variable. This variable has had a traditional form in UNIX systems: `stdhhdst`, where `std` is the abbreviation of the current time zone, hh is the offset in hours from UTC with positive offsets being west of Greenwich, and `dst` is the abbreviation of the time zone when DST is in effect. For example, the `TZ` setting in California has been written as `PST8PDT`.

The information traditionally contained in `TZ` is not sufficient for an international environment. In particular, the rule for describing when DST goes into effect is not encoded. It must be built into the system. This is a problem. Different countries have different rules for the start and end dates of DST. It may be that a program being run from a workstation in one country actually executes on a system in another country. Thus, the DST rule should be determined per process, not per system.

The POSIX.1 standard specifies two formats for the `TZ` variable. Any system can support a `TZ` string that begins with a colon (:). The meaning of such a string is implementation-defined. (This allows systems to use time

zone and DST rules not covered by the other format.) A TZ string that does
not begin with a colon must have the syntax

```
stdoffset[dst[offset][,rule]]
```

In this syntax, std and the first offset are separate tokens but are not
separated by a space. They are both required. The remaining tokens are
optional, as indicated by the brackets. The std token, and the dst token, if
present, must consist of three or more characters, none of which can be a
digit, plus sign, minus sign, or comma, and the first of which cannot be a
colon. The offset tokens have the syntax

```
hh[:mm[:ss]]
```

The hh portion of the offset is required and must consist of one or more
digits, optionally preceded by a "–" (to indicate an offset east of Greenwich)
or "+" (to indicate an offset west of Greenwich). If no sign is present, "+" is
assumed. The second offset can be omitted, in which case it is assumed to
be one more than the first offset.

The rule portion of the string gives the dates and times for starting
and ending DST. The syntax of rule is

```
start[/time],end[/time]
```

The start and end fields describe dates on which DST starts and ends.
Their associated time fields, which are optional, describe when the change
is made, in terms of current local time. The format of time is the same as that
of offset given above. If time is omitted, it defaults to 02:00:00, which is
the convention in the UNIX system (and in the United States).

A number of different formats are available to express the start and end
dates. They are:

- Mm.n.d, where the M is a literal (i.e., it is part of the string) and m, n, and
  d stand for the month, week number within the month, and day number
  within the week on which DST starts or ends. The day number must be
  between zero and 6, inclusive, with zero representing Sunday. The
  week number must be between 1 and 5, inclusive; 5 means "the last d
  day in month m". Thus, a full TZ string for the East Coast of the United
  States, in which DST begins at 2 A.M. on the first Sunday in April and
  ends at 2 A.M. on the last Sunday in October, would be

  ```
  TZ=EST5EDT6,M4.1.0/02:00:00,M10.5.0,02:00:00
  ```

  An equivalent setting for TZ, making use of the standard POSIX.1
  defaults, is

  ```
  TZ=EST5EDT,M4.1.0,M10.5.0
  ```

- Jn, where the J is a literal and n is a Julian day, in the range 1 to 365,
  inclusive. January 1st is day 1, and December 31st is day 365. There is
  no encoding for February 29th in this format.

- n, where n is simply a decimal number in the range 0 to 365, inclusive. In this format n also represents a Julian day, but January 1st is day 0, December 31st is either 365 or 364 depending on whether or not it is a leap year, and February 29th, in leap years, is 59. (In non-leap years March 1st is 59.)

Together, these formats would seem to cover all possibilities!

Every POSIX.1 process can declare the external variable tzname. This variable, like errno, is defined for your process by the system. Its declaration is:

```
extern char *tzname[2];
```

The purpose of the two character pointers is to point to the names of the std and dst time zone strings. The POSIX.1 function *tzset()* initializes tzname. Its prototype is:

```
#include <time.h>
void tzset(void);
```

A call to *tzset()* causes tzname[0] to point to a string that is a copy of std, taken from the TZ environment variable, and causes tzname[1] to point to a copy of dst. If TZ is not set in the environment, then the pointers in tzname are set to implementation-defined defaults. It would be a good idea to call *tzset()* early in a program that uses time strings, but as we shall see, it is rarely necessary.

8.4.2   More about Time Functions

To get a broken-down time, you use the *localtime()* function. This function takes as argument a pointer to a time_t object (typically returned by *time()*) and returns a pointer to a tm structure that is filled in with the corresponding broken-down time. The prototype for *localtime()* is:

```
#include <time.h>
struct tm *localtime(const time_t *timer);
```

The return value is a pointer to a static structure in which a broken-down time has been filled in, corresponding to the value of *timer. The C standard does not specify this correspondence, but for POSIX.1 systems the value stored at timer represents, as we have seen, the number of seconds since 0:00 January 1, 1970, UTC. However, the broken-down time is *not* given in terms of UTC. It is (as the function name implies) the local time. A POSIX.1 system determines the time zone and Daylight Savings Time information from the environment variable TZ. If this variable is not set, system defaults are used.

The function *gmtime()* is just like *localtime()*, except that it returns a pointer to a broken-down UTC (which used to be GMT) time. The prototype for *gmtime()* is:

```
#include <time.h>
struct tm *gmtime(const time_t *timer);
```

If you have a broken-down time and want to format it as an ASCII string in the format traditionally used by the UNIX system's date utility, you can use the *asctime()* function. This function has the following prototype:

```
#include <time.h>
char *asctime(const struct tm *timeptr);
```

It returns a pointer to a string formatted with the format

```
"%.3s %.3s%.3d %.2d:%.2d:%.2d %d\n"
```

in which the fields being formatted are the abbreviated weekday name (e.g., "Tue"); the abbreviated month (e.g., "Mar"); the day of the month; the hour, minute, and second; and the four-digit year. The abbreviations are the traditional English ones; as its name implies, *asctime()* is not internationalized. Thus, the string returned by *asctime()* might look like:

```
"Tue Aug 21 21:47:30 1990\n"
```

Note that *asctime()* includes a newline in its returned string. A common mistake is to *printf()* this string with the format `"%s\n"`, unintentionally getting two newlines.

If you want to call *asctime()*, you need a broken-down time and you'll probably get that by calling *localtime()* first. This sequence is so common that the C standard provides, and POSIX.1 supports, the function *ctime()*, which does both of these steps at once. The prototype for *ctime()* is:

```
#include <time.h>
char *ctime(const time_t *timer);
```

The expression

```
ctime(timer);
```

is equivalent to

```
asctime(localtime(timer));
```

If you want to format time strings in an internationalized way, you need to use the *strftime()* function. This function allows you to format time and date strings very flexibly. It has the prototype:

```
#include <time.h>
size_t strftime(char *s, size_t maxsize, const char *format,
                const struct tm *timeptr);
```

The argument s points to an array in which you want the formatted string to appear. The maxsize argument should be the size of the array (counting room for a null byte). The format string describes the string to be produced, using *printf()*-like conversion specifications that are shown in Figure 8.9.

%a   Replaced by the locale's abbreviated weekday name.

%A   Replaced by the locale's full weekday name.

%b   Replaced by the locale's abbreviated month name.

%B   Replaced by the locale's full month name.

%c   Replaced by the locale's appropriate date and time representation.

%d   Replaced by the day of the month as a two-digit decimal number in the range 01–31.

%H   Replaced by the hour as a two-digit decimal number in the range 00–23.

%I   Replaced by the hour as a two-digit decimal number in the range 01–12.

%j   Replaced by the day of the year as a three-digit decimal number in the range 001–366.

%m   Replaced by the month as a two-digit decimal number in the range 01–12.

%M   Replaced by the minute as a two-digit decimal number in the range 01–59.

%p   Replaced by the locale's equivalent of either A.M. or P.M.

%S   Replaced by the second as a two-digit decimal number in the range 01–59.

%U   Replaced by the week number of the year, counting Sunday as the first day of the week, as a two-digit decimal number in the range 00–53.

%w   Replaced by the weekday number as a single decimal digit in the range 0–6, with 0 = Sunday.

%W   Replaced by the week number of the year, counting Monday as the first day of the week, as a two-digit decimal number in the range 00–53.

%x   Replaced by the locale's appropriate date representation.

%X   Replaced by the locale's appropriate time representation.

%y   Replaced by the year without century as a two-digit decimal number in the range 00–99.

%Y   Replaced by the year with century as a decimal number.

%Z   Replaced by the time zone name. If the time zone cannot be determined, %Z is replaced by no characters.

%%   Replaced by a single % character.

Figure 8.9

Conversion Specifications for *strftime()*

(Recall that many of the fields formatted by *strftime()* are locale-specific, depending on the LC_TIME category of the locale.) The timeptr argument points to a tm structure in which a broken-down time can be found that is used in the string. Any characters in format other than conversion specifications are copied directly to the formatted string, just as with *printf()*. The return value of *strftime()* is the number of characters that were copied to the array at s, not counting the null byte. If this number would exceed maxsize, then zero is returned and the contents of the array are indeterminate. Note that this is one of the few functions of type int that, on error, returns zero.

For example, consider the following code fragment:

```
#define DBUFSIZE       128
char      buf[DBUFSIZE];
char      *format = "Today is %A %B %d %Y\nThe time is %H:%M:%S";
/* ... */
if (strftime(buf, DBUFSIZE, format, localtime(time(NULL))) == 0)
    strcpy(buf, "Error formatting time");
printf("%s\n", buf);
```

If the locale is set to a value appropriate for English, then this fragment will print something of the form:

```
Today is Tuesday February 13 1990
The time is 17:55:23
```

The same code, with a locale appropriate for Dutch, will print something like:

```
Today is dinsdag februari 13 1990
The time is 17:55:23
```

Of course, this shows how ridiculous it is to mix hard-coded text with the output of functions that are internationalized. If your internationalized program is going to print more text than just that provided by *strftime()*, it should use message catalogues with the appropriate national language text.

The POSIX.1 standard supports one more C standard time function. This is *mktime()*, which, in some sense, is the reverse of *localtime()*. A call to *mktime()* is passed a pointer to a broken-down time in a tm structure and converts it to a time_t that is a time as encoded by the system, e.g., in seconds since the Epoch. A prototype for *mktime()* is:

```
#include <time.h>
time_t mktime(struct tm *timeptr);
```

Note that the argument is not declared as a const pointer. This is because a call to *mktime()* can also modify the tm structure that it is passed. This is because it's possible to have a tm structure whose contents are inconsistent. For example, it could indicate a date of March 18, 1990, and a day-of-week that is Thursday (it should be Sunday) and a day-of-year that is 200 (it should be 67). Moreover, the other fields may have values outside their respective ranges. For this reason, *mktime()* ignores the `tm_wday` and `tm_yday` fields of the structure. It also accepts and converts other values that are out of range. For example, if `tm_mon` is 3, `tm_mday` is 36, and `tm_hour` is 28, *mktime()* will interpret the date as April 6th and the hour as 4:00 A.M. (unless the minute and second fields also overflow), because March 36 would be April 5, and 28 o'clock on the 5th would be 4 o'clock on the 6th. When *mktime()* returns, it not only returns the corresponding time since the Epoch, it adjusts the fields in `*timeptr` by filling in correct values for `tm_wday` and `tm_yday` and by converting any overflowed fields to correct values inside their ranges.

Any time any of the functions *ctime()*, *localtime()*, *strftime()*, or *mktime()* is called, a POSIX.1 system sets the external variable `tzname` as if *tzset()* had also been called. This is why an application rarely has to call *tzset()* explicitly.

Exercises for Chapter 8

1. Consider the following program:

```
main(argc, argv)
int argc;
char *argv[];
{
    double root;
    double x;
    if ( argc != 2 )
        exit(1);
    x = atof(*++argv);
    root = sqrt(x);
    printf("The square root of %g is %g\n", x, root);
}
```

This program is broken. How can you fix it?

2. Consider the following program:

```
#define _POSIX_SOURCE
#include <math.h>
main()
{
    printf("The square root of 3 is %g\n", sqrt(3));
}
```

What will happen if this program is compiled and executed on a system that supports standard C? What will happen if it is compiled and executed on a common usage C system? If you have access to both such types of systems, try it on both.

3. Explain why no header named in the C standard can include any other header named in the C standard. There are symbols, like NULL, that must be defined in more than one header. Explain how, if you were implementing the headers for a standard C system, you could define such symbols in only one place.

4. Explain the difference between using a typedef and using a #define to define a type. For example, consider the two fragments

```
#define ip   int *
ip       a, b;
```

and

```
typedef int *ip;
ip       a, b;
```

5. Suppose you want to *fopen()* a stream to read a FIFO. You would like to make nonblocking reads (using *getc()*) from the FIFO. That is, if the FIFO is empty you want *getc()* to return immediately and not to block. How can you arrange this?

6. Suppose you want to write to a file, using I/O functions from <stdio.h>, but if the file does not exist you want to have control over its access mode. Explain two ways that you can do this.

7. If the type time_t is defined to be unsigned long, and a long is 32 bits in length, when will the *time()* function's return value overflow?

Data Interchange Formats

The section of the POSIX.1 standard dealing with data interchange formats is somewhat anomalous. It describes no operating system interfaces. Rather, it gives the formats that conforming implementations should use in writing data to external media, to make that data transportable to other conforming implementations. There are two such formats. They are extensions of the UNIX system formats known as `tar` and `cpio`. The `tar` format was present in AT&T UNIX systems at least from 6th Edition UNIX but was replaced by `cpio` in UNIX System III. However, Berkeley UNIX systems have continued to support `tar` and not `cpio`. The POSIX.1 standard requires a conforming implementation to support both formats.

During the development of the standard, there was some disagreement within the 1003.1 committee over exactly what should be in this section, or even whether it belonged in the standard at all. The data interchange formats themselves are not very useful to writers of application programs. It is rare that a portable application will need to create archives in `tar` or `cpio` format. Such archives are usually created by system utilities, and the specification of such utilities is the job of a different POSIX committee, 1003.2. However, portability of application programs is of little value without a standard interchange and installation method. After some discussion it was decided that the formats themselves fell into a gray area that was best handled by the 1003.1 committee, while the utilities used to create or read archives in these formats would remain the responsibility of 1003.2.

The POSIX.1 standard makes no reference to 1003.2 and does not require conformance to it. The requirement in POSIX.1 is simply that a conforming implementation "shall provide a mechanism to copy files from a medium to the file hierarchy and copy files from the file hierarchy to a medium using the formats described here". The mechanism is assumed by POSIX.1 to reside in unspecified utilities that it refers to as the *format-creating utility* and the *format-reading utility*, respectively. (In practice, these will usually be the same utility.)

Yet another controversy arose over which format to support. This was a continuation of a disagreement that had been going on for years. AT&T had replaced `tar` because it suffers from serious deficiencies. However, the `cpio` format also has some problems. Each format had its adherents in the committee, continuing a dispute that has been referred to as "`tar` wars". The eventual compromise was to extend both formats in a backward-compatible way, and—as we have already observed—to require every POSIX.1 system to support both. (To make matters even more complicated, a proposed revision to the standard replaces both `tar` and `cpio` formats with a third format based on an older ANSI standard.) Incidentally, the current (as of this writing) draft of the POSIX.2 standard supports both formats with a single utility named `pax`. Ostensibly, this is an acronym for Portable Archive eXchange.

There are a number of reasons that it is useful to understand these formats. These include:

- To implement utilities, such as a `pax` utility, that create or read these formats. Only a few programmers, usually system implementors, will ever be called upon to do this. Moreover, as we shall see, it is not possible to write such utilities in a completely portable manner. They cannot be Strictly Conforming POSIX.1 Applications.

- To enable application programs to directly manipulate (read or create) such archives. You will rarely, if ever, have to do this.

- To understand the limits that these formats place on portable applications. If you want to package your application for installation or distribution in a `tar` or `cpio` archive, then you will have to recognize certain constraints. This is the most important reason for an application programmer to understand `tar` and `cpio`.

In this chapter we digress somewhat from a discussion of the POSIX.1 standard to consider the requirements of packaging a portable application. However, for the sake of completeness we also describe the structure that the POSIX.1 standard defines for `tar` and `cpio` archives.

9.1   Packaging Applications

Suppose you want to distribute a complete application in a portable package. A number of things might go into such a package, including:

- Application programs in source form. To provide complete portability, you have to distribute source code.

- Application programs in binary form. These can only be portable within a single application binary interface (ABI). An ABI describes an application programming interface (API) such as POSIX.1, along with a standard object format and calling sequence for that interface for a particular processor and operating system implementation. Standard ABIs are becoming common for the more popular microprocessors, so it is feasible to distribute an application portably in binary form, as long as you are willing to maintain several binary versions. Because of the proliferation of ABIs, the number of such versions need not be too great: one per processor/OS type, instead of one for each type of computer. But the dependency on operating systems is crucial here. Even two equivalent versions of an operating system for the same processor could have different ABIs.

- Data files. These can include online documentation, data files, and examples of ways to use the application. The files might have data of almost any type, including text, integer, and floating point data.

- Installation scripts and instructions. To write portable installation scripts, you are advised to adhere to the shell language in the proposed POSIX.2 standard. However, this is just a guideline; systems conforming to the POSIX.1 standard need not conform to any other standard, and it may be that there will be no portable way to write installation scripts that are valid for all POSIX.1 conforming systems.

9.1.1   Packaging Source Files

If you distribute your application in source form, then you need to worry about a number of issues. For the C language, the source language character set is an important issue. C uses almost all of the printable ASCII characters. (Only the backquote "`", the @ sign, and the $ sign are not used.) Not all of these characters are present on many international character sets, even for European languages. The most portable character set for languages that use the roman alphabet or variations thereof is the ISO 646 character set.

The version of the POSIX.1 standard adopted in 1988 mandated that files stored in `tar` or `cpio` archives could be stored in any form, *except that* source files had to be stored in ASCII. The 1990 revision changed that provision from ASCII to ISO 646. This presents some problems. The differences between ASCII and ISO 646:1983 are shown in Figure 9.1. The character ¤ in the table is an abstract currency symbol. In a draft revision of the ISO 646 standard, this symbol is to be replaced by the $ character.

If you look at Figure 9.1 you will notice that nine of the characters used in C source programs are not part of ISO 646. This makes it difficult for programmers using ISO 646 keyboards to create C source files. International representatives on the ANSI C committee raised this issue. The eventual

Decimal	Octal	Hex	ASCII	ISO 646
35	043	0x23	#	# or £
36	044	0x24	$	$ or ¤
64	0100	0x40	@	undefined
91	0133	0x5b	[	undefined
92	0134	0x5c	\	undefined
93	0135	0x5d	]	undefined
94	0136	0x5e	^	undefined
96	0140	0x60	'	undefined
123	0173	0x7b	{	undefined
124	0174	0x7c	|	undefined
125	0175	0x7d	}	undefined
126	0176	0x7e	~	undefined

Figure 9.1

Comparison of the ASCII and ISO 646 Character Sets

solution, chosen from a number of proposals, was to use what are known as *trigraph sequences* to represent the missing characters. These escape sequences are three-character sequences of ISO 646 characters, each of which is treated by a standard C translator as equivalent to a single corresponding C source character. The nine C trigraphs are shown in Figure 9.2. Each consists of two consecutive question marks followed by a character from ISO 646. Each trigraph is a single token and must be written with no intervening white space.

If you are archiving C source files for backup, or for transport from one machine that supports ASCII to another such machine, then there's no need to worry about using trigraphs. But if you want to put a source file in an archive that satisfies the portability requirements of POSIX.1, you must use ISO 646, and consequently you must use trigraphs. It may be that the utility you use to create your archive will support a mode in which the conversion is done automatically, or you may have to do it yourself. Of course, such a conversion program is easy to write. Figure 9.3 shows a strictly conforming POSIX.1 application that performs the transformation. The program is written as a filter: it reads from standard input and writes to standard output.

Note that this program is not itself written in ISO 646. However, it could be used (on a host that supports ASCII) to transform itself into an ISO 646 version of itself.

C Source Character	Trigraph
[	??(
]	??)
{	??<
}	??>
\	??/
|	??!
^	??'
#	??=
~	??-

Figure 9.2

C Standard Trigraphs

In principle, the reverse transformation is not needed, because any C standard compiler will perform the conversion automatically as part of the compilation process. However, the occasion may arise when you will have to take a C source file written in ISO 646 and compile it on an old-style (common usage C) compiler, which does not recognize trigraphs. For that occasion, we give the program to perform the reverse transformation in Figure 9.4.

9.1.2 Packaging Binary Executable Files

As we mentioned above, binary executables are not completely portable. This contrasts with the situation in which application packages are distributed for a proprietary architecture, such as the IBM PC and its lookalikes or the Macintosh. It is precisely because UNIX systems, and now POSIX systems, are supported on a wide variety of architectures that distribution of binary executables is a problem. However, the situation is improving.

One useful change has been the development of ABIs for major chip families. For example, the 88open consortium has developed an ABI for users of Motorola's 88000 microprocessor. Thus a single binary version of an application can be distributed for use on all computers that use this processor and adhere to the ABI. (The ABI may depend on the operating system as well as the processor.) An even more promising possibility is the eventual design and acceptance of an architecture neutral distribution format, or ANDF. The Open Software Foundation is working to develop such a format. ANDF is something like the intermediate code of a language translator: applications are translated to ANDF, distributed, and then installed on their targets by installer software that acts something like a traditional code generator.

```
#define _POSIX_SOURCE
#include <stdio.h>

#define QQ putchar('?'); putchar('?')

/*
** Store the nonportable characters in a char array. Remember
** to escape '\'. Store the corresponding replacements after
** the '??' in another char array.
*/
char    replace[] = "[]{}\\|^#~";
char    tri[] =     "()<>/!'=-";

main()
{
    int ch;
    char *p;

    while ( (ch = getchar()) != EOF )
        if ( (p = strchr(replace, ch)) == NULL )
            putchar(ch);
        else
        {
            QQ;
            putchar (*(tri + (p - replace)));
        }
    exit(0);
}
```

Figure 9.3

Inserting Trigraphs in Code

The POSIX.1 standard places no restrictions on the contents of binary files in tar or cpio archives.

9.1.3 Packaging Data Files

Your application package will almost always include some data files. These may be as simple as online copies of the documentation, or they may contain data of all sorts. Making this data portable can present substantial problems.

If a file simply contains text, then we have already seen the principal portability issue: character sets. One alternative is to distribute different versions of text files for different locales. In some cases, of course, this is

```c
#define _POSIX_SOURCE
#include <stdio.h>

#define QUES '?'

char    replace[] = "[]{}\\|^#~";  /* Escape the \ character */
char    tri[] =     "()<>/!'=-";

main()
{
    int    ch;
    char   *p;

    while ( (ch = getchar()) != EOF )
        if ( ch == QUES )
        {   /* See if a second '?' follows */
            ch = getchar();
            if ( ch == QUES )
            {   /* Yes.  See if a recognized trigraph */
                ch = getchar();
                if ( (p = strchr(tri, ch )) == NULL )
                {   /* Not a recognized trigraph */
                    putchar(QUES);
                    putchar(QUES);
                    putchar(ch);
                }
                else
                    putchar (*(replace + (p - tri)));
            }
            else
            {   /* Only one '?' */
                putchar(QUES);
                putchar(ch);
            }
        }
        else
            putchar(ch);
    exit(0);
}
```

Figure 9.4

Removing Trigraphs from Code

necessary. If you wish to distribute documents for Asian, Middle Eastern, and European locales you are faced with such a wide variety of alphabets that you have no choice. If you're just concerned with English-language text files, then if you can restrict your data to the ISO 646 character set you should have no problem.

Numeric or abstract data (e.g., values of enumerated types) presents another issue. Data portability between different and incompatible hardware platforms has always been a problem. The POSIX.1 standard helps, but it does not completely solve this problem. Part of the difficulty lies in the difference between internal and external representation of certain data types.

There is no universal internal representation of int values or of values that have floating point type (e.g., float, double). There *is* a standard (IEEE Std. 754) but it is not universally adopted, and it does not specify byte order. If you need to package data files that contain such data in a portable way, you face a formidable problem. The least portable solution is to use a binary representation, i.e., the representation that is used internally in some computers' memory. Such representations are completely unportable. The best portable solution is to convert such values into decimal representation, as a sequence of printable (ISO 646) characters, and store those character sequences.

An example will illustrate what we mean. Suppose that you need to store the value 4/7, as a float, in a data file that needs to be transported. On your machine, it has some, say, 32-bit internal representation, which is *not* exact. That is, the stored value is not exactly equal to 4/7 (which has an infinite repeating representation in both the decimal and binary systems), but it is a close approximation. But on another machine the same 32-bit pattern may represent an entirely different value; float objects might take up 48 or 64 bits on some machines. If you store your value in the archive as the ISO string "0.57142857142857" and arrange for it to be converted to the proper internal representation for the target machine when the data file is installed, you will get a value that is a good approximation of 4/7.

However, this method has its drawbacks. Suppose that you convert the 32-bit internal bit sequence that best approximates 4/7 to an ISO 646 string and then—on the same hardware—convert that string back to a 32-bit float. Will you get back the same 32 bits? Not necessarily! Thus, it is possible to lose accuracy by using string representations for certain numeric data types, when you would not lose that accuracy if you archived the binary values for restoration on identical hardware.

The best solution is to be practical and consider what portability gets you. If you are only creating an archive to back files up, or to allow them to be moved to other systems that have the same hardware or compatible data representations of all types, then using the internal representations in your files is the right choice. It's not widely portable, but it's portable over the range of targets that concerns you. The same consideration applies to the use of C trigraphs. If you are going to archive source programs for distribution only to systems that support ASCII, then converting the non–ISO 646 characters in your source files to trigraphs is silly. But for the most general distribution, it's necessary.

9.1.4 Pathnames

If you distribute your application as a collection of files, regardless of the file types, you should archive all the files with pathnames relative to the current (at the time of installation) directory. That is, none of the pathnames should start with '/' or contain '..' components. You should avoid relying on absolute pathnames for any of the installed files. An instruction of the form "Create a directory named /usr/lib/dbase and install all the files there" is a mistake; so is archiving files with pathnames like /usr/lib/dbase/phone_list. Such pathnames may conflict with existing pathnames or may conflict with local policy or requirements. The application should be able to work with all its files installed relative to an arbitrary node in the file hierarchy. If necessary, you can require users to set an environment variable with the absolute pathname of the installation directory, and the application can evaluate that variable at run time.

The tar format places a limit on pathnames. The original version of tar in the UNIX system limited pathnames to 100 bytes. (This seemed like a lot when filenames were limited to 14 bytes.) The POSIX.1 standard has extended the tar header to accommodate pathnames as long as 256 bytes, although not all pathnames of this length can be stored. In Section 9.2 we discuss the limitations of this format.

The UNIX system's cpio format has traditionally had a pathname limit of 128 bytes. This limit is not specified by the POSIX.1 extended version of cpio. However, it may be that some implementations will suffer from such limits.

Sometimes it is necessary for an application to archive special files. Both tar and cpio provide for the archiving and extraction of directories, FIFOs, and block and character special files. However, there is no portable way to create the last two file types, and a portable application should not need them. Both formats also support the archiving of links, including symbolic links (see Chapter 10, Section 10.1.1), and of contiguous or high-performance files. However, a POSIX.1 implementation is free to ignore such file types, and you should not use them.

9.2 Extended tar Format

An extended tar archive consists of a sequence of 512-byte logical blocks. Each file in the archive has a single header block, followed by any number (including possibly zero) of data blocks. After all the header and data blocks in the archive, two blocks of binary zeros must be present to indicate the end of the archive.

The header block could be represented by a C struct, but there are two reasons not to do so. Most important is that the fields in the header have byte offsets that are fixed by the standard, whereas a C implementation is free to add alignment bytes to any struct. In addition, the POSIX.1 standard does not specify field names for the fields in the tar header. Figure 9.5 shows the fields in the header, with their required lengths and byte offsets.

The fields in the tar header are all stored as ISO 646 strings of the given size. Three of them are stored as null-terminated strings: magic, uname, and gname. Three more are stored as strings that are null-terminated unless they exactly fill the available space. These are name, linkname, and prefix. The version field, which is two bytes long, must have two zero characters ("00", not null bytes, and not null-terminated). The typeflag field is a single character whose contents are discussed below. All of the remaining fields are numeric. They are stored as ISO 646 representations of octal numbers, with as many leading zeros as necessary to fill the given size.

The fields have the following meanings:

- name is used, together with prefix, to produce the pathname of the file. One of the historical problems with the tar format was that it only supported pathnames of 100 bytes. The prefix field was not present on these formats. The POSIX.1 standard specifies that the pathname of the file is reconstructed from the header as follows: if the first character of prefix is a null byte, then the pathname is name. Otherwise, the system concatenates prefix (up to the first null byte), a single implicit slash character '/', and name (also up to the first null character) to form a pathname. This pathname can (if you are fortunate) be as long as 256 bytes. The reason you need to be fortunate is that the implicit slash character is always inserted between prefix and name. Thus, you cannot have path components that span the prefix and name fields. For example, the pathname <name1>/<name2>/<name3>, where each of the <name> components is 80 bytes in length, cannot be stored, even though the total length is 242 bytes. Remember that the characters in these fields must be taken from the portable filename character set.

  If, while creating an archive, the format-creating utility cannot store a file's pathname in the space given by prefix and name, then the utility must issue a diagnostic message and will not store any header or data for the file in the archive.

- mode stores the file's nine permission bits, set-user-ID and set-group-ID bits, and a reserved bit. The format of these bits in mode, unlike the format of st_mode in the stat structure, is specified in the POSIX.1 standard. This must be so, because these modes must be portable between different implementations of POSIX.1. As the mode field is 8 bytes long and each byte holds an octal digit, there is room to represent

Field Name	Byte Offset	Length in Bytes
name	0	100
mode	100	8
uid	108	8
gid	116	8
size	124	12
mtime	136	12
chksum	148	8
typeflag	156	1
linkname	157	100
magic	257	6
version	263	2
uname	265	32
gname	297	32
devmajor	329	8
devminor	337	8
prefix	345	155

Figure 9.5

Format of a tar Header Block

24 bits in this field. However, only the 12 bits named above have formats assigned by the standard. They are:

```
TSUID    04000    /* Corresponds to S_ISUID */
TSGID    02000    /* Corresponds to S_ISGID */
TSVTX    01000    /* Reserved */
TUREAD   00400    /* Corresponds to S_IRUSR */
TUWRITE  00200    /* Corresponds to S_IWUSR */
TUEXEC   00100    /* Corresponds to S_IXUSR */
TGREAD   00040    /* Corresponds to S_IRGRP */
TGWRITE  00020    /* Corresponds to S_IWGRP */
TGEXEC   00010    /* Corresponds to S_IXGRP */
TOREAD   00004    /* Corresponds to S_IROTH */
TOWRITE  00002    /* Corresponds to S_IWOTH */
TOEXEC   00001    /* Corresponds to S_IXOTH */
```

For example, if a file's mode is (S_IRWXU | S_IRGRP | S_ISUID), **its** mode field on a tar archive would be stored as the string "00004740". The symbolic names of the bit flags are defined in the header <tar.h>.

The TSVTX bit has no portable meaning in POSIX.1, but it corresponds to a bit that has been widely used in many implementations of UNIX systems—the "sticky bit". Historically, this bit, when set in the mode of a file that is executable, would cause the text portion of the file to remain in memory after the process that had caused it to be loaded was terminated. (The *text* portion of an executable file consists of the instructions that are executable by the machine hardware.) This bit was set for program files that were likely to be used very often, such as editors, to avoid the overhead of constantly reloading the program text from disk. Because these semantics are only meaningful for regular files (and only for a few of them), the sticky bit often has been overloaded with many other implementation-specific meanings when set in the mode of directories or other types of special files. None of these meanings is POSIX.1 portable. A format-reading utility on an implementation that does not support this bit can ignore it. You should avoid setting this bit in the modes of files that you archive.

- The uid and gid fields are the numerical owner ID and group ID of the file on the hierarchy from which the archive was created. For example, if the owner ID of the file is 510, the uid field for the file would be stored as the string "00000776", because 510 is written as 776 in octal.

- The uname and gname fields are null-terminated strings that are the ISO 646 representation of the owner and group of the file on the file hierarchy from which the archive was created. They are truncated to fit, if necessary. This means that a maximum of 31 bytes plus an obligatory null byte can be stored and represents another length limitation imposed by the tar format.

- The typeflag field contains a single character that specifies the type of the file being archived. The POSIX.1 standard specifies that the following symbols are defined in <tar.h> for use in the typeflag field:

```
REGTYPE    '0'  /* File is a regular file */
AREGTYPE   '\0' /* File is a regular file */
LNKTYPE    '1'  /* File is a link */
SYMTYPE    '2'  /* Reserved for use with symbolic links */
CHRTYPE    '3'  /* File is character special */
BLKTYPE    '4'  /* File is block special */
DIRTYPE    '5'  /* File is a directory */
FIFOTYPE   '6'  /* File is a FIFO */
CONTTYPE   '7'  /* Reserved for use with contiguous files */
```

There are two different codes for regular files because, historically, different implementations have used both ASCII zero (' 0 ') and the null byte (' \0 ') for this purpose. Future implementations should use ' 0 '. The code ' 2 ' (SYMTYPE) is reserved "to represent a link to another file, of any type, whose device or file serial number differs"—in other words, for symbolic links. Many UNIX systems support them now with this code. The code ' 7 ' (CONTTYPE) is reserved "to represent a file to which an implementation has associated some high performance attribute". In practice, these "high-performance files" have been implemented as pre-allocated, contiguous files. The draft of the proposed POSIX.4 real-time standard specifies requirements for high-performance files.

The standard reserves the values ' A ' - ' Z ' for use by custom implementations. That is, implementations may use these values for typeflag to represent file types other than those in the standard. All other values of typeflag are reserved for future revisions of the POSIX.1 standard. At least three other special file types (for semaphores, shared memory, and inter-process message queues) are specified in the current draft of 1003.4. Other POSIX working groups may propose yet more special file types.

A format-reading utility on a system that does not support symbolic links should treat typeflag values of ' 2 ' as ' 1 ' (ordinary links). On a system that does not support high-performance files, a typeflag value of ' 7 ' should be treated as ' 0 '.

- linkname stores the name of a file to which the given file is linked. This field only applies to files whose typeflag is '1'. Its purpose is to save information about links in the archive. The length of this field is limited to 100 bytes, and it does not use the prefix field to produce a pathname. If the name of the linked-to file exceeds 100 bytes, then the format-creating utility is required to notify the user that this has occurred and will not store the link in the archive. This field is used for hard links only. Symbolic links, if implemented, do not use linkname.

- For regular files, the size field contains the size of the file in bytes. For files whose typeflag is LNKTYPE or SYMTYPE, the value of size must be zero. For files whose typeflag is BLKTYPE, CHRTYPE, or FIFOTYPE the POSIX.1 standard leaves unspecified the meaning of the size field. The standard does specify that the value of size for files of type FIFOTYPE shall be ignored by the format-reading utility.

For files whose typeflag is DIRTYPE, the value of size depends on the system. Some systems allocate disk space per directory. That is, there is a limit to the amount of space that may be occupied by a given subtree of the file hierarchy, and that limit may vary from one part of the hierarchy to another. On such systems, the `size` field for directories contains the maximum number of bytes that the file hierarchy rooted at that directory can contain. If the system supports such limits but there is no limit for a particular directory, that directory's `size` field shall contain zero. On systems that do not support such limits, the format-creating utility should store zero in this field and the format-reading utility should ignore the field.

For files of all types, the values of `typeflag` and `size` together tell how many data blocks follow the header, as follows: for files of type LNKTYPE, SYMTYPE, DIRTYPE, BLKTYPE, CHRTYPE, or FIFOTYPE, no data blocks are stored. In particular, archiving a FIFO merely stores its existence, not its contents. For files of all other types (including those not specified by this standard), the number of data blocks shall be (`size` + 511)/512, truncated to an integer.

- The `mtime` field represents the modification time of the file (the `st_mtime` field of the `stat` structure associated with the file) at the time it was archived. This is an ISO 646 string containing the octal representation of the number of seconds since the Epoch that the file was last modified.

- The `magic` field contains the string TMAGIC, which must be defined in the `<tar.h>` header as `"ustar"`. Counting the terminating null byte, this is a six-byte string. The POSIX.1 standard also requires that the symbol TMAGLEN be defined in `<tar.h>` as 6.

- The `version` field, as previously mentioned, contains the string TVERSION, which must be defined in the `<tar.h>` header as `"00"`. Only the two zeros, not the terminating null byte, are stored. The POSIX.1 standard also requires that the symbol TVERSLEN be defined in `<tar.h>` as 2.

- The `devmajor` and `devminor` fields are only meaningful for files whose `typeflag` is BLKTYPE or CHRTYPE. For such files they contain "information defining the device, the format of which is unspecified" by the standard. Historically, these have been the major and minor device numbers. The format-reading utility may ignore such files in an archive or may map the `devmajor` and `devminor` fields into meaningful values in a system-dependent way.

- The `chksum` field contains the octal representation of the sum of all 512 bytes in the header block, in which each byte is treated as an 8-bit unsigned value. In calculating `chksum`, the 8 bytes of `chksum` itself shall be treated as if they were 8 ISO 646 blank characters. As there are $512 = 2^9$ bytes in the header, each of which has 8 bits, the checksum must be calculated in an unsigned integer that has at least 17 bits of precision. On some systems, this means that an object of type `unsigned long` should be used in the calculation.

9.2.1   Restoring Extended `tar` Archives

Archives can be used for two distinct purposes: to transfer data from one system to another or to backup data from a system for later restoration to the same system. There are some problems in using the same format for both purposes. In particular, the information describing the user and group IDs of the files is meaningful on a given system, but may not be meaningful when transferring files from one system to another. For this reason, the POSIX.1 standard specifies different kinds of behavior when an archive is restored by a process with privileges or by a non-privileged process.

If an archive is restored using the format-reading utility and the restoring process runs without appropriate privileges, then each file is created with access permissions and ownership set as if the process had called *creat()* with a mode argument whose permission bits were those in the `mode` field of the file's header. In other words, the effective user ID of the process becomes the file's owner, the effective group ID or the parent directory's group ID becomes the file's group, and the permission bits are set to those in `mode`, modified by the process's umask. This is typically the way you would use the utility to install an application. You want the application files to be owned by whoever does the installation.

If the restoring process has appropriate privileges, however, the file modes are restored exactly as they are stored in the archive, and the owner and group are set as follows: the system's user database is searched for the name stored in the uname field. If this name is found, then the corresponding user ID from the database is used as the file's owner ID. Otherwise, the value stored in the `uid` field is used. A similar process is used with the gname field and the system group database. In other words, a privileged restore of the archive assigns file ownership and group by name if possible, and by ID otherwise. This is the way that you would like to install archives that are backups. It also allows you to preserve ownerships of files that are moved from one machine to another within an office where users keep the same login names but not necessarily the same user IDs on all machines.

9.3   Extended `cpio` Format

An extended `cpio` archive (also referred to as a byte-oriented `cpio` archive) consists of a sequence of entries. Each entry consists of a fixed-size header, a variable-size filename, and a variable-size file data portion. All of the entries

in the header are ISO 646 strings of octal digits, padded on the left with zeros
to the required length, without terminating null bytes. The most significant
octal digit appears first in each field. The format of the header is shown in
Figure 9.6.

As you can see by examining Figure 9.6, a cpio file header is 76 bytes
long. After the header, the next c_namesize bytes of the archive are the
file's pathname. This name must contain a terminating null byte, which shall
be included in the size given by c_namesize. Immediately following the
filename comes the file data, consisting of c_filesize bytes. As c_namesize
can be up to six octal digits, the cpio format supports very long pathnames.

The fields have the following meanings:

- The c_magic field contains the string "070707". This is not null-
  terminated.

- The c_dev and c_ino fields contain values that are determined in an
  unspecified manner but that shall uniquely identify the file within the
  archive. If two files in the archive are links to one another, they shall
  have the same values of c_dev and c_ino. Otherwise, no two files in
  the archive shall have the same values for both of these fields. In
  practice, these are the st_dev and st_ino fields from the file's stat
  structure.

Field Name	Length in Bytes
c_magic	6
c_dev	6
c_ino	6
c_mode	6
c_uid	6
c_gid	6
c_nlink	6
c_rdev	6
c_mtime	11
c_namesize	6
c_filesize	11

Figure 9.6

Format of a cpio Header Block

- The `c_mode` field encodes the file's type and access permissions, as the bitwise `or` of the following values:

```
C_IRUSR    000400   /* Read by owner */
C_IWUSR    000200   /* Write by owner */
C_IXUSR    000100   /* Execute by owner */
C_IRGRP    000040   /* Read by group */
C_IWGRP    000020   /* Write by group*/
C_IXGRP    000010   /* Execute by group*/
C_IROTH    000004   /* Read by others */
C_IWOTH    000002   /* Write by others */
C_IXOTH    000001   /* Execute by others */
C_ISUID    004000   /* Set uid */
C_ISGID    002000   /* Set gid */
C_ISVTX    001000   /* Reserved */
C_ISDIR    040000   /* Directory */
C_ISFIFO   010000   /* FIFO */
C_ISREG    0100000  /* Regular file */
C_ISBLK    060000   /* Block special */
C_ISCHR    020000   /* Character special */
C_ISCTG    0110000  /* Reserved for high-performance files */
C_ISLNK    0120000  /* Reserved for symbolic links */
C_ISSOCK   0140000  /* Reserved for sockets */
```

Some of the values are shown above with seven digits, but the leading digit is only there to indicate that the values are in octal. The values C_ISVTX, C_ISCTG, C_ISLNK, and C_ISSOCK have been reserved because existing implementations use the values shown. Implementations that do not support the C_ISVTX bit may ignore it. The POSIX.1 standard does not specify how implementations that do not support the three reserved file types should deal with archives that contain these types. However, the Rationale to the standard suggests that a format-reading utility on a system that does not support high-performance files should treat them as regular files and that sockets and symbolic links, if not supported, should cause a warning message to be generated and should otherwise be ignored.

Note that the standard requires no <cpio.h> header. The symbols and octal values shown above are not guaranteed to be defined anywhere. For clarity, a program that needs these values should define and use these symbols, rather than using the octal constants directly.

- The `c_uid` and `c_gid` fields contain the numerical owner ID and group ID of the file, respectively.

- The `c_nlink` field contains the number of links to the file in the hierarchy at the time that the archive was created.

- The c_rdev field contains implementation-defined data for character and block special files. It is not meaningful for other file types. Historically, systems have used the high and low bytes of this field for major and minor device numbers.

- The c_mtime field represents the modification time of the file (the st_mtime field of the stat structure associated with the file) at the time it was archived. This is exactly like the mtime field of the tar header, except that it is only 11 bytes long.

The value of c_filesize must be zero for FIFOs and directories. Its value and meaning are unspecified for other special file types. In every case, after the filename there will be c_filesize bytes of data, but only data for regular files is restored.

Immediately after the last byte of a file's data, the first byte of the next file's header appears. Thus, the cpio format is a sequence of bytes, not blocks. The end of a cpio archive is indicated by a header that describes the filename "TRAILER!!!".

9.3.1   Restoring Extended cpio Archives

Files created by restoring cpio format archives have ownership and access permissions determined in a manner similar to that used for tar archives. If an archive is restored using the format-reading utility and the restoring process runs without appropriate privileges, then—just as for tar archives— each file is created with access permissions and ownership set as if the process had called *creat()* with a mode argument whose permission bits were those in the mode field of the file's header. If the utility executes with appropriate privileges, then the user ID and group ID in the c_uid and c_gid fields are used, and the permissions are restored exactly as they are stored in the archive. There are no symbolic versions of user or group IDs in the cpio format.

If the format-reading utility is executed without appropriate privileges to create a file of a type found in an archive, the utility shall write a message to standard error and otherwise ignore the file. Typically, systems require that processes have privileges to create device special files. If the restoring process does not have the appropriate privileges to set a flag in the mode (such as C_ISVTX or C_ISUID) then the flag shall be ignored.

9.4   Future Directions

The resolution of the data interchange format dispute given in the POSIX.1 standard is not very satisfactory. A proposed change to the standard, currently part of the future revisions supplement, would replace both the tar and cpio formats with a third format, based on an existing standard, ISO 1002. This format is as controversial as the others have been, and at this writing it is too early to tell how this part of the POSIX.1 standard will evolve.

Exercises for Chapter 9

1. Type the program in Figure 9.3 into your computer, and execute it on itself. If you have a C standard conforming compiler, try to compile the resulting (trigraphed) program.

2. Why can't a format-reading utility be a strictly conforming POSIX.1 application?

3. Write a strictly conforming POSIX.1 application that reads an extended tar archive and, for each file in the archive, reports:
   - the file's type.
   - the file's mode.
   - the file's pathname, constructed from the name and prefix fields.
   - the file owner's user ID.
   - the file owner's name.
   - the file group's group ID.
   - the file group's name.
   - the file's size in bytes, as stored in the archive.
   - the file's linkname, if its type is LNKTYPE.
   - the file's modification time, formatted into a date and local time.
   - the file's devmajor and devminor fields, if the file type is BLKTYPE or CHRTYPE.

4. Write a strictly conforming POSIX.1 application that reads an extended cpio archive and, for each file in the archive, reports:
   - the file's type.
   - the file's mode.
   - the file's pathname.
   - the file owner's user ID.
   - the file group's group ID.

- the file's size in bytes, as stored in the archive.

- the file's link count.

- the file's modification time, formatted into a date and local time.

- the file's `c_dev` and `c_ino` fields.

- The value of `c_rdev` if the file's type is `C_ISBLK` or `C_ISCHR`.

Numeric values should be printed in decimal, not octal.

10

Proposed Revisions to POSIX.1

The POSIX.1 standard will change. Some changes have already been adopted: ambiguities and errors in the 1988 standard were corrected in the 1990 standard. Additional interfaces will be added, in a supplement that we have referred to as the future revisions supplement; although these are still in draft form, we describe their current state below. The description of the standard in terms of the C language will be replaced by a language-independent description. This will involve a complete rewrite of the standard, in a form that is still the subject of much discussion. When the standard is rewritten the interfaces described in this book will not be replaced; they will simply become the C language bindings to the new standard. They will have equal standing with Ada, FORTRAN, and perhaps other language bindings.

10.1 Proposed New Interfaces

We have included the changes of the 1990 revision to POSIX.1 throughout this book. It consisted of corrections to and clarifications of the original standard, but added no new functionality. The second, pending revision consists of additions to the standard and is still in somewhat immature form. Although prognostication in the standards arena is a risky business, it seems likely that some form of this revision will be adopted around 1993. In this section we briefly describe the contents of Draft 3 of this revision. Although the revision will certainly undergo more changes before it is adopted, interfaces like those given in this section will very likely be included, in some form, in a future version of POSIX.1. All references in this chapter to the future revisions supplement (or simply "the supplement") are implicitly to Draft 3.

10.1.1   Symbolic Links

The addition of symbolic links is probably the most significant feature of the future revisions supplement. A symbolic link is a type of special file. The supplement draft contains the following definition:

> **symbolic link:** A type of file that contains a pathname. The pathname is interpolated into a pathname being resolved, during pathname resolution, to create a new pathname when it is encountered.[9]

Thus, a symbolic link refers to another file, and when the symbolic link is referenced it is treated as if the file it refers to had been referenced, except under special circumstances to be described below. The other file can be any type: a regular file, a directory, a FIFO, a block or character special file, or another symbolic link. For example, suppose that the current directory contains a symbolic link named gamedir, and gamedir contains the pathname /usr/games. Then the pathname gamedir/wump would be resolved as /usr/games/wump.

Symbolic links, which are often referred to as *soft links*, originated in BSD UNIX. They behave much like ordinary links (*hard links*), but there are some important differences. One is that symbolic links can cross file systems. This was the original reason for their invention. Another difference is that a symbolic link does not have equal status with the file that it refers to. Two ordinary links to a file are "equal" in the sense that there is no way to distinguish one of them as the original or primary link. Both are simply names—directory entries—for the same underlying file. A symbolic link, on the other hand, is a file separate from the file that it references.

Symbolic links are created with the *symlink()* function, whose prototype is:

```
#include <unistd.h>
int symlink(const char *pathname, const char *slink);
```

The pathname argument specifies the contents of the symbolic link, and the slink argument names the symbolic link to be created. The file named by pathname need not exist, and no access checking for pathname is performed. Thus, a process can create symbolic links to files for which it does not have access.

Suppose that the current directory contains a symbolic link named file1 that refers to the file file2. If a program executes the call

```
stat("file1", &st);
```

what gets stored into the st structure? Because the pathname file1 is resolved to the name it refers to, file2, this function call returns the stat structure associated with file2 in st. This is the behavior you would expect of a link. However, the symbolic link file1 is a separate file. Suppose we want to discover its mode, size, or other attributes. How can we *stat()* file1 itself?

The answer is that special functions are required to refer to symbolic links. In this case, the supplement specifies the *lstat()* function to get the status of symbolic links. The rules for resolving pathnames that contain symbolic links are as follows:

- If a symbolic link is not the last component of a pathname, then the contents of the symbolic link are prefixed to the remainder of the pathname. Note that this may cause the pathname to exceed PATH_MAX bytes, in which case an error may be generated with errno set to ENAMETOOLONG. Note also that a symbolic link may contain a relative or an absolute pathname. If it is an absolute pathname, then pathname resolution continues from the process's root directory.

- If a symbolic link is the last component of a pathname, then for certain functions that are required to act on the symbolic link itself, pathname resolution is complete. For all other functions, the symbolic link is replaced by its contents, which are resolved to give the file.

For example, suppose that the directory /usr/fred contains the symbolic link link1, whose contents are "/usr/local". Suppose that the file /usr/local/dir/link2 is also a symbolic link, with contents "/etc/whatever". Then the call

```
lstat("/usr/fred/link1/dir/link2", &st);
```

returns the status of /usr/local/dir/link2, while the call

```
stat("/usr/fred/link1/dir/link2", &st);
```

returns the status of /etc/whatever.

The rules for resolving symbolic links in pathnames can cause a serious problem. Suppose that a process executes the function calls

```
symlink("link2", "link1");
symlink("link1", "link2");
```

This creates a loop in the file hierarchy. An attempt to resolve the pathname link1 would result in an infinite number of tries to replace link1 with link2 and vice versa. Clearly, there are many ways that such loops can occur.

To deal with this possibility, the supplement defines the additional errno code ELOOP. Any function that performs pathname resolution can set errno to ELOOP if the number of symbolic links encountered in resolving a path exceeds some implementation-specific limit. It is unclear whether a process will be able to determine this limit by a call to *pathconf()*.

Creating loops in the file hierarchy is dangerous, and a portable application should refrain from doing so unless there is a compelling reason. Similarly, creating links to directories can lead to confusing results. Suppose that a process's current working directory has a subdirectory named dir, and suppose that the process executes

```
chdir("dir/..");
```

You would expect this to be a no-op (i.e., to have no effect), because inside dir the pathname " . . " refers to its parent, i.e., the current directory. But suppose that dir is not a directory, but a symbolic link to another directory. Then

```
chdir("dir/..");
```

is not a no-op; it changes the process's current working directory to the parent of the directory linked to dir. For this and other reasons, symbolic links between directories should be used with caution. The same problem can occur if dir is a hard link to another directory. We mentioned in Chapter 3, Section 3.5, that a portable application should never create (hard) links to directories. Language to that effect occurs in the supplement.

An attempt to *open()* a file that is a symbolic link will result in opening the file referred to by the link. How can a process read the contents of the symbolic link itself? The supplement specifies the *readlink()* function, whose prototype is:

```
#include <unistd.h>
int readlink(const char *slink, char *buf, int bufsiz);
```

The slink argument specifies the symbolic link, buf names the buffer where the contents of the link should be stored, and bufsiz specifies the size of buf. The return value of *readlink()* is the number of bytes placed in the buffer, or –1 if an error occurs. You must refer to this byte count, because the string placed in buf is *not* null-terminated.

The *readlink()* function will not return an error if bufsiz is less than the length of the pathname in the symbolic link. It will simply return bufsiz, and the buffer will not contain the full pathname of the link. In any case, an application can always determine the length of the pathname by using *lstat()* on the link and examining the st_size field.

We have already discussed *lstat()*, but we have not yet given its prototype. Here it is:

```
#include <sys/types.h>
#include <sys/stat.h>
int lstat(const char *path, struct stat *buf);
```

A call to *lstat()* with a path argument that does not refer to a symbolic link behaves just like a call to *stat()* on the same file. If path is a symbolic link, then *lstat()* returns information about the link, and *stat()* returns information about the file referenced by the link.

The *symlink()*, *readlink()*, and *lstat()* functions are guaranteed to be reentrant with respect to signals.

The supplement requires that the header <stat.h> define a file type macro S_ISLNK(mode), which returns nonzero if mode is the st_mode field associated with a symbolic link and zero otherwise. The st_mode field associated with a symbolic link is not required to hold any other data, such as permission bits. The `st_size` member associated with a symbolic link contains the number of bytes in the pathname stored in the link. It is unspecified whether or not the remaining fields of the `stat` structure are meaningful for symbolic links. Thus, an implementation need not associate an owner ID, group ID, or modification or access times with a symbolic link.

The functions *unlink()*, *rename()*, and *rmdir()* behave like *lstat()*. That is, if passed an argument that names a symbolic link, these functions act on the link itself, rather than on the file referenced by the link. The ANSI C function *remove()* also acts on the symbolic link. On the other hand, *link()* follows the link. Thus, if `file1` is a symbolic link and a process calls

```
link("file1", "newlink");
```

then `newlink` becomes a hard link to the file referenced by `file1`. There is no portable way to create a hard link to a symbolic link. All of this follows historical practice. The supplement deviates from historical practice by requiring that *chown()* follow the link. That is, if `linkname` is a symbolic link, then the call

```
chown(linkname, owner, group);
```

changes the ownership of the file referenced by `linkname`. (It must do this, as it is unspecified whether or not `linkname` even has an owner or group.)

The symbolic link interfaces in the supplement are largely based on mature existing practice. Moreover, there is wide agreement that symbolic links are useful, and even essential. It is likely that they will be incorporated into POSIX.1 very much as we have described them here.

10.1.2 Changing Attributes of Open Files

POSIX.1 provides two ways to refer to a file to get its status: by pathname, using *stat()*, or by open file descriptor, using *fstat()*. Similarly, *pathconf()* and *fpathconf()* are two interfaces that provide the same information, either by pathname or by file descriptor.

The supplement introduces interfaces that allow a process to change the attributes of a file referred to by a file descriptor. The functions introduced are *fchmod()*, *fchown()*, and *ftruncate()*. Here are their prototypes:

```
#include <sys/types.h>
#include <sys/stat.h>
int fchmod(int fildes, mode_t mode);

#include <sys/types.h>
int fchown(int fildes, uid_t owner, gid_t group);

#include <sys/types.h>
int ftruncate(int fildes, off_t length);
```

The headers shown with each function must be included to use the function, but no decision has been made yet about which headers will have prototypes for these functions.

The *fchmod()* and *fchown()* functions behave just like *chmod()* and *chown()*, save for the way that they refer to the file. There is no *truncate()* function to correspond to *ftruncate()*. If the file referred to by fd is a regular file and has length greater than len, then the call

```
ftruncate(fd, len);
```

truncates the file to len bytes, discarding the rest. If the file has fewer than len bytes, it is unspecified whether the file is extended or whether it is unchanged. Thus, a portable application should not do this. If the file is extended, the extended portion is filled with null bytes. The behavior of *ftruncate()* if fd refers to a file that is not a regular file is unspecified.

The three functions described in this section are based on existing practice. There is not as broad a consensus regarding their utility as there is for symbolic links. Nevertheless, it is likely that they will be adopted as described here.

10.1.3 Clarification of *getgroups()* and Supplementary Groups

There is an ambiguity in the POSIX.1 specification of the *getgroups()* function and the definition of supplementary group IDs: is the process's effective group ID one of those returned by a call to *getgroups()*? Is this group ID counted in the number of supplementary groups? As we mentioned in Chapter 2, Section 2.2.1, the original standard allowed implementations to answer these questions either way, and the 1990 revision did not address the issue. The proposed revision clarifies it as follows:

- The value of NGROUPS_MAX must be at least 1, not at least zero. Thus, _POSIX_NGROUPS_MAX is changed to 1.

- The definition of NGROUPS_MAX is changed to be the maximum number of simultaneous supplementary group IDs, including the process's effective group ID.

- The effective group ID of the process will be returned in the grouplist array passed by *getgroups()*, and the return value of *getgroups()* will include this ID in its count.

This is not the only way to resolve the ambiguity, and it is not certain that these clarifications will be adopted. Another alternative is the opposite: to guarantee that the effective group ID is *not* among the list of supplementary group IDs returned by *getgroups()*. This is the behavior of System V.4.

10.1.4 Setting Effective User and Group IDs

In Chapter 2, Section 2.2, we discussed the *setuid()* function, and we mentioned there that—even on systems for which _POSIX_SAVED_IDS is defined—*setuid()* cannot generally be used to toggle the process's effective user ID between the real ID and the saved user ID. You may recall that the problem had to do with privileges: if a process has the appropriate privileges, a call to *setuid()* changes not only the process's effective user ID but its real user ID and saved user ID as well. A similar problem applies to group IDs.

The supplement proposes the following changes:

- All POSIX.1 systems will support some form of saved set-user-ID and saved set-group-ID.

- The presence or absence of the symbol _POSIX_SAVED_IDS controls the semantics of *setuid()* and *setgid()* as before.

- New functions *seteuid()* and *setegid()* are defined, with the following prototypes and semantics:

```
#include <unistd.h>
#include <sys/types.h>
int seteuid(uid_t uid);
int setegid(gid_t gid);
```

If the process has the appropriate privileges, or if uid is equal to the process's real user ID, or if uid is equal to the process's saved set-user-ID (which is now defined regardless of whether _POSIX_SAVED_IDS is in effect), then the call

```
seteuid(uid);
```

shall change the process's effective user ID to uid. The real user ID and saved set-user-ID are unaffected. Similar semantics apply to *setegid()*.

If these functions are adopted, they will solve the problem discussed in Chapter 2, Section 2.2.

10.1.5 Manipulating Environment Variables

POSIX.1 allows processes to read their environment strings by using *getenv()* or by directly manipulating the environ vector (see Chapter 2, Section 2.6). If a process wants to change, add, or delete an environment string it must go through environ, and this is not simple. The supplement proposes adding the *putenv()* and *clearenv()* functions, whose prototypes are:

```
#include <stdlib.h>
int putenv(const char *string);
int clearenv(void);
```

The string argument must point to a string of the form "name=value". If an environment variable named name is already present, then its value is replaced by value. Otherwise, name is added to the environment. Neither of these functions can be easily used to remove a single environment variable, and there is no function in the supplement that performs that function.

There are a number of pitfalls that applications using *putenv()* should be aware of. A common error is to pass a string argument that points to automatic storage. When the function that declares the storage exits, the space may be reused, with unpredictable results. Another error is to use aliases for environ. An implementation is free to change the value of environ during a call to *putenv()*, and if the application has copied environ, or is using the envp argument to *main()*, the result is unspecified.

A call to *clearenv()* clears the process's environment. Implementations are free to change environ during a call to *getenv()*, so the same warning about using copies of environ applies.

Whether these functions will be adopted as described here is unclear. Neither of them is particularly difficult to implement, but the pitfalls mentioned above make their use error-prone. At this writing, the 1003.1 committee is seeking alternatives that would have similar function.

10.1.6 Input and Output

The supplement makes one small but significant change to the semantics of *read()* and *write()*. It is most easily described by quoting from the document:

> Reads shall be atomic on ordinary files and on pipes and FIFOs: the system shall behave as if each *read()*, systemwide, was started and completed without any *read()* or *write()* being active on the same file in that interval.[10]

A similar provision is made for *write()*:

> For ordinary files, and except as noted below for pipes and FIFOs, all writes shall be atomic: the system shall behave as if each *write()*, systemwide, was started and completed without any *read()* or *write()* being active on the same file in that interval.[11]

The proviso "except as noted below" refers to the fact that writes to pipes and FIFOS are only guaranteed to be atomic if PIPE_BUF or fewer bytes are written at once.

Note that terminal special files are not covered by these changes. Multiple concurrent reads from, or writes to, terminals continue to have unpredictable behavior. This can be controlled somewhat on systems that support job control.

The *Rationale* for the supplement states that the changes described here implement the original intent of the 1003.1 committee. Thus, it is likely that they will be adopted.

There are no actions that a portable application need take to take advantage of the atomicity of reads and writes. This simply makes life easier. Suppose that an application consists of multiple processes that are all writing messages to the same log file. To guarantee that the messages will not get intermingled on a POSIX.1 system, the application could keep them to `PIPE_BUF` or fewer bytes in length and funnel them all through a FIFO. (That is, there could be one process in the application that simply reads the FIFO and writes to the log file forever.) With the proposed change, it is safe for the message writers to write directly to the log file.

10.1.7 Traversing File Trees

Some UNIX systems support a function called *ftw()* that allows a process to traverse the subtree of the file hierarchy rooted at a particular directory. The semantics of this function are somewhat complex. The supplement proposes a number of functions and data structures that act together to allow a process flexible access to all the files rooted at a directory or at a sequence of directories. This interface is not based on widespread existing practice, but on work done at Bell Labs Research. The material in this section of the supplement is in much more preliminary form than that already described, and consequently it is more likely to change before the supplement is adopted.

The interface, which we refer to as the *fts interface*, specifies the header `<fts.h>` and two data types. One, the FTS type, has unspecified contents. You should think of it as an analogue of the FILE type. (FTS stands for file tree stream.) The other is a structured type named FTSENT, with at least the following members:

```
struct FTSENT {
    char    *fts_accpath;  /* Path to access the file */
    char    *fts_path;     /* Path relative to starting file */
    unsigned short fts_info;   /* Flags for file */
    short   fts_pathlen;   /* Length of string at fts_path */
    short   fts_level;     /* Depth in hierarchy */
    short   fts_namelen;   /* Length of string at fts_name */
    FTSENT  *fts_parent;   /* Pointer to parent dir's struct */
    FTSENT  *fts_link;     /* Link structure */
    union {
        long number;
        void *pointer;
    } fts_local;           /* For application use */
    char    *fts_name;     /* Filename */
};
```

An FTSENT structure contains enough information to describe a file found during the tree traversal. There are two pathname pointers in this structure because file traversal can change the process's current working directory.

The `fts_accpath` member gives a path relative to the current directory, and the `fts_path` member gives a path relative to the root directory of the subtree that is being traversed.

Four functions make up the fts interface. Their prototypes, found in the header `<fts.h>`, are as follows:

```
FTS *fts_open( const char **pathnames, int options,
        int (*compar)(const FTSENT *f1, const FTSENT *f2) );
FTSENT *fts_read(FTS *ftsp);
int fts_set(FTS *ftsp, FTSENT *f, int options);
int fts_close(FTS *ftsp);
```

In view of the tentative nature of these proposals, we do not explain their use in detail. However, we give the general idea behind their use. A process can choose to traverse a sequence of subtrees. The `pathnames` argument points to a vector of pathnames that are the roots of the subtrees to be traversed. A call to *fts_open()* opens a file tree stream, an abstract object that can be read sequentially by *fts_read()*. Each call to *fts_read()* returns an FTSENT pointer describing the next object being traversed. Directory entries in the subtree sequence are returned twice: once before any of their descendants are traversed and once after all of their descendants have been traversed. (These are referred to as the *pre-order* and *post-order* visits.) All other objects in the subtree sequence are visited exactly once, unless a call to *fts_set()* is used to override this.

Because tree traversal requires many function calls, the tree or the files within the tree can change during the traversal process. The *fts_set()* function allows a process to revisit the most recently visited node with re-initialized entries in its FTSENT structure. The *fts_set()* function can also be used to skip a portion of a file hierarchy or to follow a symbolic link returned by a call to *fts_read()*. The *fts_close()* function closes a file tree stream and changes the calling process's current working directory back to the directory at the time *fts_open()* was called.

10.1.8 Message Catalogues and Internationalization

If an application program needs to write text messages to standard output or standard error, it can embed these messages in the source code. However, this makes internationalized use of the application impossible without changing the source code and recompiling. To be able to present messages in any language, a program can employ message identifiers that are used at run time to look up the messages in a catalogue. Then, to change language the program merely needs to change catalogues.

The supplement proposes a standard way for applications to get messages from a catalogue. The method relies on the use of locales, which we encountered in Chapter 8, and on *domains*. A domain is an abstraction that describes a set of messages that are associated with an application. You should think of each application or set of related applications as having its own domain. For example, a compiler, linker, and `lint` utility might share a domain on a system. At any given moment a process has a current domain. This is a new process attribute, to be added to the list in Figure 2.1 of Chapter 2.

A message text is determined by a locale, a domain, and a message ID. All of these are character strings. The idea is that changing the locale changes the text, but not the meaning, of the message. Thus, in the `public_messages` domain the message with ID `237.10` might be `No smoking` in the `En_US` and `En_CD` locales (English in the United States and Canada, respectively), but `Défense de fumer` in the `Fr_CD` and `Fr_FR` locales (French in Canada and France, respectively). (These are not standard locale names. There are no standard locale names. However, existing practice on many systems is to encode both language and country in the locale name.) In some other domain, the message ID `237.10` might not exist or might mean something entirely different. And because message IDs are strings rather than arithmetic types, the message ID for this message in this domain could simply be `No smoking`. Domain names and message IDs are limited to a length of `PATH_MAX` bytes.

To implement internationalized messages, the supplement introduces a new locale category (see Chapter 8, Section 8.3.1) and three new functions. The locale category is `LC_MESSAGES`, which can be set with *setlocale()*. The functions are *textdomain()*, *gettext()*, and *dgettext()*. Their prototypes are:

```
#include <header_to_be_named_later.h>
char *textdomain(const char *domainname);
char *gettext(const char *msgid);
char *dgettext(const char *domainname, const char *msgid);
```

The *textdomain()* function sets the calling process's current domain and returns a pointer to a string representing the previous domain. If the `domainname` argument is an empty string (`""`), then the domain is set to an implementation-defined default. If the argument is a `NULL` pointer, then the domain is not changed. This allows a process to query its domain without changing it.

A process retrieves a message text by calling *gettext()* with the message ID as argument. The current domain and locale are used. It may be that a process wants to retrieve a message from a domain other than the current one and does not want to change the current domain. For this purpose the process can use *dgettext()*. This function allows you to specify the domain and message ID. The `domainname` given is only used during the call to *dgettext()*.

This message interface is an invention of the 1003.1 committee. (It was proposed to 1003.1 by representatives of Uniforum.) It differs from existing message catalogue schemes, notably that specified in X/Open's XPG3 specification (see Chapter 11, Section 11.4). The difference is deliberate; the 1003.1

committee felt that the XPG3 catalogue interface does not provide the desired flexibility. The message catalogues used by XPG3 can themselves be used in the interface proposed in the supplement, so this investment would not be wasted. It is unclear whether 1003.1 will eventually adopt the X/Open message interface or the Uniforum proposal or will simply omit a message catalogue interface.

10.1.9 New Feature Test Macro

The proposed revision includes the feature test macro _POSIX1_SOURCE. The meaning of this feature test macro depends on its value. If _POSIX1_SOURCE is defined to have the value 1, then it has the same meaning and effect as defining _POSIX_SOURCE. If _POSIX1_SOURCE is defined to be 2, then it makes visible all symbols from the supplement (a superset of those symbols in 9945-1:1990).

The advantage of this symbol is that it allows a program to specify the name-space that it expects to be reserved by the implementation. For example, if the program has the line

```
#define _POSIX1_SOURCE 1     /* 1990 standard name-space */
```

then symbols like textdomain will not be made visible in any header and will not be reserved. A further advantage is that the name _POSIX1_SOURCE acknowledges the existence of other POSIX standards, with their own needs for feature test macros.

10.2 Proposed Language-Independent Interface

The POSIX.1 standard is specified in terms of C functions. This is a temporary situation. The standard will be rewritten in a way that describes its facilities in a language-independent way. This will not make the current standard obsolete. It will simply become the C language binding—one of several language bindings—to the rewritten standard.

The syntax to be used in the language-independent standard is not yet chosen, and specifying it will not be easy. It will not be simply a restatement of the existing standard with the C removed. For example, there will not necessarily be a one-to-one correspondence between interfaces in the language-independent specification and C language interfaces. Thus, the facilities covered by *fcntl()* might be specified as a collection of interfaces. Conversely, the facilities specified by *open()* and *creat()* might be specified by a single interface. Specifying the types of system and process attributes in a language-independent way is also a potential problem.

The functions described in Chapter 8 of the POSIX.1 standard (and Chapter 8 of this book) are C-specific. There may not be bindings to those functions from other languages. For example, a FORTRAN binding to POSIX.1 will not have an equivalent for *malloc()*, as dynamic memory allocation is not supported in FORTRAN. The interfaces in the other parts of the POSIX.1 standard will be supported. Again, there need not be a one-to-one relationship between, say, Ada bindings and C bindings. A single Ada function might provide the facilities given by all of the C terminal control functions.

The language-independent specification should not change the semantics of the existing standard. Thus, it should have no effect on the portability of your programs. But it may change the way we think about the standard. Essential features of the system will remain; incidental facts related to the language binding will disappear. It will be interesting to see what this standard looks like.

Related Standards

As we saw in **Chapter 8,** the specification of the POSIX.1 standard depends on the ANSI C standard. Other standards and specifications are, in turn, related to POSIX.1. These include the POSIX.1 FIPS; the remaining POSIX standards, which as of this writing are all still in draft form; and the *X/Open Portability Guide (XPG)*. The number of standards in preparation, within and without the POSIX family, is increasing rapidly. Although there is no guarantee that each working group will eventually produce an adopted standard, many of them will.

The proliferation of standards can help application developers, and also can help users, but only if it is controlled. Otherwise, the number of possible combinations of standards required to support an application, and the number of requirements that a user must specify when acquiring a system or an application, will grow to be a burden. One important concept that can help simplify the situation is the application environment profile (AEP). An AEP is a description of the facilities that a system must provide to support a particular class of application. Such a description might include (but is not limited to) headers, functions, macros, restrictions on options (e.g., requiring job control), and parameters, such as minimum required performance.

As the number of standards grows, the number of possible combinations of standards grows exponentially. The problem this presents for users is that each application might rely on its own "laundry list" of standards. A user interested in acquiring two applications might discover that they have almost but not exactly the same requirements and that the differences are incompatible. The idea behind AEPs is to keep the number of such combinations in actual use to a reasonable level.

An AEP is specific to a type of application. For example, an AEP for networked applications would point to standards specifying areas such as operating system interface (e.g., POSIX.1), remote procedure calls, protocols, name-space and directory services, etc. An AEP for batch applications might point to standards for an operating system interface and batch services. An AEP for CAD applications will need (among other things) a pointer to a graphics standard. In general, an AEP selects combinations of standards that make sense together from the point of view of an application area. An AEP might also specify gaps between the required capabilities and the existing standards, if no widely accepted standard is in place for some part of the application area's requirements.

It is important for the POSIX.1 application programmer to know about other standards and specifications for a number of reasons. One reason is that knowledge of an appropriate, widely accepted AEP can help keep your applications portable. For example, if your application needs the interfaces from POSIX.1, the C standard library, and the X Windows library (Xlib), you should determine if some AEP includes pointers to these three APIs (application programming interfaces). Another important reason to be aware of other standards and specifications is that there are interactions between some of them and POSIX.1, which can be somewhat complex. In this chapter we briefly discuss some of these standards and specifications. Perhaps the most closely related standard is the POSIX FIPS.

11.1 The POSIX.1 FIPS

A FIPS is a federal information processing standard. These standards are developed by the Department of Commerce and published in the *Federal Register*. A FIPS can be either advisory or mandatory. If it is mandatory, then it is a binding standard for acquisitions by all federal agencies for which the FIPS is relevant. (An agency can get a waiver from a mandatory FIPS if it presents suitable reasons.) An advisory FIPS constitutes a nonbinding recommendation to federal agencies. Within the Department of Commerce, the agency responsible for developing FIPSes is the National Institute of Standards and Technology, or NIST. (The NIST was formerly the National Bureau of Standards.)

In August 1988, just before the POSIX.1 standard was adopted, the NIST published an advisory POSIX.1 FIPS. This was FIPS 151 and was based on Draft 12 of 1003.1. It was adopted at almost the same time that the final POSIX.1 standard (based on Draft 13 of 1003.1) was adopted. Draft 12 and the adopted standard had many significant differences. The fact that the adopted FIPS was not based on the final standard caused some temporary difficulties, but in February 1990 FIPS 151-1, a revised POSIX.1 FIPS based on the August 1988 POSIX.1 standard, was adopted.

FIPS 151-1 does not simply specify conformance to POSIX.1. Rather, it is a separate, closely related standard. From the system implementor's point of view, it is a more restrictive standard. It differs from POSIX.1 (as originally adopted, *not* the 1990 revision) by imposing the following extra requirements:

- The symbol _POSIX_JOB_CONTROL must be defined. That is, support for job control is required.

- The symbol _POSIX_SAVED_IDS must be defined. That is, saved set-user-IDs must be supported.

- The symbol _POSIX_NO_TRUNC must be defined and not equal to –1. That is, long pathname components must cause an error.

- The symbol _POSIX_CHOWN_RESTRICTED must be defined and not equal to –1. That is, *chown()* must be restricted.

- The symbol _POSIX_VDISABLE must be defined and not equal to –1. That is, it must be possible for each asynchronous terminal device to disable special characters.

- The value of NGROUPS_MAX must be at least 8. That is, each process can have as many as 8 supplementary group IDs.

- The group ID of a newly created file must be set to the group ID of the directory in which the file is created.

- If a call to *read()* or *write()* is interrupted by a caught signal after some data has been transferred, then the call must return the number of bytes transferred so far.

- A login shell must define the environment variables HOME and LOGNAME.

Each of these requirements is a restriction on a POSIX.1 option. As a consequence, a FIPS-conforming system is always POSIX.1 conforming, but not necessarily vice versa. For example, a POSIX.1 system on which long pathname components are truncated is not FIPS conforming.

The POSIX.1 FIPS does not define what a FIPS-conforming application is. We can speak informally of such an application as one that requires no features other than those specified in the FIPS and in the relevant language standards and that does not require any system limits to have values greater than the minima given by the FIPS. With this definition, we see that the situation is reversed for application programs: a strictly conforming POSIX.1 application is always FIPS conforming, but not necessarily vice versa. This is because a FIPS-conforming program can assume more about its environment than a strictly conforming POSIX.1 application can. For example, a FIPS-conforming program can rely on the presence of job control and, consequently, can reliably send and handle job control signals like SIGSTOP. A program that assumes the availability of job control is *not* a strictly conforming POSIX.1 application.

11.1.1   Portable Application Programs and the POSIX.1 FIPS

Because of the long bureaucratic delays involved in producing a FIPS, changes in the POSIX.1 standard will not be immediately reflected by changes in the POSIX.1 FIPS. FIPS 151-1 does not reflect any of the changes made in the 1990 revision. Most of these changes are additional requirements (e.g., definitions of the types size_t and ssize_t), and thus, vendors can conform to the FIPS and 9945.1-1990 simultaneously. However, a system that conforms to the POSIX.1 FIPS must support the *cuserid()* function as specified by 1003.1. This conflicts with the historical implementation of *cuserid()* (see Chapter 2, Section 2.3).

Applications that aim for maximum portability should use only those facilities that are guaranteed to be supported on any system that conforms to either of 1003.1-1988, 9945.1-1990, or the POSIX.1 FIPS. This is actually not so difficult. Such programs should:

- Avoid using *cuserid()*.

- Work with any combination of the POSIX.1 options.

- Assume nothing about the return value of *read()* or *write()* calls interrupted by signals.

- Be prepared for getenv("HOME") and getenv("LOGNAME") to return NULL. A process can determine the login name by calling *getlogin()* and can determine the home directory associated with the login name by calling *getpwuid()*, with its real user ID as argument and using the returned pointer to extract the pw_dir member of a passwd structure.

- Be prepared for the group ID of newly created files to be either that of the parent directory or the effective group ID of the process.

We return to this subject in Chapter 12, Section 12.6.

11.2   The TCOS Project

The POSIX.1 working group is one of many such groups working under the sponsorship of the IEEE's Technical Committee on Operating Systems, or TCOS. Figure 11.1 shows the structure of these groups.

Clearly, the TCOS standards effort extends far beyond POSIX.1. However, POSIX.1 holds a special place, not only because it was the first of these

Number	Area
1003.0	Guide to the POSIX Open System Environment
1003.1	System Interface
1003.2	Shell and Utilities
1003.3	Test Methods
1003.4	Real Time and Other Extensions to 1003.1
1003.5	Ada Bindings to 1003.1
1003.6	Security
1003.7	System Administration
1003.8	Transparent File Access
1003.9	FORTRAN Bindings to 1003.1
1003.10	Supercomputing AEP
1003.11	Transaction Processing AEP
1003.12	Protocol Independent Network Access
1003.13	Real-Time AEP
1003.14	Multiprocessing AEP
1003.15	Supercomputing Batch Services
1003.16	C Language Bindings to 1003.1
1201.1	Windowing Toolkit
1201.2	Recommended Practice for Driveability and User Portability
1201.?	Xlib
1224	X.400 API
1237	Remote Procedure Call
1238	Common OSI and FTAM API

Figure 11.1

TCOS Committees as of August 1990

standards to be adopted (and at this writing remains the only one) but also because it is central to many of the other efforts. Many of the other draft standards assume POSIX.1 as a base. An important exception is POSIX.2.

11.3   Interactions with 1003.2

The POSIX 1003.2 committee is charged with developing a standard for
portable shell application programs. This standard specifies the basic facilities
of the shell itself and the utilities that shell programs can use. (In general, the
POSIX.2 standard is concerned with the use of utilities in shell scripts, not
their interactive use.) Our description of the standard is based on Draft 9, the
latest version that is complete as of this writing.

The shell described in POSIX.2 is based on the Bourne shell. In addition,
POSIX.2 specifies the syntax and semantics of about 70 utilities. These include
such utilities as grep, awk, cat, and date. Most of the POSIX.2 utilities are
familiar from UNIX systems and have semantics that are based on either
their AT&T or Berkeley versions (or, in some cases, a combination of the
two). A few are inventions of the POSIX.2 committee.

The most important relationship between POSIX.1 and POSIX.2 is a
negative one: neither standard requires adherence to the other. That is, a
system can conform to POSIX.1 without conforming to POSIX.2 (indeed,
without supporting any sort of command interpreter at all), and conversely a
system can conform to POSIX.2 without conforming to POSIX.1. For example,
a UNIX Version 7 system could conform to POSIX.2 with minor modifications
to the kernel and substantial changes to the utilities. With a suitable set of
utilities, so could MS-DOS systems. Neither of these systems conforms to
POSIX.1.

Nevertheless, there is a lot of interaction between the two standards,
and in practice many systems will conform to both. A number of the POSIX.2
utilities are specified in terms of corresponding POSIX.1 functions. For
example, the semantics of the chown utility are given in terms of the
POSIX.1 *chown()* function, and the mkdir utility is specified by reference to
the POSIX.1 description of *mkdir()*. Here is an extract from the POSIX.2 Draft
10 specification of the mkdir utility:

> For each *dir* operand, the mkdir utility performs actions equivalent to the
> POSIX.1 *mkdir()* function, called with the following arguments:
>
> (1)   The *dir* argument is used as the *path* argument.
>
> (2)   The value of the bitwise inclusive OR of S_IRWXU, S_IRWXG and
>   S_IRWXO is used as the *mode* argument.[12]

This does not mean that a POSIX.2 conforming system must support
a *mkdir()* C interface for application programs. It must simply support a
utility that behaves *as if* it were implemented with such an interface. This
is a relationship between the standards, but not between the systems that
conform to them.

11.3.1 Name-Spaces

A second interaction concerns name-spaces. Although the POSIX.2 standard is a shell and command interface standard, it specifies certain C interfaces as options. They are shown in Figure 11.2. On systems with C standard support these interfaces must have prototypes in specified headers. Some of these headers are also used in POSIX.1. For example, the *system()* function must have a prototype in <stdlib.h>, and *popen()* and *pclose()* must have prototypes in <stdio.h>. However, the POSIX.1 standard restricts the name-space from its headers visible to a program that defines the feature test macro _POSIX_SOURCE. (See Chapter 1, Section 1.7.) To make the additional identifiers visible, C programs that are compiled for a POSIX.2 environment must define the feature test macro _POSIX2_SOURCE.

Two of the headers shown in Figure 11.2, <regex.h> and <glob.h>, are not POSIX.1 headers. The symbols defined in those headers do not affect the name-space of POSIX.1 applications. We include them here just to be complete.

```
#include <stdlib.h>
int system(const char *cmd);

#include <stdio.h>
FILE *popen(const char *cmd, const char *mode);
int pclose(FILE *stream);

#include <regex.h>
int regcomp(regex_t *preg, const char *pattern, int cflags);
int regexec(const regex_t *preg, const char *string,
    size_t nmatch, regmatch_t *pmatch, int eflags);
void regfree(regex_t *preg);

#include <unistd.h>
int fnmatch(const char *pattern, const char *string,
    int flag);
int getopt(int argc, const char *argv[],
    const char *optstring);
extern char *optarg;
extern int optind, opterr, optopt;

#include <glob.h>
int glob(const char *pattern, int flags,
    const int (*errfunc)(), glob_t *pglob);
void globfree(glob_t *pglob);
```

Figure 11.2

C Functions Defined by the POSIX.2 Draft Standard

A description of the semantics of the functions named in Figure 11.2 is beyond the scope of this book. However, as it's pretty infuriating to find these functions mentioned without any description, we give a very abbreviated summary of their use. This is to satisfy curiosity only; the reader who needs to use these interfaces should consult the 1003.2 draft standard.

- `system(cmd)` forks a shell that executes the command line in the string `cmd` and returns the exit status of the shell.

- `popen(cmd, mode)` forks a shell that executes the command line in the string `cmd`, opens a pipe for reading or writing depending on `mode`, associates a stream with the pipe, and directs the standard input or output (depending on `mode`) of the command to the pipe. `pclose(stream)` closes a stream opened by *fopen()* and returns the exit status of the shell.

- *regcomp()*, *regexec()*, and *regfree()* are used to match regular expressions. The call `regcomp(&reg, pattern, flags)` compiles the regular expression in `pattern` and stores the compiled result in `reg`. The call `regexec(&reg, string, nmatch, &match, eflags)` matches `string` against the compiled regular expression in `reg`. It may optionally store information about matched substrings in `match`. The call `regfree(&reg)` frees any memory allocated by the call to *regcomp()* for `reg`.

- The call `fnmatch(pattern, string, flag)` returns zero if `string` matches the pattern `pattern` when filename pattern-matching rules are used and returns nonzero otherwise. The `flag` option controls whether or not `'/'` characters are matched in `string`.

- The call `getopt(argc, argv, optstring)` returns the next option character in the command line represented by `argc` and `argv`. The `optstring` argument describes the valid option characters. The external variables `optarg`, `optind`, `opterr`, and `optopt` are used to store global data set by *getopt()*. They are essentially extra return values.

- The call `glob(pattern, flags, func, &globstruct)` generates a vector of pathnames that match `pattern` and stores a pointer to the vector in a member of the `globstruct` structure. The call `globfree(&globstruct)` frees any memory allocated by a call to *glob()* that filled `globstruct`.

The POSIX.2 draft standard also specifies system limits for a number of values that can vary from one implementation to another. POSIX.2 follows the convention established by POSIX.1: there are "minimum maxima" that are absolute constants and actual maxima that are the limits for a particular implementation. Each implementation must make its limits available to an application at run time. The symbols are defined in the header `<limits.h>`.

Symbol	Description
BC_BASE_MAX	Maximum value of input or output base allowed by the bc utility.
BC_DIM_MAX	Maximum number of elements in an array allowed by the bc utility.
BC_SCALE_MAX	Maximum number of digits to the right of the decimal point in a value manipulated by the bc utility.
COLL_ELEM_MAX	The maximum number of bytes that can be used to define one collation element in the definition of a collation sequence.
EXPR_NEST_MAX	The maximum number of expressions that can be nested within parentheses accepted by the expr utility.
LINE_MAX	The maximum length in bytes of an input line (including the newline) that is guaranteed to be accepted by a utility that processes text files. This applies to all utilities that do not impose explicit limits of their own, except for sort (see below).
PASTE_FILES_MAX	The maximum number of file operands that will be accepted by the paste utility.
RE_DUP_MAX	The maximum number of repeated occurrences of a regular expression that matches the pattern \{m,n\}.
SED_PATTERN_MAX	The maximum number of bytes in the pattern space used by the sed utility.
SENDTO_MAX	The maximum length in bytes of the body of a message accepted by the sendto utility.
SORT_LINE_MAX	The maximum length in bytes of input lines accepted by the sort utility.

Figure 11.3

Symbolic Limits Made Visible in <limits.h> When _POSIX2_SOURCE Is Defined

If a C program on a POSIX.2 conforming system defines _POSIX2_SOURCE, then the additional symbols shown in Figures 11.3 and 11.4 are visible to the program. Note that, because they all end with the reserved suffix _MAX, they could in principle be visible even without the definition of _POSIX2_SOURCE.

To partially satisfy the curious reader, Figure 11.3 gives a brief description of the meaning of the symbols. A detailed description of their semantics

Symbol	Value
_POSIX2_BC_BASE_MAX	99
_POSIX2_BC_DIM_MAX	2048
_POSIX2_BC_SCALE_MAX	99
_POSIX2_COLL_ELEM_MAX	4
_POSIX2_EXPR_NEST_MAX	32
_POSIX2_LINE_MAX	2048
_POSIX2_PASTE_FILES_MAX	12
_POSIX2_RE_DUP_MAX	255
_POSIX2_SED_PATTERN_MAX	20480
_POSIX2_SENDTO_MAX	90000
_POSIX2_SORT_LINE_MAX	20480

Figure 11.4

Minimum Values for Symbolic Limits in
<limits.h>, Made Visible When
_POSIX2_SOURCE Is Defined

is beyond the scope of this book. (Indeed, it would turn into a description of POSIX.2, a subject worth a book in its own right.)

In Chapter 1, we described the POSIX.1 implementation options and the symbols that denoted their presence or absence (e.g., _POSIX_JOB_CONTROL). The POSIX.2 standard provides similar options and symbols. They are shown in Figure 11.5. As in POSIX.1, these symbols, if defined, are found in <unistd.h>.

The existence of these symbols is relevant to POSIX.1: the POSIX.2 standard specifies additional semantics for the POSIX.1 function *sysconf()*, in order to allow a process to determine these values at run time. For example, a process executing on a POSIX.2 system that needs to know the largest value of scale that can be used by the bc utility on the system can get this value as the return value of the call

```
sysconf(_SC_BC_SCALE_MAX);
```

The symbols passed as arguments to *sysconf()* are shown in Figure 11.6. They follow the POSIX.1 convention of starting with _SC_.

Note that the name-space occupied by the POSIX.2 symbols shown in Figure 11.2 is not part of the reserved name-space; as we have noted, that

Symbol	Description
_POSIX2_C_DEV	If defined and not -1, then the system supports the C Language Development Utilities Option.
_POSIX2_FORT_DEV	If defined and not -1, then the system supports the FORTRAN Development Utilities Option.
_POSIX2_SW_DEV	If defined and not -1, then the system supports the Software Development Utilities Option.
_POSIX2_VERSION	A value of the form 19xxxxL, indicating the year and month of the adoption of the standard to which the current system conforms.

Figure 11.5

Symbols for POSIX.2 Options in `<unistd.h>`, Made Visible When `_POSIX2_SOURCE` Is Defined

Name	Used to Find
_SC_BC_BASE_MAX	BC_BASE_MAX
_SC_BC_DIM_MAX	BC_DIM_MAX
_SC_BC_SCALE_MAX	BC_SCALE_MAX
_SC_COLL_ELEM_MAX	COLL_ELEM_MAX
_SC_EXPR_NEST_MAX	EXPR_NEST_MAX
_SC_LINE_MAX	LINE_MAX
_SC_PASTE_FILES_MAX	PASTE_FILES_MAX
_SC_RE_DUP_MAX	RE_DUP_MAX
_SC_SED_PATTERN_MAX	SED_PATTERN_MAX
_SC_SENDTO_MAX	SENDTO_MAX
_SC_SORT_LINE_MAX	SORT_LINE_MAX
_SC_2_FORT_DEV	_POSIX2_FORT_DEV
_SC_2_SW_DEV	_POSIX2_SW_DEV
_SC_2_VERSION	_POSIX2_VERSION

Figure 11.6

Additional Argument Values for *sysconf()*, Defined in `<unistd.h>` and Made Visible When `_POSIX2_SOURCE` Is Defined

occupied by the symbols in Figures 11.3 through 11.6 is reserved. Thus, if your application defines the symbol _POSIX2_SOURCE, the extra precautions that you must take are simply to avoid defining the identifiers system, popen, etc., that appear in Figure 11.2.

Another relationship between the two standards is that the semantics of *system()*, *popen()*, and *pclose()* are specified by POSIX.2 in a way that differs from some historical implementations. This difference is based on the availability of *waitpid()* in POSIX.1. (The same effect can be achieved on existing BSD systems by using the *wait3()* function.) The *system()* function invokes a shell and passes its argument string to the shell to be executed as a command. For example, the statement

```
system("date");
```

causes the date utility to be executed, which writes the current date and time to standard output. The following semantic requirement for *system()* is specified in POSIX.2: "The *system()* function shall not affect the termination status of any child of the calling process other than the process(es) it itself creates".

Many existing implementations of *system()* do not satisfy this requirement. The problem arises as follows: suppose a process calls *fork()* to create a child process, and the parent then calls *system()* to execute a command. The *system()* function must return the exit status of the shell that it invokes. The format of this exit status must be that of an int passed through the status argument to a *wait()* call. If *system()* calls *wait()* to get the shell status, and the previously *fork()*ed child exits before the shell does, the *wait()* call will have to discard this status and wait again. When *system()* returns, if the calling process tries to *wait()* for the first child it created, it will fail.

This problem can be fixed by using *waitpid()* instead of *wait()*. Figure 11.7 shows a correct implementation of *system()* on a POSIX.1 conforming system that has a shell named /bin/sh. The code in this figure is a modified version of an example given in the *Rationale* in Draft 9 of 1003.2. There it is presented as an example of how to implement *system()* on top of POSIX.1. There is *no requirement* that *system()* be implemented in this way.

Note that POSIX.2 requires that the *system()* function ignore SIGINT and SIGQUIT and that it block SIGCHLD. This explains the manipulation of the signals and signal mask in the code in Figure 11.7.

11.4 Other POSIX Standards

In this section we briefly discuss some of the committees we have not yet mentioned and the work they are doing. We offer this information principally to allow you to plan intelligently based on the best guess of what direction POSIX standards will take. For example, if you need to write a portable application that requires support for semaphores, you should know that the 1003.4 committee is developing a standard for semaphore interfaces.

```
#include <unistd.h>
#include <sys/types.h>
#include <signal.h>

int system(const char *cmd)
{
    pid_t pid;
    pid_t rpid;
    int status;
    struct sigaction sa,
                     saveintr,
                     savequit;
    sigset_t saveblock;

    if ( cmd == NULL )
        return(1);
    sa.sa_handler = SIG_IGN;
    sigemptyset(&sa.sa_mask);
    sa.sa_flags = 0;
    sigaction(SIGINT, &sa, &saveintr);
    sigaction(SIGQUIT, &sa, &savequit);
    sigaddset(&sa.sa_mask, SIGCHLD);
    sigprocmask(SIG_BLOCK, &sa.sa_mask, &saveblock);
    if ( (pid = fork()) == 0 )
    {
        sigaction(SIGINT, &saveintr, (struct sigaction *)NULL);
        sigaction(SIGQUIT, &savequit, (struct sigaction *)NULL);
        sigprocmask(SIG_SETMASK, &saveblock, (sigset_t *)NULL);
        execl("/bin/sh", "sh", "-c", cmd, (char *)0);
        _exit(127);
    }
    else if ( pid < 0 )
    {
        status = -1;
    }
    else
    {   /* Parent: wait for child, return exit status */
        rpid = waitpid(pid, &status, 0);
        if ( waitpid(pid, &status, 0) == -1 )
            status = -1;
    }
    sigaction(SIGINT, &saveintr, (struct sigaction *)NULL);
    sigaction(SIGQUIT, &savequit, (struct sigaction *)NULL);
    sigprocmask(SIG_SETMASK, &saveblock, (sigset_t *)NULL);
    return(status);
}
```

Figure 11.7

POSIX.2 Conforming Implementation of *system()* Using POSIX.1

11.4.1   The POSIX Guide: 1003.0

The 1003.0 committee, despite its low number, was formed relatively recently. It is not going to produce a standard, but a document: the *Guide to POSIX Open System Environments*. This document will cover a number of issues that span the different standards. Internationalization is one. The guide will also draw up profiles that include parts of more than one standard. One of the most important tasks of the 1003.0 working group is to describe how to produce profiles for POSIX standards.

The 1003.0 committee has given a draft definition of an *open system*, one of the buzzwords of the industry whose status has been like that of the word *democracy*: everyone claims to be one, but nobody wants to say what it really means. According to 1003.0, an open system is "one that implements sufficient open specifications for interfaces, services and supporting formats to enable properly engineered applications software:

- to be ported across a wide range of systems (with minimal changes),

- to interoperate with other applications on local and remote systems, and

- to interact with users in a style which facilitates user portability".*

There are some key phrases in this definition. One is "open specification". An open specification is one that is maintained by a process of public consensus. it must be consistent with international standards. This allows specifications that were developed in a proprietary way, such as the FOR-TRAN or C languages or the UNIX system, to qualify, if their maintenance is based on a public process.

11.4.2   Shell and Tools: 1003.2

We have already discussed the work of this committee in the context of its considerable interactions with POSIX.1. We have not yet mentioned the proposed 1003.2a standard, the user portability extension (UPE). The UPE is an attempt to develop standards for such interactive programs as the vi editor and the more pager. The idea behind UPE is that users become "portable" when the utilities that they use interactively behave the same way on all systems.

There are few interactions between UPE and POSIX.1. UPE is in the middle stages of development, and there is some controversy about the tools that it has chosen. For example, some members of the POSIX community would prefer to standardize on the emacs editor. Others would prefer to include both emacs and vi, and still others would prefer that neither be standardized. Despite this, UPE is in ballot at this writing.

---

* Thanks to Jim Isaak for providing me with this definition.

11.4.3   Verification of Conformance: 1003.3

The 1003.3 committee develops standards for measuring conformance to other POSIX standards. This turns out to be a rather complex task. The committee attempts to describe those aspects of a POSIX standard that can be tested for conformance on a system. The method consists of developing *assertions* for each standard.

An assertion is a declarative statement about the correct behavior of a POSIX interface, header, or other construct. Here are some examples of possible assertions for the POSIX.1 standard:

- The *chdir()* function has a result of type int.

- When a signal is caught by a signal-handling function established with a call to *sigaction()*, the caught signal is added to the process's signal mask.

- When an I/O error occurs during a call to *read()*, –1 is returned and errno is set to EIO.

The 1003.3 committee has developed over 2,000 assertions for POSIX.1. These constitute a draft POSIX.3 standard and form the basis for test suites that can be used to measure an implementation's conformance to the POSIX.1 standard. At least three test suites have already been developed that use these assertions. One, the NIST PCTS (Posix conformance test suite), was developed by the federal government. It is used to certify conformance to FIPS 151-1, rather than to POSIX.1, and is the only official tool for measuring such conformance. A second test suite, VSX, was developed for X/Open by Unisoft. It measures conformance to the *XPG3* specification (see Section 11.5, below), which includes POSIX.1. A third, the IBM PCTS, was developed for IBM by Mindcraft, Inc. It can measure conformance either to the FIPS or to the 1990 revision of POSIX.1. The latest release of AT&T's System V verification suite (SVVS) includes the NIST PCTS.

The 1003.3 committee also develops general principles for conformance testing. For example, consider the three assertions shown above. The first of these assertions cannot be portably tested unless there is an external declaration or a prototype for *chdir()* in scope. On a common usage C support implementation, neither of these need be present. On a C standard support implementation, a prototype must be present. This is an example of a *conditionally testable* assertion. The second assertion should be testable on any implementation. The third assertion cannot be portably tested; there is no portable way to make an I/O error occur during a system call. The 1003.3 committee has a general assertion classification scheme that can be used in conformance testing for any standard.

At this writing, the assertion list for POSIX.1 is in ballot, and the 1003.3 committee is developing assertions for the 1003.2 draft standard. Perhaps the most important aspect of the work done by 1003.3 is simply the idea that methods of standards conformance testing should themselves be standardized.

11.4.4   Real-Time Systems: 1003.4

A real-time system is one that can guarantee bounded response time to requests for services. Traditional UNIX systems are not real-time, because any process can be blocked indefinitely. There have been many implementations of real-time operating systems on top of (or underneath) UNIX systems. Unfortunately, these attempts have not followed a single pattern. Thus, there is no mainstream existing practice on which to base a standard. Most real-time UNIX-based applications are therefore not portable. This is the problem that POSIX.4 is trying to solve.

The draft POSIX.4 standard is quite mature. It is currently in Draft 9 and has progressed to ballot. The interfaces in 1003.4 are being specified in C, although a future version of the standard will have a language-independent description. The 1003.4 committee has specified 11 areas where standard interfaces are required for real-time application programs. These are:

- Binary semaphores

- Process memory locking

- Shared memory

- Priority scheduling

- Asynchronous event notification

- Timers

- Interprocess communication

- Synchronized (as opposed to synchronous) I/O

- Asynchronous I/O

- Real-time (high-performance) files

- Threads

We briefly describe what each of these areas covers.

A *binary semaphore* is an operating system mechanism whereby processes can guarantee mutually exclusive access to a shared resource such as a line printer. To oversimplify slightly, a binary semaphore is a flag that a process can test and set. If the flag is set, the associated resource is in use, and the process blocks until the resource is released. If the flag is not set, the process sets the flag, uses the resources, and clears the flag. It is important that the test-and-set operation be atomic and that a single semaphore can be shared among all the processes that need the resource. UNIX System V has a set of interfaces for handling semaphores, but they are quite cumbersome. The proposed POSIX.4 mechanism is an invention of the 1003.4 committee. It is very much in the spirit of the UNIX system: each semaphore is associated with a special file, so semaphores can be manipulated by functions like *unlink()* and *open()*. As a result, the POSIX.4 standard as currently drawn changes the semantics of POSIX.1 functions. There are also special POSIX.4 functions, such as *makesem()*.

Process memory locking involves arranging for a process's text, or data, or both, to be kept in memory rather than paged or swapped out. This is another area in which some UNIX systems have existing interfaces, but there is no widespread consensus and POSIX.4 has invented new ones.

Shared memory deals with arranging for multiple processes to share a portion of their address space, so that changes to a shared variable in one process are recognized by another. There is an existing System V interface for shared memory, but it is not used in 1003.4, which has proposed a mechanism based on special files.

Priority scheduling deals with the issue of how processes arrange priorities for use of the processor(s). POSIX.1 does not address this issue. Traditionally, UNIX systems have supported the *nice()* function, which gives processes a very limited ability to reduce or (if they are privileged) increase their own priority. Real-time systems may need a way to dynamically change not only priorities, but also the scheduling algorithms themselves, under application control.

Asynchronous event notification is closely related to signal-handling. The difference between a signal and an event (as used in 1003.4) is that events may be queued until the process requests them, rather than forcing an immediate transfer of control. Multiple occurrences of an event are left on the queue.

Timers are generalizations of the *sleep()* and *alarm()* interfaces of POSIX.1. For example, there is a proposed *nanosleep()* function in POSIX.4 that can block the calling process for times measured to a much finer granularity than whole seconds. (Despite the name, the granularity is not necessarily a nanosecond.)

Interprocess communication, also called IPC, deals with message queues between processes. Again, the POSIX.4 committee chose to pass up an existing System V interface and propose a mechanism based on special files.

Synchronized I/O is an I/O package in which a write operation does not return until the data is guaranteed to be written to the external medium. Traditional UNIX system I/O is not synchronized. It is *synchronous*, which means that a write operation does not return until it is complete. However, completion in this case may merely mean that the data has been transferred to a system buffer and that the physical write operation may still be scheduled for the future. This is the only type of I/O that POSIX.1 guarantees. A system crash after a *write()* but before the data is written from system buffers can leave files in an unpredictable state.

Asynchronous I/O describes an I/O package in which a read or write call can return before the operation is complete—that is, even before the data has been transferred to or from the process's address space. Completion of the I/O will cause an event to be generated for the process.

Real-time files are simply files that can be accessed very quickly. Typically, a real-time file system has provisions for pre-allocation of contiguous file space for a file.

Threads are sometimes called lightweight processes. A process can consist of multiple threads that execute concurrently. These can share a few, or most, of the process's attributes. For example, all the threads of a process might share a common address space. On a system with more than one processor, a multi-threaded process can execute several threads simultaneously. The threads proposal in the current draft of 1003.4 is less mature than the rest of the draft standard. It will be balloted separately, as 1003.4a.

The relationship between POSIX.1 and POSIX.4 is complex and the subject of some controversy. The main issue is, do the interfaces of POSIX.4 constitute an extension to POSIX.1 or are they an independent standard? Originally, POSIX.4 was viewed as an extension. That is, a POSIX.4-conforming system would have to be a POSIX.1-conforming system. However, some members of the POSIX community think this is unnecessary. One side of the argument is that many real-time systems are embedded; there is no need for an *open()* function in an implementation that has no file system, such as one that controls your microwave oven or an unmanned spacecraft. The other side says that such systems need not be POSIX systems; POSIX is intended to be a standardization and generalization of UNIX systems, and unrelated environments should not place themselves under the POSIX umbrella.

The POSIX.13 working group is developing real-time AEPs. It may turn out that some of these AEPs will specify only a subset of POSIX.1, while others will require conformance to all of POSIX.1 as well as some portion of POSIX.4.

We have seen that POSIX.4 specifies additional semantics for some POSIX.1 functions. There are more interactions between these two standards, and—not surprisingly—name-space issues are among them. For instance, because POSIX.4 specifies three new special file types (semaphore special files, shared memory special files, and IPC special files), the <stat.h> header will require three new macros to test for these file types. To satisfy the POSIX.1 name-space rules they will have to be protected by a feature test macro. But the situation is more complex. Systems will be permitted to implement and conform to portions of the POSIX.4 standard. For example, a system will be able to claim conformance to the shared memory, process locking, and timers portions of the standards. Each of these has name-space implications. Thus, POSIX.4 anticipates having a separate feature test macro for each of the 11 parts of its standard.

11.4.5   Other POSIX Committees

The work of the remaining POSIX committees is still in early stages. There is some sentiment to the effect that the issues before these committees have not achieved any kind of stability in the industry and that it is therefore too early to settle on standards. Others feel that this is precisely the time to choose standards, before too many implementations do the same things in different and incompatible ways. Because the work of these committees is in such an early stage, we content ourselves with brief descriptions of their tasks.

The 1003.5 committee is developing Ada bindings to POSIX.1. This will not be a separate standard; it will be another interface to the (language-independent) POSIX.1 standard. It should include interfaces that have the equivalent functionality of all the C interfaces in the present standard, except the C-specific library given in Chapter 8. An important feature of the Ada binding is that it will not have a one-to-one correspondence with the C binding. For example, because Ada specifies tasking as part of the process, the *fork()/exec()* method of starting a new process and program is not appropriate. Instead, a single Ada *Start_Process* primitive will be required.

The 1003.6 committee is concerned with issues of system security. Historically, UNIX systems have not been greatly concerned with security. The single level of security provided by the superuser mechanism is not adequate for most purposes where security really matters. Rather, it should be possible to provide users with appropriate privileges for certain purposes without giving them unrestricted access to the system.

The requirements envisioned by 1003.6 will include both program interfaces and utilities. The program interfaces will be specified in a language-independent manner. The specific elements being addressed by 1003.6 include:

- Least privilege. This will specify the discrete privileges that are necessary for a conforming 1003.6 system, so that processes can have exactly the privileges they need and no more.

- Discretionary access control (DAC). This describes access controls for objects (such as files) that are under the control of the creator of the object. An example of DAC is an access control list. Such a list explicitly enumerates the user IDs that can have access to the object. It further restricts, but does not replace, the basic POSIX.1 access scheme.

- Mandatory access control (MAC). This describes access controls for objects that are under the control of the system or the system's security administrator. An example of a MAC is a hierarchy of categories for objects. Each user ID can have read access to all objects created with the same or lower categories and gives write access for the objects it creates to all objects with the same or higher categories ("write up, read down").

- Auditability mechanism. This describes the actions that need to be audited and the mechanism by which the system keeps track of them.

The 1003.7 committee is concerned with standards for system administration of POSIX systems. This will include utilities and program interfaces, to be specified in a language-independent manner. The current form of the 1003.7 standard is quite unusual; it is an "object-oriented" standard. That is, it addresses certain kinds of objects and actions on those objects. For example, one class of object might be "user". Operations on such an object could be "install", "remove", "change command interpreter", and so forth. Another class of objects could be "file system". Operations on objects of this class could include "mount", "check consistency", and so forth. Because this proposal is not based on any existing practice, it may change considerably before a standard is adopted.

Originally, the 1003.8 committee was the "networking" committee. That subject has proven sufficiently thorny to have been broken up among a number of working groups. Currently, 1003.8 is concerned with standards for transparent file access. One of the issues confronting 1003.8 is whether transparent access to files will support all of the semantics of POSIX.1 file access. This is not true of most of the current network file systems, such as NFS. One of the 1003.8 splinter groups is 1003.12, which is concerned with protocol independent application interfaces for networks. This group, in its infancy, is faced with a number of existing incompatible interfaces and will have to either choose between them or make up something new.

The 1003.9 committee is developing a Fortran binding to POSIX.1. Like the Ada binding, this will not be a separate standard. However, the 1003.5 standard is being written as a stand-alone document, while 1003.9 makes many references to 1003.1. This group has made considerable progress and as of this writing is preparing their draft standard for its first ballot.

The 1003.10 committee is charged with developing a "supercomputing AEP". This group actually is evolving into two subgroups. One is producing a profile for applications that require supercomputing support. The other is developing a standard for batch computing. This standard is currently based on the Network Queueing System developed at NASA Ames. It will specify extensions to POSIX.1 for such features as checkpoint/restart and batch system administration.

The 1003.11 committee is charged with developing a transaction processing support AEP. Historically, UNIX systems have not been widely used for transaction processing applications, and thus there is no single widespread mode of transaction processing on UNIX-like systems. For this reason the work of this committee may prove difficult.

11.4.6 The 1201 Committee

The IEEE's Technical Committee on Operating Systems, which sponsors all of the 1003 working groups, has also started a new set of working groups with the number 1201. The individual groups will be numbered 1201.x, and there are at this writing three such groups. Their focus is on user interfaces. This is a very competitive area at the moment, with such proprietary systems as Motif, Open Look, and NextStep vying for acceptance.

One of the 1201 subgroups is charged with developing standards for Xlib, the X Windows package that was developed at MIT and has become a de facto standard for window systems on many UNIX-based workstations. The Xlib working group is considering simply proposing the adoption of X Windows Release 3 or Release 4 as a standard.

11.5   The *X/Open Portability Guide*

X/Open Ltd. is an organization whose members are vendors of computer equipment. Originally it was formed by a group of European companies, but it currently has a membership of over 20 companies from around the world. The goal of X/Open is to promote open systems by getting its members to agree on common standards. Yet, X/Open is not a standards-making body. Rather, it provides guides and attempts to promote existing industry standards. From its inception it has used the UNIX system as one basis for its guides.

X/Open publishes a document called the *X/Open Portability Guide*, or *XPG*. This guide is a specification; it does not describe a standard, but an interface that is recommended for portability. The third edition of this guide, referred to as *XPG3*, is in seven volumes, which cover the following subjects.

Volume 1 covers the shell and utilities. It covers much the same ground as POSIX.2. The shell and utilities are modeled on those found on UNIX systems.

Volume 2 covers system interfaces and headers, expressed in C. It is the *XPG* equivalent of POSIX.1. This volume includes a message catalogue interface that differs from the Uniforum proposal in the future revisions supplement. It includes all of the original POSIX.1 functions and many more functions from UNIX System V.

Volume 3 covers "supplementary definitions". This includes a number of topics, but the main content of this volume is the terminal interface specification. This is based on the *curses* package that was developed at Berkeley and is now distributed with many UNIX systems. The *curses* functions allow programs to manipulate the cursor on displays in a relatively device-independent way. They are optional in *XPG*. That is, an X/Open conforming vendor need not support them. There is no POSIX equivalent for this package.

Volume 4 specifies standards for two programming languages: C and COBOL. The C specification includes an early draft of the ANSI standard and a discussion of the `lint` utility and of general C portability principles. Support of these features is optional.

Volume 5 covers data management. It specifies interface standards for ISAM (indexed sequential access methods) and for SQL (structured query language, widely used in database applications). Support of these features is optional.

Volume 6 covers window management. It uses Release 2 of X11, the X Windows package that was developed at MIT and is widely used on UNIX workstations. This is an outdated release of X Windows. (Release 3 of X11 is in wide use now, and Release 4 is becoming widely used. Unfortunately, Release 4 is not entirely upward compatible with Release 3.) Support of *XPG* window management is optional.

Volume 7 covers networking. It describes a transport interface, XTI, that is *not* in wide use on UNIX systems in the United States. Support of XTI is optional.

As you can see, the *XPG* specification is much broader than the POSIX.1 standard. In fact, the *XPG* constitutes a large application environment profile.

X/Open has announced its intention to support POSIX, including the POSIX.2 standard when that is adopted. Volume 2 of *XPG3*, covering system interfaces and headers, includes all of (original) POSIX.1 as a subset. Thus, *XPG3* is an extension of POSIX.1. It also includes many functions not in POSIX.1, such as *signal()* and *ulimit()*. System administration functions such as *mknod()*, which are specifically excluded from the POSIX.1 effort, are included in *XPG3*.

If you need to develop an application that uses full-screen cursor addressing, you cannot write it as a strictly conforming POSIX.1 application. There simply are no POSIX.1 functions that suit the purpose. Probably the most portable choice in this case is to use *curses*. If you need a more powerful user interface, such as one that uses a mouse and windows, then you have no serious hope of portability until the 1201 committee finishes its job, which likely will be some years from now. In the next chapter we discuss the issue of relative portability: what to do when your application needs a facility that is not portable.

General C Portability Considerations

In the Preface to this book we made the distinction between internal and external program portability. The rest of this book has been devoted to external portability in the POSIX.1 context. In this chapter we briefly discuss some C portability techniques, including internal portability, and give some general techniques you can use to help ensure the portability of your C programs. It is not our purpose to give an exhaustive discussion of this subject. That would require a book to itself, and indeed such books exist.* Rather, we cover a few simple but useful points that every C programmer should be aware of and a few points where the C standard has created new portability concerns.

12.1   What C Does Not Guarantee

Some of the semantics of C are implementation-defined. Clearly, a portable program should not depend on those semantics. What could be simpler? But that's easier said than done. Let's review some of these dependencies.

12.1.1   Questions of Sign and Sign Extension

Are objects of type `char` signed or unsigned? As is well known, this varies from one implementation to another. The following code fragment will give different results on different machines:

---

* For example, *C Traps and Pitfalls,* by Andrew Koenig, Addison-Wesley, 1989, or *Portability and the C Language,* by Rex Jaeschke, Hayden Books, 1989.

```
char ch;
ch = -1;
if ( ch == -1 )
    printf("Yes\n");
else
    printf("No\n");
```

The first statement apparently assigns –1 to ch. After this assignment, many C compilers will treat the value in ch as –1, but many others will treat it as 255. (On a computer with 8-bit bytes that uses two's-complement arithmetic, the signed 8-bit representation of –1 and the unsigned 8-bit representation of 255 are both 0xff.) The problem only arises when you attempt to use the value in an expression. For example, the conditional expression (ch == -1) in the code is ambiguous. This is because the constant –1 is of type int and the value of ch is promoted to int before the comparison is made. There are two ways that this promotion may be made: with or without sign extension. If sign extension is used, then ch will be promoted to the integer –1. Otherwise, it will (on 8-bit byte, two's-complement systems) be promoted to the integer 255.

A special case of this bug is the following classic error: consider the function *getchar()*, which gets characters from standard input. It has a result of type int, but because it's used to read characters people often store the result in a char variable. This can lead to disaster in two different ways. Consider this fragment:

```
#include <stdio.h>
char ch;
while ( (ch = getchar()) != EOF )
    process_character();
```

How will this loop terminate? Clearly, when ch is equal to EOF. On most systems EOF is #defined to be –1 in <stdio.h>, and *getchar()* is implemented to return the int –1 when end-of-file is reached on standard input. If this code is executed on a system where chars are unsigned, the loop will *never* terminate; ch can never compare equal to EOF on such a system. But if the code is executed on a system with signed chars, the loop may exit prematurely! This is because standard input may contain a byte that has the same bit representation as ((char)EOF). Reading this byte will cause the condition to evaluate as true and terminate the loop. The reason that *getchar()* is specified as returning an int is to enable it to return all possible char values *and* an additional one, EOF.

Remember that objects of type char are integral types in C; they store numbers. (And char constants are of type int. The constant 'a' can [on ASCII systems] be viewed as just an arcane way to write 97.) The only numbers that you can portably store in a char variable are zero through 127. ANSI C provides the types signed char and unsigned char, and their use will solve some of these problems—but not all of them, and then only on ANSI systems; signed is not a keyword in common usage C.

12.1.2 Pointers

The title of this section is enough to make some C programmers groan, but in fact C's use of pointers and pointer arithmetic is one of the language's most powerful features. However, it also allows for nonportable constructs. One of them arises in the confusion of array names and pointers. Consider the following construct:

```
char string1[] = "hello";
string1[0] = 'H';
```

After this code, `string1` is a 6-byte array with contents `"Hello"`. (The sixth byte is null.) This code is correct and portable. Suppose now we use a pointer instead of an array:

```
char *string2 = "hello";
string2[0] = 'H';          /* Or if you prefer: *string2 = 'H'; */
```

Code like this can be found in many programs and works on many systems, but it is not portable! It violates a constraint of the ANSI C standard. The reason has to do with the semantics of the two declarations. The statement

```
char string1[] = "hello";
```

means: allocate an array of 6 bytes, initialize them with `'h'`, `'e'`, `'l'`, `'l'`, `'o'`, `'\0'`, and use `string1` as a name for the address of the `'h'`. The statement

```
char *string2 = "hello";
```

means something slightly different: allocate 6 bytes somewhere, compile the same 6 characters into them as before, allocate enough more space to hold a `char` pointer, call that space `string2`, and store into it the address of the first of those 6 characters, `'h'`. The situation is shown in Figure 12.1.

The problem is that the 6 allocated bytes in the second declaration constitute a string constant. The C standard permits string constants to be stored in read-only memory, and the results of attempting to modify a string constant in ANSI C are undefined. The initializer for the array is *not* a string constant, even though it looks like one. It is just a shorthand way to list the initial `char` values of an array. It is equivalent to

```
char string1[] = {'h', 'e', 'l', 'l', 'o', '\0'};
```

Another C pointer pitfall arises from the fact that pointers to different types are themselves different types. Many C programs assume that pointers to different types can be freely mixed. This is not so. Suppose you have declared the following two pointers:

```
char *pch;
long *plong;
```

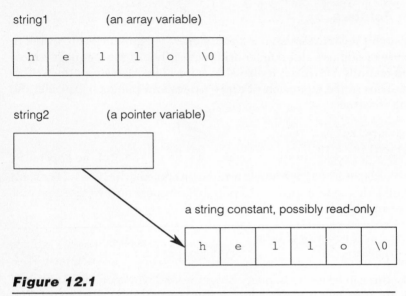

Figure 12.1

The Effect on Memory of Two Declarations

Can you portably assign one of these values to the other? Definitely not. First, they might not be the same size. Pointers to different types of objects need not be the same size. This may seem arcane, but in fact there are very common implementations of C on segmented architectures in which pointers to functions have an internal form that is different from pointers to data objects. Even when the pointers are the same size, one might have alignment requirements that the other does not. Use type casts! For example:

```
pch = (char *)plong; or plong = (long *)pch;
```

In ANSI C, the type void * can be used as a generic pointer: a pointer declared to be of type void * is assignment-compatible with a pointer of any other type. In common usage C, the type char * is commonly (but nonportably) used for this purpose. Thus, the *malloc()* function, which has a result of type void * in ANSI C, is declared to return a char * on many older systems. If you are going to use char * as a generic pointer, use a cast. For example, don't say:

```
long *buf;
buf = malloc(NUMLONGS * sizeof(long));
```

Instead, say:

```
long *buf;
buf = (long *)malloc(NUMLONGS * sizeof(long));
```

A great deal of confusion surrounds the NULL pointer in C. A pointer whose value is NULL is guaranteed to not point to a legitimate address. If you assign to a pointer variable a constant expression whose value is zero, that will be a NULL pointer. But that is not the same as the address zero! Suppose we have declared the char pointer pch as above and an int variable named n as well. The statement

```
pch = (char *)0;
```

does what you expect; it assigns a NULL pointer to pch. But the apparently equivalent sequence

```
n = 0;
pch = (char *)n;
```

may not assign a NULL pointer to pch. The reason is as follows: the internal representation of NULL may or may not be all zero bits. If it is not, then when the compiler sees a constant expression whose value is zero being assigned to a pointer variable, it converts that constant at compile time to the representation of NULL. But no such automatic conversion takes place at run time. As the internal representation of NULL *is* zero on most machines, this nonportable code will often work. That's unfortunate; if a nonportable construct rarely works, you will find it and fix it quickly, but if you port it to ten machines and it works on all of them, when it fails on the eleventh machine you'll have a hard time tracking it down.

12.1.3 Byte Order and Structure Alignment

Byte order problems are well known. The issue is this: on byte-addressable machines, an arithmetic object of multibyte type (e.g., an int or a float) occupies several addresses. Is the most significant byte at the lowest or highest address of the object? Architectures of both types exist. Consider the following code:

```
int n;
char ch;
n = 1;
ch = *( (char *)&n );
```

On a PDP-11, this code assigns ch the value 1, the numerical value of the least significant byte of the int 1. This is because on the PDP-11 the least significant byte appears first, and &n is the address of the first byte of n. On an MC68000, the same code assigns ch the value zero, because the lowest address is the address of the most significant byte, which is zero. It's distressingly easy to write C code that depends on byte order, especially if (as above) you mix pointer types. (The expression &n has the type "pointer to int".) Casts will not protect you here.

A related issue has to do with elements in structures and unions. A C compiler is free to pad structures and unions as it sees fit. Because some architectures have alignment requirements for certain types (e.g., ints must be located at even addresses), padding is sometimes necessary. If you want to know the offset of a structure or union member it's not sufficient to count up all the space occupied by preceding members. Some have argued for an *offsetof* compile-time operator in C, similar to *sizeof*, but it does not yet exist. If you need to figure out the offset of a member, do something like this: given the structure definition

```
struct item {
    char    init;
    int     year;
    long    code;
    char    name[NAMELEN];
    int     type;
} item;
```

suppose you need the offset of the type member. You can compute it as a difference of pointers:

```
offset_of_type = ((char *) &item.type) - ((char *)&item.init);
```

You *must* cast the pointers to type char *. Pointer arithmetic is only allowed between pointers to the same type of object and is scaled by the size of the object. Incidentally, this is why pointer arithmetic between void pointers is not permitted in ANSI C. If the pointers

```
void *p1;
void *p2;
```

are declared, and both have values (e.g., from calls to *malloc()*), the pointer difference

```
p2 - p1
```

is undefined. It would have to be scaled by the size of an object of type void, but there are no such objects and there is no such size. At least one supposed ANSI C compiler allows this construct, scaling by 1 as if the pointers were char pointers. So you shouldn't rely on compilers finding this bug for you.

The issues of byte order and structure alignment are part of the larger problem of data portability. We addressed this issue in Chapter 9, Section 9.1.3. It bears repeating here: C makes no guarantees about the internal representation of data. Data items that are stored on some medium in their internal representation are not portable. Programs that make assumptions about the internal representation of data items (e.g., shifting right instead of dividing) are not portable.

12.1.4 Order of Evaluation

As is well known, the order of evaluation of function arguments is not specified. The same is true for sub-expressions. Evaluation of sub-expressions can have side effects, so if you write statements like:

```
i += ++i + i++;
```

you can't expect anything reasonable to happen. Side effects in function arguments can have the same confusing consequences. We executed the following program on four different computers, all UNIX systems:

```
int func(int n, int m)
{
    return n - m;
}

main()
{
    int i = 1;
    int n;

    n = func(i++, i++);
    printf("%d\n", n);
}
```

Two of the systems printed –1, one of them printed 1, and one of them printed zero. The values of –1 and 1 can be easily understood. If arguments are evaluated left to right and passed as they are evaluated, then func(2, 3) is called. If right to left, then func(3, 2) is called. But it is also conforming for both of the side effects to be evaluated before either argument is passed, giving a call to func(3, 3).

12.1.5 Integral Promotions

Here is a short C program. What does it print?

```
unsigned short s1;
long l1;

main()
{
    l1 = -1;
    s1 = 1;
    if ( l1 >= s1 )
        printf("unsigned\n");
    else
        printf("value\n");
}
```

How do you evaluate the conditional expression? The two variables must be converted to some common type. Historically, C compilers have performed these conversions in two different ways. The rule called *unsigned-preserving* calls for converting both arguments to an unsigned type that is wide enough to hold both of them—in this case, unsigned long. The difference would then be greater than or equal to zero under any circumstances, because it is an unsigned expression. (Unsigned arithmetic in C is modular; it never results in an overflow or underflow.) The rule called *value-preserving* calls for widening a narrow unsigned type (such as unsigned short) to a signed type, if the wider type can represent all of the possible values of the original type. Thus, s1 would be promoted to a signed int or long, and then the subtraction would be done. These two rules give two different results. Indeed, we compiled and executed this program using two C compilers on the same computer and got output of "unsigned" one time and "value" the other.

To make things more complex, the ANSI C standard mandates value-preserving rules. This is true despite the fact that most UNIX C compilers use unsigned-preserving rules. Section 3.2.1.1 of the C standard states:

> A char, a short int, or an int bit field, or their signed or unsigned varieties, or an object that has enumeration type, may be used in an expression wherever an int or unsigned int may be used. If an int can represent all values of the original type, the value is converted to an int; otherwise it is converted to an unsigned int.[13]

These problems can always be avoided by the use of casts. In every case, you should have a clear idea of how you want the arithmetic to be performed, and if you have such an idea you can code it. Thus, the above program should be rewritten with either

```
if ( 11 >= (int)s1 )        /* signed arithmetic */
```

or

```
if ( (unsigned)11 >= s1 )   /* unsigned arithmetic */
```

12.2 Types

You may have noticed that the POSIX.1 standard makes heavy use of typedefed types in its declarations. This is part of a strategy that is sometimes referred to as *delayed commitment*. The idea is to put off as long as possible the association of a variable with a type. For example, if the st_uid field of the stat structure were required to be of type unsigned short (as it is on many UNIX systems), then a POSIX system would be limited in the range of user IDs it could assign. If it were specified as unsigned long, then a POSIX system would be forced to allocate more space for these fields than it might need. By using a typedef, the standard allows implementations to choose the type they use while allowing applications to be portable.

You can use the same technique in your own code. Suppose that you are writing an application that requires a variable of some integral type. Suppose that the range of values needed in this integral type may vary or is unpredictable. Instead of choosing a type, use a `typedef`, and put the `typedef` in a header file (yes, this is really a file!) of your own:

```
#include "my_app.h"
range_type range;
```

And in `my_app.h`, something like:

```
typedef unsigned long range_type;
```

(Do not use a type name that ends in `_t`; such names are reserved!) Later, if you need to port this code and the type `unsigned long` is inappropriate for values of type `range_type`, you simply have to change the header. Such code is not strictly portable, because a change is required, but the change is restricted to a single, easily found line.

C is not a strongly typed language. In many contexts, it allows expressions to mix different types, enforcing compatibility of these types by default conversions. For example, we have noted that on some compilers, if a signed integral object is compared to an unsigned integral object, the signed object may be converted to unsigned before the comparison is made. This can have some surprising consequences: the expression

```
-1 >= sizeof(int)
```

evaluates as true on most systems! This is because the *sizeof* operator evaluates at compile time to an unsigned constant (actually, a constant of type `size_t`, which is an unsigned integral type), so—on systems with unsigned-preserving rules—the –1 is converted to an unsigned value. On most architectures it will convert to a very large value indeed.

This behavior may seem unexpected, but how is it nonportable? The porting problem arises in the way that signed values are converted to unsigned. On a two's-complement system, signed integers are converted to unsigned ones by "doing nothing". The bit pattern is simply treated as an unsigned binary integer. Such systems are so common, especially in the small and midrange computer worlds, that you may never have encountered any other behavior. But other representations of integers exist. When –1 is converted to an unsigned integer on such systems, there's no telling what you'll get.

12.3 Function Argument Promotions

C has default promotion rules for function arguments. For example, if you pass a `float` as a function argument, it is converted to a `double`. A `char` or `short` is converted to an `int` before being passed. (Note that, on ANSI C systems, *in the presence of a prototype for the function, these promotions are not made.* See Chapter 8, Section 8.1.) The reasons for these promotions have to do with the architecture of the PDP–11, on which C was nurtured.

Suppose that you're working on a system on which `long`s and `int`s are the same size. (Such systems are very common.) Suppose further that you have a function *func()* that expects an argument of type `long`. Now, what happens if you call the function like this?

```
func('0');
```

On an ASCII system, this will pass the `int` value 48 (ASCII '0' = 48, promoted to `int`), and because an `int` and a `long` are indistinguishable, *func()* receives the value 48. But suppose you move the code to a machine on which `short`s and `int`s are the same size and are smaller than `long`s. (Such systems are also very common.) What will this code do now? It will still pass an `int` 48, but *func()* will get something else. (Exactly what it gets depends on byte order and what else happens to be on the stack, or in the registers, or wherever arguments are passed.) If you are not using ANSI C, make sure to cast your non-`int` function arguments to the correct type. Be aware, however, that casts do not suppress the default promotions. The call

```
func( (char)'0' );              /* Silly thing to do! */
```

is identical to the previous call; it still promotes its argument. If your function expects a `long`, cast your argument to type `long`. If your function expects a `char`, you've made a portability mistake; on most implementations it won't get one.

A common error is to call *lseek()* with a second argument that is implicitly an `int`:

```
(void) lseek(fd, 10, SEEK_SET);              /* Error */
```

This code attempts to position the file pointer for `fd` at offset 10. But if the type of the second argument, `off_t`, is not the same size as the type `int`, the call will not work. The correct version is:

```
(void) lseek(fd, (off_t)10, SEEK_SET);      /* Correct */
```

12.4   ANSI C or Common Usage C?

At this writing, the number of ANSI C compilers is still rather small. However, there is little doubt that ANSI C compilers will soon become preferred and widely available. Should you write your programs in ANSI C or in old-style C?

Strictly speaking, use of old-style C is more portable. After all, ANSI C does support old-style function declarations and definitions. It is almost[*]

---

[*] Almost, but not quite, because there are a number of "quiet changes" in ANSI C—that is, changes in the semantics of the language that will cause old-style programs to compile as before but to run differently. An example of such a quiet change is the shift from unsigned-preserving to value-preserving promotion rules described in Section 12.1.5, above.

backward compatible. Nevertheless, if you have the chance to take advantage of function prototypes you should. You can use conditional compilation to protect yourself; see the example testing _ _STDC_ _ in Chapter 8, Section 8.1.

12.5 Verification

How can you tell if your program is portable? Trial and error is not a good method, as the number of available systems may be far fewer than the number you eventually want your code to run on. One useful technique is to use software tools.

The most well known tool for checking portability of C programs is lint. The lint utility comes with most UNIX systems and will find many nonportable constructs that C compilers permit. Use lint if it is available. It will save you much grief.

However, there is a lot that lint will not do. Although it checks your function calls against certain standard libraries, it does not know about most of the POSIX.1 functions. It does not check that all the appropriate headers are included. Nor can lint know what environment you want your programs to run in. After all, a program can be entirely portable in X/Open environments but fail to run in POSIX.1 environments that do not support all of X/Open. Other tools exist that can perform some of these checks.

One of these tools, developed by AT&T, tests whether or not a program is portable among System V Release 4 environments. Unfortunately, it only runs on a relatively small number of machines and is not extendable to other standards. Another tool, the C Portability Verifier, was developed by Mindcraft Inc. to test portability of programs among any one of a number of environments. It can check for POSIX.1, POSIX.2, FIPS 151-1, ANSI C, or *XPG3* portability or any combination thereof. It runs on a wide variety of UNIX-based systems.

12.6 Relative Portability, or Practical Nonportability

Suppose that you want your application to run in as many environments as possible. What should you do? Ideally, you would only use external interfaces that are supported everywhere, but there are very few such interfaces. For example, you might want to write an application that runs on both UNIX-like systems and MS-DOS-like systems. But if the application is at all complex, this may be very difficult. These environments have little in common.

Practical considerations dictate that you will sometimes need to use nonportable constructs. When this occurs, you can still use good coding style, structured code, and common sense to minimize the portability problems. For example, you should keep all of the nonportable code in a separate source file, if possible. You should try to adhere to a well-known specification when there is no applicable standard. For example, if your application requires a graphical user interface, you might need to choose between Motif, Open Look, NextStep, and SunViews. Any of these choices is better than inventing an interface of your own.

Figure 12.2 shows a diagram that illustrates the relative relationship of three specifications: POSIX.1, ANSI C, and *XPG3*. You can see from the figure that POSIX.1 is contained in *XPG3*; much of ANSI C is contained in POSIX.1. Thus, if you can restrict yourself to using only ANSI C functions that are also supported by POSIX.1 (see Chapter 8, Figure 8.2), your programs will be supported in ANSI C environments, POSIX.1 environments, and *XPG3* environments. Such programs can be strictly conforming POSIX.1 applications.

Other standards and specifications could be added to this picture, although they would make it rather cluttered. We could add FIPS 151-1. It bears a strange relationship to POSIX.1: it supports the same interfaces (if we ignore *cuserid()*) but has fewer restrictions. Thus, it would extend slightly outside POSIX.1. We could add POSIX.2 (C interfaces), which would be entirely inside *XPG3* but have no overlap with POSIX.1 or ANSI C. We could

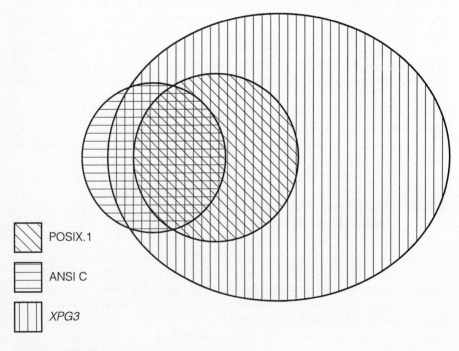

POSIX.1

ANSI C

XPG3

Figure 12.2

Relative Relationships of Three Standards and Specifications also add such proprietary products as System V Release 4, 4.4BSD, and OSF/1. All of these would entirely include POSIX.1 and some but not all of *XPG3* as well. Note that *XPG3* includes much more than C interfaces.

Maximum portability is gained by using facilities that are in as many of the standards as possible. If you need to use a non-POSIX.1 function, try to find a suitable ANSI C or *XPG3* function that will do the job. The chances are greater that any given environment will have such a function. But if there is a POSIX.1 function that will do the job, use it. Support for the POSIX.1 standard is very widespread. It is at the heart of most other UNIX-like standards, of most proprietary systems, and of a federal standard. It is itself an international standard. If it is not already so, adherence to POSIX.1 will soon be the key to writing truly portable programs.

A

POSIX.1 Functions

This appendix gives an **ANSI C–style prototype** for each function defined in the POSIX.1 standard, except for those functions that are also part of the C standard. The functions are arranged in alphabetical order for ease of reference. We do not attempt to explain the semantics of the functions here. However, we give the return type and values on success and failure. For each function, we also show the headers that should be included when that function is used. Recall that implementations claiming support for ANSI standard C must have prototypes declared for all POSIX.1 functions. Implementations claiming common usage C support must have external declarations for all functions that do not return a "plain" int. The comment `/* proto */` following a header indicates that the given header is the one in which the function's prototype or external declaration is given. The prototypes for *getcwd()*, *read()*, and *write()* are given as in the revised 1990 standard, rather than the originally adopted standard.

We also give the portable values of `errno` that each function can set. Because the conditions that give rise to a particular value of `errno` are common to many functions, we do not list the condition that returns a given value of `errno` unless it is unusual. Remember that implementations are free to set other values of `errno` for error conditions not covered by the POSIX.1 standard.

access

```
#include <unistd.h>   /* proto */
int access(const char *path, int mode);
```

Tests whether the real (not effective) user ID of the calling process has the requested mode of access to the named file. Returns zero if the requested access is granted, –1 otherwise.

access *(continued)*

Error codes:
EACCES: if permissions are denied.
ENAMETOOLONG
ENOENT
ENOTDIR
EROFS

alarm

```
#include <unistd.h>  /* proto */
unsigned int alarm(unsigned int seconds);
```

Schedules a SIGALRM to be generated for the calling process in seconds seconds. Returns the number of seconds remaining on any previously scheduled alarm or zero if there is no scheduled alarm.

Error codes: none.

cfgetispeed

```
#include <termios.h> /* proto */
speed_t cfgetispeed(const struct termios *termios_p);
```

Returns the input baud rate (the code defined in <termios.h>, e.g., B1200) stored in the indicated termios structure.

Error codes: none.

cfgetospeed

```
#include <termios.h> /* proto */
speed_t cfgetospeed(const struct termios *termios_p);
```

Returns the output baud rate stored in the indicated termios structure.

Error codes: none.

cfsetispeed

```
#include <termios.h> /* proto */
int cfsetispeed(struct termios termios_p, speed_t
   speed);
```

Stores the specified input baud rate in the named termios structure. Returns zero on success, –1 if an error occurs.

Error codes: none.

cfsetospeed

```
#include <termios.h> /* proto */
int cfsetospeed(struct termios termios_p, speed_t
    speed);
```

Stores the specified output baud rate in the named `termios` structure. Returns zero on success, –1 if an error occurs.

Error codes: none in the standard.

chdir

```
#include <unistd.h> /* proto */
int chdir(const char *path);
```

Changes the current working directory of the calling process to the named directory. Returns zero on success, –1 if an error occurs.

Error codes:
EACCES
ENAMETOOLONG
ENOTDIR
ENOENT

chmod

```
#include <sys/types.h>
#include <sys/stat.h> /* proto */
int chmod(const char *path, mode_t mode);
```

Changes the access permission of the named file to `mode`. Returns zero on success, –1 if an error occurs.

Error codes:
EACCES
ENAMETOOLONG
ENOTDIR
ENOENT
EPERM
EROFS

chown

```
#include <unistd.h> /* proto */
#include <sys/types.h>
int chown(const char *path, uid_t owner, gid_t
    group);
```

chown *(continued)*

Changes the owner ID of the file to owner and the group ID of the file to group. Returns zero on success, –1 if an error occurs.

Error codes:
EACCES
ENAMETOOLONG
ENOTDIR
ENOENT
EPERM
EROFS
EINVAL

close

```
#include <unistd.h> /* proto */
int close(int fildes);
```

Closes the given file descriptor. Returns zero on success, –1 if an error occurs.

Error codes:
EBADF
EINTR

closedir

```
#include <sys/types.h>
#include <dirent.h> /* proto */
int closedir(DIR *dirp);
```

Closes the directory stream associated with dirp. Returns zero on success, –1 if an error occurs.

Error codes:
EBADF

creat

```
#include <sys/types.h>
#include <sys/stat.h>
#include <fcntl.h> /* proto */
int creat(const char *path, mode_t mode);
```

Creates and opens for writing the named regular file with the given mode. Returns a nonnegative file descriptor on success, –1 if an error occurs.

Error codes:
EACCES
EEXIST
EINTR
EISDIR
EMFILE
ENAMETOOLONG
ENFILE
ENOENT: if a component of the path prefix does not exist or
                       path points to an empty string.
ENOSPC
ENOTDIR
EROFS

ctermid

```
#include <stdio.h>
#include <unistd.h> /* proto */
char *ctermid(char *s);
```

Returns a pointer to a string that, when used as a pathname, refers to
the current controlling terminal for the process. (If s is not NULL,
then s is returned.)

Error codes: none.

cuserid   *(obsolescent)*

```
#include <stdio.h>
#include <unistd.h> /* proto */
char *cuserid(char *s);
```

This function has been removed from the POSIX standard in the 1990
revision. Its original POSIX specifications: returns a pointer to a
character representation of the owner (effective user ID) of the
current process and also stores it in the buffer at s. If this cannot be
determined, then returns NULL if s is NULL, otherwise puts '\0' at
*s and returns s.

Error codes: none.

dup

```
#include <unistd.h> /* proto */
int dup(int fildes);
```

Duplicates the given file descriptor. Returns a nonnegative file descriptor that refers to the same open file description as fildes on
success, or −1 if an error occurs.

dup *(continued)*

Error codes:
EBADF
EMFILE

dup2

```
#include <unistd.h> /* proto */
int dup2(int fildes, int fildes2);
```

Closes `fildes2` if open, and then duplicates `fildes` with the lowest available file descriptor that is greater than or equal to `fildes2`. Returns the file descriptor on success, or –1 if an error occurs.

Error codes:
EBADF
EMFILE

execl

```
#include <unistd.h> /* proto */
int execl(const char *path, const char *arg0, ...);
```

The last argument must be (char *) 0.

Overlays the calling process with the executable image in `path`, which is invoked with an argument vector of `arg0`, ... Returns –1 if an error occurs. Does not return if successful.

Error codes:
E2BIG: if arg list plus environment strings are too long.
EACCES
ENAMETOOLONG
ENOENT
ENOEXEC
ENOTDIR
ENOMEM

execle

```
#include <unistd.h> /* proto */
int execle(const char *path, const char *arg0, ...);
```

The second-to-last argument must be (char *) 0 and the last argument must be char **envp, a pointer to the array of environment strings.

Overlays the calling process with the executable image in `path`, which is invoked with an argument vector of `arg0`, ... and an environment given by envp. Returns –1 if an error occurs. Does not return if successful.

Error codes:

E2BIG: if arg list plus environment strings are too long.
EACCES
ENAMETOOLONG
ENOENT
ENOEXEC
ENOTDIR
ENOMEM

execlp

```
#include <unistd.h> /* proto */
int execlp(const char *file, const char *arg0, ...);
```
The last argument must be (char *)0.

Overlays the calling process with an executable image in a file found by
appending file to each of the path prefixes in the PATH environment variable, until an executable image is found. The program is
invoked with an argument vector of arg0, ... Returns –1 if an
error occurs. Does not return if successful.

Error codes:

E2BIG: if arg list plus environment strings are too long.
EACCES
ENAMETOOLONG
ENOENT
ENOTDIR
ENOEXEC
ENOMEM

execv

```
#include <unistd.h> /* proto */
int execv(const char *path, char * const argv[]);
```
Overlays the calling process with the executable image in path, which
is invoked with an argument vector of argv. Returns –1 if an error
occurs. Does not return if successful.

Error codes:

E2BIG: if arg list plus environment strings are too long.
EACCES
ENAMETOOLONG
ENOENT
ENOEXEC
ENOTDIR
ENOMEM

execve

```
#include <unistd.h> /* proto */
int execve(const char *path, char * const argv[],
    char * const *envp);
```

Overlays the calling process with the executable image in `path`, which is invoked with an argument vector of `argv` and an environment given by `envp`. Returns –1 if an error occurs. Does not return if successful.

Error codes:

E2BIG:	if arg list plus environment strings are too long.
EACCES	
ENAMETOOLONG	
ENOENT	
ENOEXEC	
ENOTDIR	
ENOMEM	

execvp

```
#include <unistd.h> /* proto */
int execvp(const char *file, char * const argv[]);
```

Overlays the calling process with an executable image in a file found by appending `file` to each of the path prefixes in the `PATH` environment variable, until an executable image is found. The program is invoked with an argument vector of `argv`. Returns –1 if an error occurs. Does not return if successful.

Error codes:

E2BIG:	if arg list plus environment strings are too long.
ENAMETOOLONG	
ENOENT	
ENOEXEC	
ENOTDIR	
ENOMEM	

_exit

```
#include <unistd.h> /* proto */
void _exit(int status);
```

Terminates the calling process and closes all open files. Does not return.

Error codes: none.

fcntl

```
#include <sys/types.h>
#include <unistd.h>
#include <fcntl.h> /* proto */
int fcntl(int fildes, int cmd, ...);
```

Controls or returns open file attributes in a way that depends on the value of cmd. Returns a value that, if *fcntl()* is successful, depends on the value of cmd. If cmd is F_DUPFD, then a file descriptor is returned. If cmd is F_GETFL, then the value of certain flags and access modes (not negative) is returned. In all other cases a value other than –1 is returned. If *fcntl()* fails, it returns –1.

Error codes:

EACCES:	if trying to set lock on locked portion of file.
EAGAIN:	may be returned instead of EACCES.
EBADF	
EINTR	
EINVAL	
EMFILE	
ENOLOCK:	if setting a lock would exceed the system lock limit.
EDEADLK:	if setting a lock might cause a deadlock condition.

fdopen

```
#include <stdio.h> /* proto */
FILE *fdopen(int fildes, const char *type);
```

Opens a stream whose underlying file descriptor is fildes. Returns a pointer to the stream if successful, NULL if not.

Error codes: none.

fileno

```
#include <stdio.h> /* proto */
int fileno(FILE *stream);
```

Returns a nonnegative integer that is the underlying file descriptor of stream if successful, –1 otherwise.

Error codes: none.

fork

```
#include <sys/types.h>
#include <unistd.h> /* proto */
pid_t fork(void);
```

fork *(continued)*

Creates a new (child) process that is a copy of the calling (parent) process. Returns zero to the child process and a nonzero child process ID to the parent process if successful. Returns –1 otherwise.

Error codes:

EAGAIN: if the system lacks the necessary resources to create another process *or* if the limit on the number of processes that can be owned by a single user ID would be exceeded.

ENOMEM: if the process requires more space (typically swap or paging space, not physical memory) than the system is able to supply.

fpathconf

```
#include <unistd.h> /* proto */
long fpathconf(int fildes, int name);
```

Returns the current value of the named variable for the given file descriptor. If the current value is not defined for the file descriptor, returns –1 and does not change errno. On error, returns –1 and sets errno.

Error codes:
EINVAL
EBADF

fstat

```
#include <sys/types.h>
#include <sys/stat.h> /* proto */
int fstat(int fildes, struct stat *buf);
```

Gets the file status information of the open file referred to by fildes and stores it in the stat structure at buf. Returns zero if successful, –1 otherwise.

Error codes:
EBADF

getcwd

```
#include <unistd.h> /* proto */
char *getcwd(char *buf, size_t size);
```

Stores an absolute pathname for the calling process's current working directory in buf. Returns buf if successful, NULL otherwise.

Error codes:

EINVAL:	if the value of size is ≤ 0.
ERANGE:	if the value of size is > 0 but less than the length of the pathname plus 1.
EACCES	

getegid

```
#include <sys/types.h>
#include <unistd.h> /* proto */
gid_t getegid(void);
```

Returns the effective group ID of the calling process.

Error codes: none.

getenv

```
#include <stdlib.h>
#include <unistd.h> /* proto */
char *getenv(const char *name);
```

Returns a pointer to a string containing the environment value for the specified name if successful, NULL otherwise.

Error codes: none.

geteuid

```
#include <sys/types.h>
#include <unistd.h> /* proto */
uid_t geteuid(void);
```

Returns the effective user ID of the calling process.

Error codes: none.

getgid

```
#include <sys/types.h>
#include <unistd.h> /* proto */
gid_t getgid(void);
```

Returns the real group ID of the calling process.

Error codes: none.

getgrgid

```
#include <grp.h> /* proto */
struct group *getgrgid(gid_t gid);
```

Searches the group database for an entry whose group ID is gid. Returns a pointer to a struct group filled in with such an entry if successful. Otherwise, returns NULL.

Error codes: none.

getgrnam

```
#include <grp.h> /* proto */
struct group *getgrnam(const char *name);
```

Searches the group database for an entry whose group name is name. Returns a pointer to a struct group filled in with such an entry if successful. Otherwise, returns NULL.

Error codes: none.

getgroups

```
#include <sys/types.h>
#include <unistd.h> /* proto */
int getgroups(int gidsetsize, gid_t *grouplist);
```

Fills the grouplist array with the calling process's supplementary group IDs. Returns the number of supplementary group IDs associated with the calling process if successful, –1 otherwise. If grouplist is a NULL pointer, then returns the number of supplementary group IDs but does not store them anywhere.

Error codes:
EINVAL: if gidsetsize is not zero but is less than the number of supplementary group IDs.

getlogin

```
#include <unistd.h> /* proto */
char *getlogin(void);
```

Returns a pointer to a string containing the user's login name, or returns NULL if the login name cannot be found.

Error codes: none.

getpgrp

```
#include <sys/types.h>
#include <unistd.h> /* proto */
pid_t getpgrp(void);
```

Returns the process group ID of the calling process.

Error codes: none.

getpid

```
#include <sys/types.h>
#include <unistd.h> /* proto */
pid_t getpid(void);
```

Returns the process ID of the calling process.

Error codes: none.

getppid

```
#include <sys/types.h>
#include <unistd.h> /* proto */
pid_t getppid(void);
```

Returns the process ID of the parent process of the calling process.

Error codes: none.

getpwnam

```
#include <pwd.h> /* proto */
struct passwd *getpwnam(const char *name);
```

Searches the user database for an entry whose user name is name.
Returns a pointer to a struct passwd filled in with such an entry
if successful. Otherwise, returns NULL.

Error codes: none.

getpwuid

```
#include <pwd.h> /* proto */
struct passwd *getpwuid(uid_t uid);
```

Searches the user database for an entry whose user ID is uid. Returns a
pointer to a struct passwd filled in with such an entry if successful. Otherwise, returns NULL.

Error codes: none.

getuid

```
#include <sys/types.h>
#include <unistd.h> /* proto */
uid_t getuid(void);
```

Returns the real user ID of the calling process.

Error codes: none.

isatty

```
#include <unistd.h> /* proto */
int isatty(int fildes);
```

Returns 1 if fildes is a valid open file descriptor associated with a terminal, and returns zero otherwise.

Error codes: none.

kill

```
#include <sys/types.h>
#include <signal.h> /* proto */
int kill(pid_t pid, int sig);
```

Sends signal sig to the process or process group specified by pid. Returns zero if successful, –1 otherwise.

Error codes:

EINVAL:	if sig is invalid or unsupported.
EPERM	
ESRCH	

link

```
#include <unistd.h> /* proto */
int link(const char *path1, const char *path2);
```

Creates a link named path2 to the file named path1. Returns zero if successful, –1 otherwise.

Error codes:

EACCES	
EEXIST:	if path2 names an existing file.
EMLINK	
ENAMETOOLONG	
ENOENT	
ENOSPC:	if the directory that would contain the link cannot be extended.

ENOTDIR

EPERM: if path1 names a directory and the calling process
                     does not have appropriate privileges or if the
                     implementation does not support links
                     between directories.

EROFS

EXDEV: if path1 and path2 are on different file systems
                     and the implementation does not support links
                     across file systems.

lseek

```
#include <unistd.h> /* proto */
#include <sys/types.h>
off_t lseek(int fildes, off_t offset, int whence);
```

Moves the file pointer of the open file description associated with
fildes to the location specified by offset, relative to whence.
Returns the resulting offset location in bytes from the beginning of
the file if successful, or ((off_t) -1) otherwise.

Error codes:

EBADF

EINVAL

ESPIPE

mkdir

```
#include <sys/types.h>
#include <sys/stat.h> /* proto */
int mkdir(const char *path, mode_t mode);
```

Creates the directory named by path, with the specified mode. Returns
zero if successful, –1 otherwise.

Error codes:

EACCES

EEXIST

EMLINK: if the link count of the parent would exceed
                     LINK_MAX.

ENAMETOOLONG

ENOENT

ENOSPC

ENOTDIR

EROFS

mkfifo

```
#include <sys/types.h>
#include <sys/stat.h> /* proto */
int mkfifo(const char *path, mode_t mode);
```

Creates the FIFO named by path with the specified mode. Returns zero
if successful, −1 otherwise.

Error codes:
EACCES
EEXIST
ENAMETOOLONG
ENOENT
ENOSPC
ENOTDIR
EROFS

open

```
#include <sys/types.h>
#include <sys/stat.h>
#include <fcntl.h> /* proto */
int open(const char *path, int oflag, ...);
```

Opens the named file with the specified flags. If O_CREAT is set in
oflags, then the mode of the file to be created must be passed as a
third argument. Returns a nonnegative open file descriptor if
successful, −1 otherwise.

Error codes:
EACCES
EEXIST
EINTR
EISDIR
EMFILE
ENAMETOOLONG
ENFILE
ENOENT
ENOSPC
ENOTDIR
ENXIO: if the named file is a FIFO, O_NONBLOCK and
O_WRONLY are set, and no process has the file
open for reading.

EROFS

opendir

```
#include <sys/types.h>
#include <dirent.h> /* proto */
DIR *opendir(const char *dirname);
```

Opens a directory stream for the named directory. Returns a pointer to a DIR object if successful, NULL otherwise.

Error codes:
EACCES
ENAMETOOLONG
ENOENT
ENOTDIR
EMFILE
ENFILE

pathconf

```
#include <unistd.h> /* proto */
long pathconf(const char *path, int name);
```

Returns the current value of the named variable for the given path. If the current value is not defined for the path, returns –1 and does not change errno. On error, returns –1 and sets errno.

Error codes:
EINVAL
EACCES
ENAMETOOLONG
ENOENT
ENOTDIR

pause

```
#include <unistd.h> /* proto */
int pause(void);
```

Blocks the calling process until a signal is delivered. Returns –1 (if it returns at all).

Error codes:
EINTR

pipe

```
#include <unistd.h> /* proto */
int pipe(int fildes[2]);
```

pipe *(continued)*

Creates a pipe, with reading and writing file descriptors stored in
fildes[0] and fildes[1], respectively. Returns zero if successful, –1 otherwise.

Error codes:
EMFILE
ENFILE

read

```
#include <unistd.h> /* proto */
ssize_t read(int fildes, void *buf, size_t nbyte);
```

Reads up to nbyte bytes from the file associated with fildes, storing
them in the buffer at buf. Returns the number of bytes actually
read if successful, –1 otherwise.

Error codes:

EAGAIN: if O_NONBLOCK is set for the file descriptor and the
             process would block trying to read.

EINTR

EIO: if, on a job control system, the process is in the
             background, is ignoring or blocking SIGTTIN,
             and is attempting to read from its controlling
             terminal.

readdir

```
#include <sys/types.h>
#include <dirent.h> /* proto */
struct dirent *readdir(DIR *dirp);
```

Reads the next directory entry from the stream associated with dirp,
storing it in a struct dirent. Returns a pointer to the struct
dirent if successful, NULL otherwise.

Error codes:

EBADF: if dirp doesn't refer to an open DIR stream.

rename

```
#include <unistd.h> /* proto */
int rename(const char *old, const char *new);
```

Renames the existing file old as new. Returns zero if successful, –1
otherwise.

Error codes:

EACCES	
EBUSY:	if old or new refers to a directory that is in use by the system or another process.
EEXIST:	if new refers to a non-empty directory.
ENOTEMPTY:	if new refers to a non-empty directory.
EINVAL:	if old is a path prefix of new.
EISDIR	
ENAMETOOLONG	
ENOENT	
ENOSPC	
ENOTDIR	
EROFS	
EXDEV:	if old and new are on different file systems.

rewinddir

```
#include <sys/types.h>
#include <dirent.h> /* proto */
void rewinddir(DIR *dirp);
```

Rewinds the directory stream associated with dirp.

Error codes: none.

rmdir

```
#include <unistd.h> /* proto */
int rmdir(const char *path);
```

Unlinks the directory named by path. Returns zero if successful, –1 otherwise.

Error codes:

EACCES	
EBUSY:	if path is being used by another process.
EEXIST:	if path is a non-empty directory.
ENOTEMPTY:	if path is a non-empty directory.
ENAMETOOLONG	
ENOENT	
ENOTDIR	
EROFS	

setgid

```
#include <sys/types.h>
#include <unistd.h> /* proto */
int setgid(gid_t gid);
```

Sets the group ID of the calling process to gid. Returns zero if
successful, –1 otherwise.

Error codes:
EINVAL
EPERM

setpgid

```
#include <sys/types.h>
#include <unistd.h> /* proto */
int setpgid(pid_t pid, pid_t pgid);
```

Sets to pgid the process group ID of the process whose process ID is
pid. Returns zero if successful, –1 otherwise.

Error codes:
EACCES
EINVAL
ENOSYS: if the implementation does not support *setpgid()*.
EPERM: if pid is the process ID of a process group leader; if
                   pid is the process ID of a child of the caller
                   that is not in the caller's session; or if pgid is
                   neither the process group of process pid nor
                   the process group of any other process in the
                   caller's session.

setsid

```
#include <sys/types.h>
#include <unistd.h> /* proto */
pid_t setsid(void);
```

Changes the session of the caller to a new session, with a new process
group of which the caller is the only member. Returns the process
group ID of the caller if successful, ((pid_t) -1) otherwise.

Error codes:
EPERM: if the caller is already a process group leader, or if
                   the process ID of the caller matches the process
                   group ID of some other process.

setuid

```
#include <sys/types.h>
#include <unistd.h> /* proto */
int setuid(uid_t uid);
```

Changes the real, effective, and saved user IDs of the calling process to uid. Returns zero if successful, –1 otherwise.

Error codes:

EINVAL
EPERM

sigaction

```
#include <signal.h> /* proto */
int sigaction(int sig, const struct sigaction *act,
    struct sigaction *oact);
```

Arranges for the signal-handling action associated with sig to be that specified in the struct sigaction stored at act. Stores the previous action in the structure at oact. Returns zero if successful, –1 otherwise.

Error codes:

EINVAL

sigaddset

```
#include <signal.h> /* proto */
int sigaddset(sigset_t *set, int signo);
```

Adds signo to the sigset_t pointed to by set. Returns zero if successful, –1 otherwise.

Error codes:

EINVAL

sigdelset

```
#include <signal.h> /* proto */
int sigdelset(sigset_t *set, int signo);
```

Removes signo from the sigset_t pointed to by set. Returns zero if successful, –1 otherwise.

Error codes:

EINVAL

sigemptyset

```
#include <signal.h> /* proto */
int sigemptyset(sigset_t *set);
```

Removes from the sigset_t pointed to by set all the POSIX.1 signals
supported by the implementation. The effect on other signals is
implementation-defined. Returns zero if successful, –1 otherwise.

Error codes: none.

sigfillset

```
#include <signal.h> /* proto */
int sigfillset(sigset_t *set);
```

Adds to the sigset_t pointed to by set at least all the POSIX.1 signals
supported by the implementation. The effect on other signals is
implementation-defined. Returns zero if successful, –1 otherwise.

Error codes: none.

sigismember

```
#include <signal.h> /* proto */
int sigismember(const sigset_t *set, int signo);
```

Returns 1 if signo is a member of set, zero if not, or –1 if an error
occurs.

Error codes:
EINVAL

siglongjmp

```
#include <setjmp.h> /* proto */
void siglongjmp(sigjmp_buf env, int val);
```

Transfers control to the *sigsetjmp()* call that set the contents of env. The
environment and signal mask stored in env are restored. The
sigsetjmp() returns val, unless val is zero (in which case the
sigsetjmp() returns 1). The *siglongjmp()* function does not return.

Error codes: none.

sigpending

```
#include <signal.h> /* proto */
int sigpending(sigset_t *set);
```

Stores in set the set of signals pending for the current process. Returns
zero if successful, –1 otherwise.

Error codes: none.

sigprocmask

```
#include <signal.h> /* proto */
int sigprocmask(int how, const sigset_t *set,
    sigset_t *oset);
```

Modifies the calling process's signal mask according to how and set.
Stores the previous mask in oset. Returns zero if successful, –1
otherwise.

Error codes:
EINVAL

sigsetjmp

```
#include <setjmp.h> /* proto */
int sigsetjmp(sigjmp_buf env, int savemask);
```

Stores the current environment and signal mask in env. Returns zero if
called directly, 1 if branched to by a *siglongjmp()* call whose val
argument is zero, or val otherwise.

Error codes: none.

sigsuspend

```
#include <signal.h> /* proto */
void sigsuspend(const sigset_t *sigmask);
```

Atomically changes the calling process's signal mask to that stored in
sigmask and blocks the calling process until a signal is delivered.
If *sigsuspend()* returns at all, it returns –1 and sets errno.

Error codes:
EINTR

sleep

```
#include <unistd.h> /* proto */
unsigned int sleep(unsigned int seconds);
```

Blocks the calling process for at least seconds seconds. Returns the
amount of time unslept due to receipt of a signal, or zero if the
sleep was completed.

Error codes: none.

stat

```
#include <sys/types.h>
#include <sys/stat.h> /* proto */
int stat(const char *path, struct stat *buf);
```

Gets the file status information of the named file and stores it in the
   stat structure at buf. Returns zero if successful, –1 otherwise.

Error codes:
EACCES
ENAMETOOLONG
ENOENT
ENOTDIR

sysconf

```
#include <unistd.h> /* proto */
long sysconf(int name);
```

Returns the value of the named variable on the system. If the value is
   not defined on the system, returns –1 and does not change errno.
   On error, returns –1 and sets errno.

Error codes:
EINVAL

tcdrain

```
#include <termios.h> /* proto */
int tcdrain(int fildes);
```

Blocks the calling process until output on the terminal device referred
   to by fildes has drained. Returns zero if successful, –1 otherwise.

Error codes:
EBADF
EINTR

tcflow

```
#include <termios.h> /* proto */
int tcflow(int fildes, int action);
```

Stops or restarts output, or requests stop or restart of input, to or from
   the terminal device referred to by fildes. Returns zero if
   successful, –1 otherwise.

Error codes:
EBADF
EINVAL
ENOTTY

tcflush

```
#include <termios.h> /* proto */
int tcflush(int fildes, int queue_selector);
```

Flushes unread input or untransmitted output or both, according to
queue_selector, on the terminal device associated with fildes.
Returns zero if successful, –1 otherwise.

Error codes:
EBADF
EINVAL
ENOTTY

tcgetattr

```
#include <termios.h> /* proto */
int tcgetattr(int fildes, struct termios *termios_p);
```

Gets the terminal attributes of the device associated with fildes and
stores them at termios_p. Returns zero if successful, –1 otherwise.

Error codes:
EBADF
ENOTTY

tcgetpgrp

```
#include <termios.h> /* proto */
pid_t tcgetpgrp(int fildes);
```

Returns the process group ID of the foreground process group associated with the terminal on success, –1 otherwise.

Error codes:
EBADF
ENOSYS: if this is not a job control system and does not
                       support the *tcgetpgrp()* function.
ENOTTY

tcsendbreak

```
#include <termios.h> /* proto */
int tcsendbreak(int fildes, int duration);
```

Generates a break condition for at least 0.25 seconds if duration is zero, or for an implementation-dependent interval if duration is nonzero, on the terminal device associated with fildes. Returns zero if successful, –1 otherwise.

Error codes:
EBADF
ENOTTY

tcsetattr

```
#include <termios.h> /* proto */
int tcsetattr(int fildes, int optional_actions,
    const struct termios *termios_p);
```

Sets the attributes of the terminal device associated with fildes according to the contents of the structure at termios_p. Returns zero if partially or completely successful, –1 otherwise.

Error codes:
EBADF
EINVAL
ENOTTY

tcsetpgrp

```
#include <termios.h> /* proto */
int tcsetpgrp(int fildes, pid_t pgrp_id);
```

Sets the foreground process group for the terminal associated with fildes to the process group with ID pgrp_id. Returns zero if successful, –1 otherwise.

Error codes:
EBADF
EINVAL
ENOSYS: if this is not a job control system and does not
                     support the *tcsetpgrp()* function.

ENOTTY
EPERM

time

```
#include <time.h> /* proto */
time_t time(time_t *tloc);
```

Returns the number of seconds since the Epoch and—if `tloc` is not NULL—stores the same value at `tloc`.

Error codes: none.

times

```
#include <sys/times.h> /* proto */
clock_t times(struct tms *buffer);
```

Stores the process's user and system CPU times, and those of its children, in `buffer`. Returns the elapsed real time in clock ticks since an arbitrary point in the past, if successful, and returns `((clock_t) -1)` otherwise.

Error codes: none.

ttyname

```
#include <unistd.h> /* proto */
char *ttyname(int fildes);
```

Returns a pointer to a pathname of the terminal associated with `fildes` if successful, NULL otherwise.

Error codes: none.

tzset

```
#include <time.h> /* proto */
void tzset(void);
```

Sets time conversion information according to the TZ environment variable.

Error codes: none.

umask

```
#include <sys/types.h>
#include <sys/stat.h> /* proto */
mode_t umask(mode_t cmask);
```

Sets the calling process's file mode creation mask to `cmask`. Returns previous value of the file mode creation mask.

Error codes: none.

uname

```
#include <sys/utsname.h> /* proto */
int uname(struct utsname *name);
```

Stores information identifying the current system in the utsname structure at name. Returns a nonnegative value if successful, –1 otherwise.

Error codes: none.

unlink

```
#include <stdio.h> /* proto */
int unlink(const char *path);
```

Removes the link named by path. If this is the last link for the file, frees the space occupied by the file. Returns zero if successful, –1 otherwise.

Error codes:

EACCES
EBUSY
ENAMETOOLONG
ENOENT
ENOTDIR
EPERM: if the file named by path is a directory and either the process does not have the appropriate privileges or the system does not support using *unlink()* on directories.

EROFS

utime

```
#include <sys/types.h>
#include <utime.h> /* proto */
int utime(const char *path, const struct utimbuf
    *times);
```

Sets the file access and modification times of the named file according to the values in the buffer pointed to by times. Returns zero if successful, –1 otherwise.

Error codes:

EACCES
ENAMETOOLONG
ENOENT
ENOTDIR
EPERM
EROFS

wait

```
#include <sys/types.h>
#include <sys/wait.h> /* proto */
pid_t wait(int *stat_loc);
```

Blocks the calling process until information is available about a terminated child process. Returns the process ID of the child process whose status is being reported in *stat_loc if successful, –1 otherwise.

Error codes:
ECHILD
EINTR

waitpid

```
#include <sys/types.h>
#include <sys/wait.h> /* proto */
pid_t waitpid(pid_t pid, int *stat_loc, int options);
```

Gets information about a particular child process, or about any child process, that has terminated or stopped. Returns the process ID of the child process whose status is being reported in *stat_loc, zero if WNOHANG was set in options and the caller has at least one child process specified by pid for which status is unavailable, or –1 otherwise.

Error codes:
ECHILD

write

```
#include <unistd.h> /* proto */
ssize_t write(int fildes, const void *buf, size_t
    nbyte);
```

Writes nbyte bytes from buf to the file associated with fildes. Returns the number of bytes actually written if successful, –1 otherwise.

Error codes:

EAGAIN:	if O_NONBLOCK is set and writing would block the caller.
EFBIG:	if the write would make the file exceed an (implementation-defined) maximum size.
EINTR	
EIO	
ENOSPC	
EPIPE:	if fildes refers to a pipe and no process has the pipe open for reading.

B

ANSI C Functions in POSIX.1

This appendix gives the prototypes for each function from the C standard that has been included in the POSIX 1003.1 standard. The functions are arranged in alphabetical order for ease of reference. We give the return type and values on success and failure. For each function, we also show the headers that should be included when that function is used. Recall that implementations claiming support for ANSI standard C must have prototypes declared for all POSIX functions. The comment /* proto */ following a header indicates that the given header is the one in which the function's prototype is given. In addition, we give a brief explanation of the semantics of the function; however, you should not use this appendix as a semantic reference for these functions!

ANSI C supports an errno construct compatible with POSIX.1.* However, the only values of errno specified in ANSI C are EDOM and ERANGE. These always have the same meaning. EDOM indicates a *domain error*: the value supplied as argument to the function is not in the function's domain. ERANGE indicates a *range error*: the result of the function call cannot be represented as a value of the return type (which, in these cases, is usually double). If the function can cause these errors, we so indicate.

The following considerations always hold for functions declared in the <math.h> header. If a domain error occurs, the return value is implementation-defined and errno is set to EDOM. If a range error consisting

---

* It is not identical; in ANSI C errno must be a modifiable lvalue but need not be an int. For example, it could be defined as the contents of an address returned by some function:

```
extern int *_errno();
#define errno *_errno()
```

of an overflow occurs, the return value is the macro HUGE_VAL (defined in <math.h>) with the same sign that the correct value would have, and errno is set to ERANGE. If a range error consisting of an underflow occurs, the return value is zero; it is implementation-defined whether errno is set to ERANGE when underflow occurs.

The character-handling functions (all the functions whose names start with *is,* such as *isupper()*) have locale-dependent behavior: the set of argument values for which these functions return nonzero includes a standard set of values, plus an extra set that depends on the current locale. In every case, if the current locale is the "C" locale then this extra set is empty.

abort

```
#include <stdlib.h> /* proto */
void abort(void);
```

Terminates the current process abnormally. The POSIX.1 standard specifies the following extra semantics for *abort()*:

- The status made available to *wait()* or *waitpid()* by a process terminated by *abort()* shall be that of a process terminated by the SIGABRT signal.

abs

```
#include <stdlib.h> /* proto */
int abs(int j);
```

Returns the absolute value of j. Note that if the absolute value of j cannot be represented as an int, the result is undefined.

acos

```
#include <math.h> /* proto */
double acos(double x);
```

Returns the arc cosine of x in the range $[0, \pi]$.

Error codes:
EDOM
ERANGE

asctime

```
#include <time.h> /* proto */
char *asctime(const struct tm *timeptr);
```

Returns a 26-byte string (including newline and null byte) containing the date and time, converted from *timeptr.

asin

```
#include <math.h> /* proto */
double asin(double x);
```

Returns the arc sine of x in the range $[-\pi/2, \pi/2]$.

Error codes:
EDOM
ERANGE

assert

```
#include <assert.h> /* macro definition */
void assert(int expression);
```

The *assert()* function is always defined as a macro, not an actual
function. If expression evaluates to false (zero) then *assert()* issues a
diagnostic to standard error and terminates the program. If the
symbol NDEBUG is defined at the point where the header
<assert.h> is included, then a call to *assert()* does nothing and
expression is not evaluated.

atan

```
#include <math.h> /* proto */
double atan(double x);
```

Returns the arc tangent of x in the range $[-\pi/2, \pi/2]$.

Error codes:
EDOM
ERANGE

atan2

```
#include <math.h> /* proto */
double atan2(double y, double x);
```

Returns the arc tangent of y/x in the range $[-\pi, \pi]$. The sign of both
arguments is used to determine the quadrant of the result.

Error codes:
EDOM
ERANGE

atof

```
#include <stdlib.h> /* proto */
double atof(const char *nptr);
```

atof *(continued)*

> Returns the value of the initial portion of the string at nptr, converted
> to a double.

atoi

```
#include <stdlib.h> /* proto */
int atoi(const char *nptr);
```

> Returns the value of the initial portion of the string at nptr, converted
> to an int.

atol

```
#include <stdlib.h> /* proto */
long atol(const char *nptr);
```

> Returns the value of the initial portion of the string at nptr, converted
> to a long.

bsearch

```
#include <stdlib.h> /* proto */
void *bsearch(const void *key, const void *base,
   size_t nmemb, size_t size, int (*compar)(const
   void *, const void *));
```

> Returns a pointer to a member of the sorted array pointed to by base
> that matches the value pointed to by key, or NULL if there is no
> such member.

calloc

```
#include <stdlib.h> /* proto */
void *calloc(size_t nmemb, size_t size);
```

> Returns a pointer to space for an array of nmemb objects each of size
> size and with all bits set to zero. If the space cannot be allocated,
> returns a NULL pointer.

ceil

```
#include <math.h> /* proto */
double ceil(double x);
```

> Returns the double that is the smallest integer value not less than its
> argument.

clearerr

```
#include <stdio.h> /* proto */
void clearerr(FILE *stream);
```

Clears the error indicator on stream, so that *ferror()* on the stream will return zero.

cos

```
#include <math.h> /* proto */
double cos(double x);
```

Returns the cosine of x.

cosh

```
#include <math.h> /* proto */
double cosh(double x);
```

Returns the hyperbolic cosine of x.

Error code:
ERANGE

ctime

```
#include <time.h> /* proto */
char *ctime(const time_t *timer);
```

Returns a pointer to a 26-byte string in the same form as *asctime()*. The call ctime(timer) is equivalent to the call asctime(localtime(timer)); POSIX.1 imposes the following extra semantics on *ctime()*:

- Whenever *ctime()* is called, the time zone names contained in the external variable tzname shall be set as if the *tzset()* function had been called.

exit

```
#include <stdlib.h>
void exit(int status);
```

Terminates the calling program. All open files are closed. All open streams are flushed and closed.

exp

```
#include <math.h> /* proto */
double exp(double x);
```

Returns the exponential e^x of its argument.

Error code:
ERANGE

fabs

```
#include <math.h> /* proto */
double fabs(double x);
```

Returns the absolute value of its argument.

fclose

```
#include <stdio.h> /* proto */
int fclose(FILE *stream);
```

Flushes and closes stream. Returns zero if the stream was successfully closed, EOF otherwise.

feof

```
#include <stdio.h> /* proto */
int feof(FILE *stream);
```

Returns nonzero if the end-of-file indicator is set for stream, zero otherwise.

ferror

```
#include <stdio.h> /* proto */
int ferror(FILE *stream);
```

Returns nonzero if the error indicator is set for stream, zero otherwise.

fflush

```
#include <stdio.h> /* proto */
int fflush(FILE *stream);
```

Flushes stream. Returns EOF if a write error occurs, zero otherwise.

fgetc

```
#include <stdio.h> /* proto */
int fgetc(FILE *stream);
```

Returns the next character (as an unsigned char converted to an int) from the specified stream, or EOF if the stream is at end-of-file.

fgets

```
#include <stdio.h> /* proto */
char *fgets(char *s, int n, FILE *stream);
```

Gets a string from stream, up to the next newline or end-of-file, and stores it at s. Returns s if successful, NULL if an error occurs or if stream is at end-of-file.

floor

```
#include <math.h> /* proto */
double floor(double x);
```

Returns the largest integer not greater than x, as a double.

fmod

```
#include <math.h> /* proto */
double fmod(double x, double y);
```

If y is nonzero, then *fmod()* returns the value $x - i*y$ for the unique integer i such that $x - i*y$ has the same sign as x and magnitude less than the magnitude of y. If y is zero, the behavior is implementation-defined.

fopen

```
#include <stdio.h>
FILE *fopen(const char *filename, const char *mode);
```

Opens a stream on the named file, in the specified access mode. Returns a pointer to a FILE describing the open stream, or NULL if the stream cannot be opened.

fprintf

```
#include <stdio.h>
int fprintf(FILE *stream, const char *format, ...);
```

Writes formatted output to the named stream. Returns the number of characters transmitted to stream if successful, or a negative value otherwise.

fputc

```
#include <stdio.h> /* proto */
int fputc(int c, FILE *stream);
```

Writes a single byte to stream. Returns the character written, or EOF if a write error occurs.

fputs

```
#include <stdio.h> /* proto */
int fputs(const char *s, FILE *stream);
```

Writes the string s to stream. Returns a nonnegative value if successful, or EOF if a write error occurs.

fread

```
#include <stdio.h> /* proto */
size_t fread(void *ptr, size_t size, size_t nmemb,
    FILE *stream);
```

Reads up to nmemb objects of size size from stream, storing them at ptr. Returns the number of objects successfully read.

free

```
#include <stdlib.h> /* proto */
void free(void *ptr);
```

Releases the memory located at ptr if it was previously allocated by *malloc(), calloc(),* or *realloc().*

freopen

```
#include <stdio.h>
FILE *freopen(const char *filename, const char *mode,
    FILE *stream);
```

Flushes and closes stream if open, and then opens stream as a stream on filename with access mode mode. Returns stream if successful, or NULL otherwise.

frexp

```
#include <math.h> /* proto */
double frexp(double val, int *exp);
```

If val is zero, returns zero and stores zero in *exp. Otherwise, returns the unique value x and stores the unique integer in *exp, such that $1/2 \leq x < 1$ and val equals x times two to the power *exp.

fscanf

```
#include <stdio.h>
int fscanf(FILE *stream, const char *format, ...);
```

Performs a formatted read from stream into the named locations according to format. Returns the number of input items assigned if successful, or EOF if an input error or failure occurred before any input items were converted.

fseek

```
#include <stdio.h>
int fseek(FILE *stream, long offset, int whence);
```

Flushes stream if necessary and sets the stream pointer according to offset and whence. Returns zero if successful, nonzero if the request was invalid.

ftell

```
#include <stdio.h>
long ftell(FILE *stream);
```

Returns the current file position indicator for stream if successful, –1L otherwise.

Error codes: An implementation-defined positive value in case of failure.

fwrite

```
#include <stdio.h> /* proto */
size_t fwrite(const void *ptr, size_t size, size_t
    nmemb, FILE *stream);
```

Writes nmemb objects of size size starting at location ptr to stream. Returns the number of objects successfully written. Unless an error occurs, this will be nmemb.

getc

```
#include <stdio.h> /* proto */
int getc(FILE *stream);
```

Reads and returns the next character (as an unsigned char converted to an int) from the specified stream, or EOF if the stream is at end-of-file or an error occurs.

getchar

```
#include <stdio.h> /* proto */
int getchar(void);
```

Reads and returns the next character from stdin, or EOF if stdin is at end-of-file or an error occurs.

getenv

```
#include <stdlib.h> /* proto */
char *getenv(const char *name);
```

Returns a pointer to the string associated with name, if it could be found in the environment, or NULL otherwise. This function is specified in 1003.1 as well as in the C standard, and it is described in Appendix A.

gets

```
#include <stdio.h> /* proto */
char *gets(char *s);
```

Gets a string from stdin, up to the next newline or end-of-file, and stores it at s. Returns s if successful, NULL if an error occurs or if stream is at end-of-file.

gmtime

```
#include <time.h> /* proto */
struct tm *gmtime(const time_t *timer)
```

Returns a pointer to a struct tm that contains a broken-down time converted from the value of timer, expressed as Universal Co-ordinated Time (or UCT, which used to be called Greenwich Mean Time, or GMT). If UCT is not available (e.g., because the current time zone is unknown), then a NULL pointer is returned. The

POSIX.1 standard imposes the following extra semantics on the *gmtime()* function:

- The fields in the returned structure shall be related to the `time_t` value of the argument by the formula:

```
timer = tm_sec + 60*tm_min + 3600*tm_hour +
86400*tm_day + 31536000*(tm_year - 70) +
((tm_year - 69)/4)*86400
```

This is equivalent to specifying that the argument is interpreted as the number of seconds since January 1, 1970, 0:00:00 UCT—the *Epoch* in POSIX.1 terminology.

isalnum

```
#include <ctype.h> /* proto */
int isalnum(int c);
```

Returns nonzero if and only if either *isalpha()* or *isdigit()* returns nonzero for c.

isalpha

```
#include <ctype.h> /* proto */
int isalpha(int c);
```

Returns nonzero if and only if *isupper()* or *islower()* returns nonzero for c, or if c is one of an implementation-defined set of characters for which *iscntrl()*, *isdigit()*, *ispunct()*, and *isspace()* all return zero.

iscntrl

```
#include <ctype.h> /* proto */
int iscntrl(int c);
```

Returns nonzero if and only if c is a control character.

isdigit

```
#include <ctype.h> /* proto */
int isdigit(int c);
```

Returns nonzero if and only if c is any of '0', '1', '2', '3', '4', '5', '6', '7', '8', or '9'.

isgraph

```
#include <ctype.h> /* proto */
int isgraph(int c);
```

Returns nonzero if and only if c is any printing character other than
   ' ' (space).

islower

```
#include <ctype.h> /* proto */
int islower(int c);
```

Returns nonzero if and only if c is any lower-case letter or is one of an
   implementation-defined set of characters for which *iscntrl()*,
   isdigit(), *ispunct()*, and *isspace()* all return zero.

isprint

```
#include <ctype.h> /* proto */
int isprint(int c);
```

Returns nonzero if and only if c is any printing character including ' '
   (space).

ispunct

```
#include <ctype.h> /* proto */
int ispunct(int c);
```

Returns nonzero if and only if c is any character other than ' ' (space)
   or a character for which *isalnum()* returns nonzero.

isspace

```
#include <ctype.h> /* proto */
int isspace(int c);
```

Returns nonzero if and only if c is any standard white-space character
   (' ', '\f', '\n', '\r', '\t', or '\v') or is any one of an
   implementation-defined set of characters for which *isalnum()*
   returns zero.

isupper

```
#include <ctype.h> /* proto */
int isupper(int c);
```

Returns nonzero if and only if c is any upper-case letter or is one of an
implementation-defined set of characters for which *iscntrl()*,
isdigit(), *ispunct()*, and *isspace()* all return zero.

isxdigit

```
#include <ctype.h> /* proto */
int isxdigit(int c);
```

Returns nonzero if and only if c is any of '0', '1', '2', '3', '4',
'5', '6', '7', '8', '9', 'a', 'b', 'c', 'd', 'e', 'f', 'A', 'B',
'C', 'D', 'E', or 'F'.

ldexp

```
#include <math.h> /* proto */
double ldexp(double x, int exp);
```

Returns $x * 2^{exp}$.

Error code:
ERANGE

localtime

```
#include <time.h> /* proto */
struct tm *localtime(const time_t *timer);
```

Returns a pointer to a struct tm that contains a broken-down time
converted from the value of timer, expressed as local time. The
POSIX.1 standard imposes the following extra semantics on the
localtime() function:

- The contents of the environment variable TZ override the default
  time zone.

- A call to *localtime()* shall set the external variable tzname as if the
  tzset() function had been called.

- If the time zone UCT0 is in effect, then the fields in the returned
  structure shall be related to the time_t value of the argument by
  the formula:

```
timer = tm_sec + 60*tm_min + 3600*tm_hour +
86400*tm_day + 31536000*(tm_year - 70) +
((tm_year - 69)/4)*86400
```

log

```
#include <math.h> /* proto */
double log(double x);
```

Returns the natural logarithm of x.

Error codes:
EDOM
ERANGE

log10

```
#include <math.h> /* proto */
double log10(double x);
```

Returns the base-ten logarithm of x.

Error codes:
EDOM
ERANGE

longjmp

```
#include <setjmp.h> /* proto */
void longjmp(jmp_buf env, int val);
```

Transfers control with an environment specified by jmp_buf to the location of the corresponding *setjmp()*. Does not return a value, but val becomes the return value of the corresponding *setjmp()* (unless val is zero, in which case the *setjmp()* returns 1).

malloc

```
#include <stdlib.h> /* proto */
void *malloc(size_t size);
```

Allocates space for an object of size size and returns a pointer to the space; returns NULL if such space is not available.

mktime

```
#include <time.h> /* proto */
time_t mktime(struct tm *timeptr);
```

Returns the calendar time from struct tm *timeptr encoded as a value of type time_t. If the time cannot be represented, then (time_t) -1 is returned. The POSIX.1 standard imposes the following extra semantics on the *mktime()* function:

- The contents of the environment variable TZ override the default time zone.
- A call to *mktime()* shall set the external variable tzname as if the *tzset()* function had been called.
- If the time zone UCT0 is in effect, then the fields in the structure pointed to by the argument shall be related to the returned time_t value by the formula:
  ```
  return value = tm_sec + 60*tm_min + 3600*tm_hour +
  86400*tm_day + 31536000*(tm_year - 70) + ((tm_year
  - 69)/4)*86400
  ```

modf

```
#include <math.h> /* proto */
double modf(double value, double *iptr);
```

Returns the fractional part of value, with the same sign as that of value. Stores the integral part of value (represented as a double) in *iptr.

perror

```
#include <stdio.h> /* proto */
void perror(const char *s);
```

Prints the string at s, followed by a diagnostic message that depends on the value of errno, on stderr.

pow

```
#include <math.h> /* proto */
double pow(double x, double y);
```

Returns x raised to the power y.

Error codes:
EDOM
ERANGE

printf

```
#include <stdio.h> /* proto */
int printf(const char *format, ...);
```

Writes formatted output to stdout. Returns the number or characters transmitted, or a negative value if an output error occurs.

putc

```
#include <stdio.h> /* proto */
int putc(int c, FILE *stream);
```

Writes the single byte whose value is (char)c to stream. Returns the
value c, or EOF if an error occurs.

putchar

```
#include <stdio.h> /* proto */
int putchar(int c);
```

Writes the single byte whose value is (char)c to stdout. Returns the
value c, or EOF if an error occurs.

puts

```
#include <stdio.h> /* proto */
int puts(const char *s);
```

Writes the string at s to stdout. Returns a nonnegative value, or EOF if
an error occurs.

qsort

```
#include <stdlib.h> /* proto */
void qsort(void *base, size_t nmemb, size_t size,
           int (*compar)(const void *, const void *));
```

Sorts in place the nmemb objects of size size located at base, using the
quicksort algorithm to sort and the *compar()* function to compare
objects.

rand

```
#include <stdlib.h> /* proto */
int rand(void);
```

Returns a pseudo-random integer in the range zero to RAND_MAX
(which is defined in <stdlib.h> and must be at least 32,767).

realloc

```
#include <stdlib.h> /* proto */
void *realloc(void *ptr, size_t size);
```

Allocates space for an object of size size and returns a pointer to the
space; returns NULL if such space is not available. The space at ptr

must have been allocated by *malloc()*, *calloc()*, or *realloc()* and the contents of this space, up to the minimum of size and the previously allocated space, are copied to the newly allocated space.

remove

```
#include <stdio.h> /* proto */
int remove(const char *filename);
```

Removes the named file from the file system. Returns zero if the remove operation succeeds and nonzero if it fails.

rename

```
#include <stdio.h> /* proto */
int rename(const char *old, const char *new);
```

Changes the name of file old to new. Returns zero if the remove operation succeeds and nonzero if it fails. This function is specified in 1003.1 as well as in the C standard, with extra semantics to deal with POSIX.1 pathnames, and is described in Appendix A.

rewind

```
#include <stdio.h> /* proto */
void rewind(FILE *stream);
```

Sets the stream pointer of stream to zero.

scanf

```
#include <stdio.h> /* proto */
int scanf(const char *format, ...);
```

Performs a formatted read from stdin into the named locations according to format. Returns the number of input items assigned, or EOF if an error occurs before any conversion.

setbuf

```
#include <stdio.h> /* proto */
void setbuf(FILE *stream, char *buf);
```

Sets buf as the buffer for stream.

setjmp

```
#include <setjmp.h> /* macro definition */
int setjmp(jmp_buf env);
```

Saves the current execution environment in env. Returns zero if it is invoked directly, nonzero if it is returning from a call to *longjmp()*. The precise return value depends on the value of the val parameter to *longjmp()*. The *setjmp()* function is always defined as a macro.

setlocale

```
#include <locale.h> /* proto */
char *setlocale(int category, const char *locale);
```

Sets part of the program locale specified by category according to locale. Returns a pointer to the string associated with the specified category for the specified locale. If the request fails, NULL is returned. If a NULL pointer (*not* the same as a pointer to an empty string!) is given as the value of locale, then *setlocale()* returns a pointer to the string associated with the specified category for the process's current locale. The POSIX.1 standard specifies the following additional semantics for *setlocale()*:

* If the locale argument points to an empty string (""); category is any of the values LC_CTYPE, LC_COLLATE, LC_TIME, LC_NUMERIC, or LC_MONETARY; and the corresponding environment variable is defined, then the value of the string associated with the environment variable shall be used instead of "".

* If the corresponding environment variable is not set but the LANG environment variable is set, then the string associated with LANG shall be used in place of the category.

sin

```
#include <math.h> /* proto */
double sin(double x);
```

Returns the sine of x.

sinh

```
#include <math.h> /* proto */
double sinh(double x);
```

Returns the hyperbolic sine of x.

Error code:

ERANGE

sprintf

```
#include <stdio.h>
int sprintf(char *s, const char *format, ...);
```

Writes a formatted string to the array at s. Returns the number of
characters written to the array at s, not including the terminating
null character.

sqrt

```
#include <math.h> /* proto */
double sqrt(double x);
```

Returns the nonnegative square root of x.

Error code:
EDOM

srand

```
#include <stdlib.h> /* proto */
void srand(unsigned int seed);
```

Sets the seed for the random number generator *rand()*.

sscanf

```
#include <stdio.h> /* proto */
int sscanf(char *s, const char *format, ...);
```

Performs a formatted read from the string at s into the named locations
according to format. Returns the number of input items assigned
if successful or EOF if an input error or failure occurred before any
input items were converted.

strcat

```
#include <string.h> /* proto */
char *strcat(char *s1, const char *s2);
```

Concatenates a copy of the string at s2 to the end of the string at s1.
Returns s1.

strchr

```
#include <string.h> /* proto */
char *strchr(const char *s, int c);
```

Returns a pointer to the first occurrence of (char) c in s, or NULL if c
does not occur in s.

strcmp

```
#include <string.h> /* proto */
int strcmp(const char *s1, const char *s2);
```

Returns zero if s1 and s2 point to identical strings, a positive value if
the string pointed to by s1 is greater than the string pointed to by
s2, and a negative value otherwise. String comparison is based on
the sign of the difference of the first pair of nonidentical characters
in the string.

strcpy

```
#include <string.h> /* proto */
char *strcpy(char *s1, const char *s2);
```

Copies the string at s2 to s1. Returns s1.

strcspn

```
#include <string.h> /* proto */
size_t strcspn(const char *s1, char *s2);
```

Returns the length of the initial portion of s1 consisting entirely of
characters not included in s2.

strftime

```
#include <time.h> /* proto */
size_t strftime(char *s, size_t maxsize, const char
   *format, const struct tm *timeptr);
```

Returns the total number of characters, not including the terminating
null character, placed into the array at s. If the total number of
characters including the null character that would be placed in s by
the request exceeds maxsize, then *strftime()* returns zero. The
POSIX.1 standard imposes the following additional semantics on
strftime():

- Whenever *strftime()* is called, the value of the external variable
  tzname shall be set as if *tzset()* had been called.

strlen

```
#include <string.h> /* proto */
size_t strlen(const char *s);
```

Returns the number of characters in s, not including the terminating
null character.

strncat

```
#include <string.h> /* proto */
char *strncat(char *s1, const char *s2, size_t n);
```

Concatenates a copy of the string at s2 to the end of the string at s1, but no more than n bytes. Returns s1.

strncmp

```
#include <string.h> /* proto */
int strncmp(const char *s1, const char *s2, size_t n);
```

Returns a value based on the comparison of not more than n characters of the strings pointed to by s1 and s2, but will not compare past a null byte. The return value is zero if the compared portions of the strings are identical, positive if the compared portion of s1 is greater than that of s2, and negative otherwise.

strncpy

```
#include <string.h> /* proto */
char *strncpy(char *s1, const char *s2, size_t n);
```

Copies the string at s2 to s1, but stops after at most n bytes. Returns s1.

strpbrk

```
#include <string.h> /* proto */
char *strpbrk(const char *s1, const char *s2);
```

Returns a pointer to the first occurrence in s1 of any character in the string pointed to by s2, or NULL if there is no such occurrence.

strrchr

```
#include <string.h> /* proto */
char *strrchr(const char *s, int c);
```

Returns a pointer to the last occurrence of (char) c in s, or NULL if c does not occur in s.

strspn

```
#include <string.h> /* proto */
size_t strspn(const char *s1, const char *s2);
```

Returns the length of the initial portion of s1 consisting entirely of characters included in s2.

strstr

```
#include <string.h> /* proto */
char *strstr(const char *s1, const char *s2);
```

Returns a pointer to the first occurrence in s1 of a substring identical to the string pointed to by s2, not including s2's null character. If there is no such occurrence, then *strstr()* returns NULL.

strtok

```
#include <string.h> /* proto */
char *strtok(const char *s1, const char *s2);
```

Returns a pointer to the first character of the next token in s1, using the characters in s2 as token delimiters. If there is no such token, *strtok()* returns NULL.

tan

```
#include <math.h> /* proto */
double tan(double x);
```

Returns the tangent of x.

Error codes:
EDOM
ERANGE

tanh

```
#include <math.h> /* proto */
double tanh(double x);
```

Returns the hyperbolic tangent of x.

time

```
#include <time.h> /* proto */
time_t time(time_t *timeptr);
```

Returns the current calendar time, which is also stored in *timeptr. For POSIX.1 implementations, this is measured in seconds since the Epoch. This function is specified in POSIX.1 as well as in the C standard, and it is described in Appendix A.

tmpfile

```
#include <stdio.h> /* proto */
FILE *tmpfile(void);
```

Opens a stream for writing. The stream will be closed and removed upon normal program termination. Returns a pointer to a FILE describing the stream.

tmpnam

```
#include <stdio.h> /* proto */
char *tmpnam(char *s);
```

Returns a pointer to a string that is not the name of an existing file. If s is not NULL, then the filename is written at s and s is returned.

tolower

```
#include <ctype.h> /* proto */
int tolower(int c);
```

If c is an upper-case letter and a corresponding lower-case letter exists, then the lower-case letter is returned. Otherwise, the argument is returned unchanged.

toupper

```
#include <ctype.h> /* proto */
int toupper(int c);
```

If c is a lower-case letter and a corresponding upper-case letter exists, then the upper-case letter is returned. Otherwise, the argument is returned unchanged.

ungetc

```
#include <stdio.h> /* proto */
int ungetc(int c, FILE *stream);
```

Pushes (unsigned char)c back onto stream. At least one character of pushback is guaranteed. Returns the character pushed back onto stream. If the pushback fails, then EOF is returned.

Error Numbers

This appendix gives the symbolic values of errno that must be supported by all POSIX.1 implementations and also gives their meanings. Recall that an implementation is free to add other values of errno and to use the values given below for errors not covered in the POSIX standard. However, a conforming implementation must use the specified errno values for those errors that are described in the standard.

E2BIG   Argument list too long.

This error is generated by an *exec()* function if the total amount of space needed by a process's argument list and environment exceeds ARG_MAX bytes.

EACCES   Permission denied.

This error is generated when a process attempts to access a file in a way for which it does not have permission.

EAGAIN   Resource temporarily unavailable; try again.

This error is generated by temporary conditions when later calls to the same function might complete normally.

EBADF   Bad file descriptor.

This error is generated when a function uses a file descriptor that does not refer to an open file, is out of range (e.g., negative), or refers to a file for which the request is inappropriate (e.g., a read request on a file only open for writing, or vice versa).

EBUSY   Resource unavailable.

This error is generated when a process requests a resource that is being used by another process in a way that conflicts with the request. For example, a call to *rmdir()* a directory that is being used by another process may generate an EBUSY error.

ECHILD   No child process.

This error is generated when *wait()* or *waitpid()* tries to wait for a child process, and either no child processes exist, all have been waited for, or—in the case of *waitpid()*—a process ID was specified that is not the process ID of an unwaited-for child.

EDEADLK   Resource deadlock would result.

This error is generated when a request would result in a deadlock.

EDOM   Domain error.

This error is generated when an input argument is outside the domain of a mathematical function. EDOM is defined in the C standard.

EEXIST   File exists.

This error is generated when an existing file is specified in a context in which it is forbidden, e.g., *mkdir()* of a path that names an existing file or directory.

EFAULT   Bad address.

This error is generated when the system detects an invalid address while attempting to access a function argument. Not all POSIX implementations can reliably detect this error.

EFBIG   File too large.

This error is generated by a request that would cause the size of a file to exceed an implementation-defined maximum file size.

EINTR   Function interrupted by signal.

This error is generated when a request is interrupted by a signal that is caught, and for which the signal handler performs a normal return.

EINVAL   Invalid argument.

This error is generated when the argument to a function is not a valid value, e.g., an undefined signal to *kill()*.

EIO   I/O error.

This error usually indicates a hardware problem. It is generated when the physical transfer of data to or from the medium fails.

EISDIR   Is a directory.

This error is generated when a request specifies a file that is a directory when a nondirectory file is required, e.g., *rename()* when the first argument is a file and the second is a directory.

EMFILE   Too many open files by this process.

This error is generated when a request would cause the process to have more than the maximum permitted number of open file descriptors per process (OPEN_MAX). The attempt may be indirect, e.g., via an *opendir()* call.

EMLINK   Too many links.

This error is generated when a request would cause a file to have more than the maximum number of links (LINK_MAX).

ENAMETOOLONG   Filename too long.

This error is generated when the length of a pathname exceeds PATH_MAX, or the length of a path component exceeds NAME_MAX and _POSIX_NO_TRUNC is in effect for the file.

ENFILE   Too many open files in the system.

This error is generated when a request would cause the system to have more simultaneously open files than it can handle. Such a condition should be temporary.

ENODEV   No such device.

This error is generated by an inappropriate request to a device, such as a request to read from a printer.

ENOENT   No such file.

This error is generated when a request names a pathname of a file that does not exist (and ought to) or when a pathname is an empty string.

ENOEXEC   Not an executable file.

This error is generated when a request is made for the execution of a file that has the appropriate execute permission but is not in executable format.

ENOLCK   No locks available.

This error is generated when a request to impose a file or record lock would exceed the system-imposed limit on the number of such locks.

ENOMEM   Not enough memory.

This error is generated when a *fork()* or *exec()* request would require more memory than is physically available or more than the system will allow to be allocated.

ENOSPC   No space left on device.

This error is generated when a request would extend a regular file or a directory, but there is not sufficient free space left on the device.

ENOSYS   Function not supported.

This error is generated when a request is made to use a function that is not supported by the implementation, e.g., *setpgid()* on a system that does not support job control.

ENOTDIR   Not a directory.

This error is generated when a request requires a pathname that specifies a directory but the pathname given does not name a directory.

ENOTEMPTY   Directory not empty.

This error is generated if a request requires the name of an empty directory but the name of a directory with entries other than dot or dot-dot was supplied.

ENOTTY   Inappropriate I/O control operation.

This error is generated when a request is made for a control operation on a file or special file that does not support the operation, e.g., *tcsetattr()* on an ordinary file or a directory.

ENXIO   No such device or address.

This error is generated by an input or output request on a special file that refers to a nonexistent device or exceeds the limits of the device, or by a request for a device that is not currently available.

EPERM   Operation not permitted.

This error is generated by a request to perform an operation that is limited to a process with appropriate privileges or to the owner of the specified resource.

EPIPE   Broken pipe.

This error is generated by a request to write on a pipe or FIFO that is not open for reading by any process.

ERANGE   Result too large.

This error is generated by a call to a function in which the return value is too large to be represented in the available space. ERANGE is defined in the C standard.

EROFS   Read-only file system.

This error is generated by a request that would result in the modification of a file or directory on a file system that is read-only.

ESPIPE   Invalid seek.

This error is generated by an *lseek()* request on a pipe or FIFO.

ESRCH   No such process.

This error is generated when a request specifies a process or process group and there is no process or process group with the specified ID.

EXDEV   Invalid link.

This error is generated by a request to create a link on another file system.

D

Headers and Their Contents

This appendix gives the symbols that a POSIX.1 program compiled in an ANSI C environment can expect to have defined if it includes a given header. We list all the headers required by either POSIX.1 or ANSI C. If a program is executing in a common usage C environment but has defined the feature test macro _POSIX_SOURCE, then the same symbols will be visible.

Some of the symbols given here are not referenced by any POSIX.1 function. Nevertheless, they affect POSIX.1 programs because they occupy part of the name-space that is otherwise reserved for application programmers. Such symbols are listed in parentheses. When we give a structure, we do not list its members, as these do not affect the name-space available to the programmer. The portable contents of all structures referenced by POSIX.1 functions are given in the text.

The symbols L_cuserid in <stdio.h> and *cuserid()* in <unistd.h> are special. No implementation is required to define these symbols, but they are permitted. Therefore, they should be considered part of the reserved name-space, but should not be used.

<assert.h>

Function or Macro:

assert()

<ctype.h>

Functions or Macros:

isalnum()	*isgraph()*	*ispunct()*	*isxdigit()*
isalpha()	*islower()*	*isspace()*	*tolower()*
iscntrl()	*isprint(*	*isupper()*	*toupper()*
isdigit()			

<dirent.h>

Functions:		**Type:**	**Structure:**
closedir()	*readdir()*	DIR	dirent
opendir()	*rewinddir()*		

<errno.h>

Macros:

E2BIG	EFBIG	ENODEV	ENOTTY
EACCES	EINTR	ENOENT	ENXIO
EAGAIN	EINVAL	ENOEXEC	EPERM
EBADF	EIO	ENOLCK	EPIPE
EBUSY	EISDIR	ENOMEM	ERANGE
ECHILD	EMFILE	ENOSPC	EROFS
EDEADLK	EMLINK	ENOSYS	ESPIPE
EDOM	ENAMETOOLONG	ENOTDIR	ESRCH
EEXIST	ENFILE	ENOTEMPTY	EXDEV
EFAULT			

External variable:

errno

<fcntl.h>

Functions:	**Macros:**		
creat()	FD_CLOEXEC	F_SETFD	F_WRLCK
fcntl()	F_DUPFD	F_SETFL	O_ACCMODE
open()	F_GETFD	F_SETLK	O_APPEND
	F_GETFL	F_SETLKW	O_CREAT
	F_RDLCK	F_UNLCK	O_EXCL

O_NOCTTY	O_RDONLY	O_TRUNC	**Structure:**
O_NONBLOCK	O_RDWR	O_WRONLY	flock

(`<float.h>`)

Macros:

(DBL_DIG)	(FLT_EPSILON)	(LDBL_DIG)
(DBL_EPSILON)	(FLT_MANT_DIG)	(LDBL_EPSILON)
(DBL_MANT_DIG)	(FLT_MAX)	(LDBL_MANT_DIG)
(DBL_MAX)	(FLT_MAX_10_EXP)	(LDBL_MAX)
(DBL_MAX_10_EXP)	(FLT_MAX_EXP)	(LDBL_MAX_10_EXP)
(DBL_MAX_EXP)	(FLT_MIN)	(LDBL_MAX_EXP)
(DBL_MIN)	(FLT_MIN_10_EXP)	(LDBL_MIN)
(DBL_MIN_10_EXP)	(FLT_MIN_EXP)	(LDBL_MIN_10_EXP)
(DBL_MIN_EXP)	(FLT_RADIX)	(LDBL_MIN_EXP)
(FLT_DIG)	(FLT_ROUNDS)	

`<grp.h>`

Functions:	**Structure:**
getgrgid()	group
getgrnam()	

`<limits.h>`

Macros; those shown in *italics* will be omitted from `<limits.h>` when the corresponding value is indeterminate.

ARG_MAX	*MAX_INPUT*	(SHRT_MAX)	_POSIX_MAX_CANON
(CHAR_BIT)	(MB_LEN_MAX)	SSIZE_MAX	_POSIX_MAX_INPUT
(CHAR_MAX)	*NAME_MAX*	STREAM_MAX	_POSIX_NAME_MAX
CHILD_MAX	NGROUPS_MAX	(UCHAR_MAX)	_POSIX_NGROUPS_MAX
(INT_MAX)	*OPEN_MAX*	(UINT_MAX)	_POSIX_OPEN_MAX
(INT_MIN)	*PATH_MAX*	(ULONG_MAX)	_POSIX_PATH_MAX
LINK_MAX	*PIPE_BUF*	(USHRT_MAX)	_POSIX_PIPE_BUF
(LONG_MAX)	(SCHAR_MAX)	_POSIX_ARG_MAX	_POSIX_SSIZE_MAX
(LONG_MIN)	(SCHAR_MIN)	_POSIX_CHILD_MAX	_POSIX_STREAM_MAX
MAX_CANON			

`<locale.h>`

Functions:	Macros:		Structure:
(localeconv())	LC_ALL	LC_MONETARY	(lconv)
setlocale()	LC_COLLATE	LC_NUMERIC	
	LC_CTYPE	LC_TIME	

`<math.h>`

Functions:			Macro:
acos()	fabs()	pow()	HUGE_VAL
asin()	floor()	sin()	
atan()	fmod()	sinh()	
atan2()	frexp()	sqrt()	
ceil()	ldexp()	tan()	
cos()	log10()	tanh()	
cosh()	log()		
exp()	modf()		

`<pwd.h>`

Functions:	Structure:
getpwnam()	passwd
getpwuid()	

`<setjmp.h>`

Functions:		Types:
longjmp()	siglongjmp()	jmp_buf
setjmp()	sigsetjmp()	sigjmp_buf

`<signal.h>`

Functions:			Macros:
kill()	sigdelset()	(signal())	SA_NOCLDSTOP
(raise())	sigemptyset()	sigpending()	SIG_DFL
sigaction()	sigfillset()	sigprocmask()	SIG_ERR
sigaddset()	sigismember()	sigsuspend()	

SIG_IGN	SIGHUP	SIGSEGV	SIGUSR1
SIGABRT	SIGILL	SIGSTOP	SIGUSR2
SIGALRM	SIGINT	SIGTERM	SIG_BLOCK
SIGCHLD	SIGKILL	SIGTSTP	SIG_SETMASK
SIGCONT	SIGPIPE	SIGTTIN	SIG_UNBLOCK
SIGFPE	SIGQUIT	SIGTTOU	

Types: **Structure:**

(sig_atomic_t)   sigaction
sigset_t

(<stdarg.h>)

Macros:

(va_arg)   (va_list)

(va_end)   (va_start)

(<stddef.h>)

Macros: **Types:**

NULL   (ptrdiff_t)

(offsetof)   size_t

                (wchar_t)

<stdio.h>

Functions:

clearerr()	*fprintf()*	*getchar()*	*setbuf()*
fclose()	*fputc()*	*gets()*	*setvbuf())*
fdopen()	*fputs()*	*perror()*	*sprintf()*
feof()	*fread()*	*printf()*	*sscanf()*
ferror()	*freopen()*	*putc()*	*tmpfile()*
fflush()	*fscanf()*	*putchar()*	*tmpnam()*
fgetc()	*fseek()*	*puts()*	*ungetc()*
(fgetpos())	*(fsetpos())*	*remove()*	*(vfprintf())*
fgets()	*ftell()*	*rename()*	*(vprintf())*
fileno()	*fwrite()*	*rewind()*	*(vsprintf())*
fopen()	*getc()*	*scanf()*	

`<stdio.h>` *(continued)*

Macros:

			Type:
BUFSIZ	(L_tmpnam)	_IOFBF	(fpos_t)
EOF	NULL	_IOLBF	
FILENAME_MAX	SEEK_CUR	_IONBF	**Structure:**
FOPEN_MAX	SEEK_END	stderr	FILE
L_ctermid	SEEK_SET	stdin	
(L_cuserid)	TMP_MAX	stdout	

`<stdlib.h>`

Functions:		**Macros:**	**Types:**
abort()	*malloc()*	EXIT_FAILURE	(div_t)
abs()	*(mblen())*	EXIT_SUCCESS	(ldiv_t)
(atexit())	*(mbstowcs())*	(MB_CUR_MAX)	size_t
atof()	*(mbtowc())*	NULL	(wchar_t)
atoi()	*qsort()*	(RAND_MAX)	
atol()	*rand()*		
bsearch()	*realloc()*		
calloc()	*srand()*		
(div())	*(strtod())*		
exit()	*(strtol())*		
free()	*(strtoul())*		
getenv()	*(system())*		
(labs())	*(wcstombs())*		
(ldiv())	*(wctomb())*		

`<string.h>`

Functions:			**Macro:**
(memchr())	*(strcoll())*	*strncpy()*	NULL
(memcmp())	*strcpy()*	*strpbrk()*	
(memcpy())	*strcspn()*	*strrchr()*	**Type:**
(memmove())	*(strerror())*	*strspn()*	size_t
(memset())	*strlen()*	*strstr()*	
strcat()	*strncat()*	*strtok()*	
strchr()	*strncmp()*	*(strxfrm())*	
strcmp()			

`<sys/stat.h>`

Functions:	Macros:		Structure:
chmod()	S_IRGRP	S_ISGID	stat
fstat()	S_IROTH	S_ISREG	
mkdir()	S_IRUSR	S_ISUID	
mkfifo()	S_IRWXG	S_IWGRP	
stat()	S_IRWXO	S_IWOTH	
umask()	S_IRWXU	S_IWUSR	
	S_ISBLK	S_IXGRP	
	S_ISCHR	S_IXOTH	
	S_ISDIR	S_IXUSR	
	S_ISFIFO		

`<sys/times.h>`

Function:	Type:	Structure:
times()	clock_t	tms

`<sys/types.h>`

Types:

dev_t	nlink_t	size_t
gid_t	off_t	ssize_t
ino_t	pid_t	uid_t
mode_t		

`<sys/utsname.h>`

Function:	Structure:
uname()	utsname

`<sys/wait.h>`

Functions:	Macros:		
wait()	WEXITSTATUS	WIFSTOPPED	WNOHANG
waitpid()	WIFEXITED	WSTOPSIG	WUNTRACED
	WIFSIGNALLED	WTERMSIG	

`<tar.h>`

Macros:

AREGTYPE	REGTYPE	TMAGLEN	TSVTX
BLKTYPE	SYMTYPE	TOEXEC	TUEXEC
CHRTYPE	TGEXEC	TOREAD	TUREAD
CONTTYPE	TGREAD	TOWRITE	TUWRITE
DIRTYPE	TGWRITE	TSGID	TVERSION
FIFOTYPE	TMAGIC	TSUID	TVERSLEN
LNKTYPE			

`<termios.h>`

Functions:

cfgetispeed()	*tcdrain()*	*tcgetattr()*
cfgetospeed()	*tcflow()*	*tcsendbreak()*
cfsetispeed()	*tcflush()*	*tcsetattr()*
cfsetospeed()		

Macros:

B0	CLOCAL	IGNPAR	TCOON
B50	CS5	INLCR	TCSADRAIN
B75	CD6	INPCK	TCSADFLUSH
B110	CS7	ISIG	TCSANOW
B134	CS8	ISTRIP	TOSTOP
B150	CSIZE	IXOFF	VEOF
B200	CSTOPB	IXON	VEOL
B300	ECHO	NCCS	VERASE
B600	ECHOE	NOFLSH	VINTR
B1200	ECHOK	OPOST	VKILL
B1800	ECHONL	PARENB	VMIN
B2400	HUPCL	PARMRK	VQUIT
B4800	ICANON	PARODD	VSTART
B9600	ICRNL	TCIFLUSH	VSTOP
B19200	IEXTEN	TCIOFF	VSUSP
B38400	IGNBRK	TCIOFLUSH	VTIME
BRKINT	IGNCR	TCOOFF	

Types:	Structure:
cc_t	termios
speed_t	
tcflag_t	

`<time.h>`

Functions:	Macros:	Structure:
asctime()	CLK_TCK	tm
(clock())	(CLOCKS_PER_SEC)	
ctime()	NULL	**External variable:**
(difftime())		tzname
gmtime()	**Types:**	
localtime()	clock_t	
mktime()	size_t	
strftime()	time_t	
time()		
tzset()		

`<unistd.h>`

Functions:

_exit()	*execlp()*	*getpgrp()*	*setgid()*
access()	*execv()*	*getpid()*	*setpgid()*
alarm()	*execve()*	*getppid()*	*setsid()*
chdir()	*execvp()*	*getuid()*	*seuid()*
chown()	*fork()*	*isatty()*	*sleep()*
close()	*fpathconf()*	*link()*	*sysconf()*
ctermid()	*getcwd()*	*lseek()*	*tcgetpgrp()*
(cuserid())	*getegid()*	*pathconf()*	*tcsetpgrp()*
dup()	*geteuid()*	*pause()*	*ttyname()*
dup2()	*getgid()*	*pipe()*	*unlink()*
execl()	*getgroups()*	*read()*	*write()*
execle()	*getlogin()*	*rmdir()*	

<unistd.h> *(continued)*

Macros:

F_OK	_POSIX_CHOWN_RESTRICTED
NULL	_POSIX_JOB_CONTROL
R_OK	_POSIX_NO_TRUNC
SEEK_CUR	_POSIX_SAVED_IDS
SEEK_END	_POSIX_VDISABLE
SEEK_SET	_POSIX_VERSION
STDERR_FILENO	_SC_ARG_MAX
STDIN_FILENO	_SC_CHILD_MAX
STDOUT_FILENO	_SC_CLK_TCK
W_OK	_SC_JOB_CONTROL
X_OK	_SC_NGROUPS_MAX
_PC_CHOWN_RESTRICTED	_SC_OPEN_MAX
_PC_LINK_MAX	_SC_SAVED_IDS
_PC_MAX_CANON	_SC_STREAM_MAX
_PC_MAX_INPUT	_SC_TZNAME_MAX
_PC_NAME_MAX	_SC_VERSION
_PC_NO_TRUNC	
_PC_PATH_MAX	**Types:**
_PC_PIPE_BUF	size_t
_PC_VDISABLE	ssize_t

<utime.h>

Function:	**Structure:**
utime()	utimbuf

Signal-Safe Reentrant Functions

T his appendix gives the list of functions that are "safe" with respect to signals. Recall from Chapter 5, Section 5.9, that a function is considered safe with respect to signals if it can be invoked without restriction from a signal handler. Any POSIX.1 or ANSI C function not in this list will, if invoked from a signal handler, have undefined behavior if the interrupted function is also a POSIX.1 or ANSI C function that is not on this list. A portable program should avoid using such functions in a signal handler.

The following functions are required by POSIX.1 to be safe with respect to signals:

access()	dup()	getgroups()	pathconf()
alarm()	dup2()	getpgrp()	pause()
cfgetispeed()	execle()	getpid()	pipe()
cfgetospeed()	execve()	getppid()	read()
cfsetispeed()	_exit()	getuid()	rename()
cfsetospeed()	fcntl()	kill()	rmdir()
chdir()	fork()	link()	setgid()
chmod()	fstat()	lseek()	setpgid()
chown()	getegid()	mkdir()	setsid()
close()	geteuid()	mkfifo()	setuid()
creat()	getgid()	open()	sigaction()

sigaddset()	*sleep()*	*tcgetpgrp()*	*uname()*
sigdelset()	*stat()*	*tcsendbreak()*	*unlink()*
sigemptyset()	*sysconf()*	*tcsetattr()*	*ustat()*
sigfillset()	*tcdrain()*	*tcsetpgrp()*	*utime()*
sigismember()	*tcflow()*	*time()*	*wait()*
sigpending()	*tcflush()*	*times()*	*waitpid()*
sigprocmask()	*tcgetattr()*	*umask()*	*write()*
sigsuspend()			

If a function not on this list is interrupted by a signal that invokes a signal handler that, in turn, invokes another function not on this list, problems could arise. The reason is that POSIX.1 interfaces not on this list are not guaranteed to be implemented in a reentrant manner. Moreover, any two of those functions may, in principle, share data, such as `static` variables. In such a case, two functions that share a single data item might be simultaneously active, with unpredictable results.

Other standards and specifications impose the same requirements on other functions. The C standard requires that the following function be safe with respect to signals:

signal()

The *X/Open Portability Guide, Issue 3*, requires that the following functions be safe with respect to signals:

abort()	*chroot()*	*exit()*	*longjmp()*

A strictly conforming POSIX.1 application cannot make use of *chroot()* or *signal()* and should not rely on the safety of *abort()*, *exit()*, or *longjmp()* when invoked from a signal handler.

Access to Standards

This appendix tells **where you can get copies** of standards, proposed standards, and de facto standards that bear some relationship to POSIX.1, in their current versions.

POSIX.1 (ANSI/IEEE 1003.1-1990, ISO/IEC 9945-1:1990)

Copies of this standard are available from the IEEE:

Publication Sales
IEEE Service Center
P.O. Box 1331
445 Hoes Lane
Piscataway, NJ 08855-1331

Phone: (201) 981-0060

Other POSIX Standards

As of this writing, all of these are proposed standards, in various stages of development. You can order them from:

IEEE Computer Society
Attn: Assistant Director/Standards
1730 Massachusetts Avenue, NW
Washington, DC 20036

Phone: (202) 371-0101

After a draft has progressed to the balloting stage, it can also be ordered from the IEEE Service Center at the New Jersey address given above.

ANSI Standards

You can order the C standard, X3.159-1989, or any other ANSI or ISO standard from:

American National Standards Institute (ANSI)
Sales Department
1430 Broadway
New York, NY 10018

Phone: (212) 642-4900

If you want to request an official interpretation of some part of the ANSI C standard, you can do so from:

X3 Secretariat
CBEMA
311 First St., NW
Suite 500
Washington, DC 20001-2178

Attn: Manager of Standards Processing

X/Open Portability Guide

XPG3 can be ordered from Prentice-Hall publishers, which distributes it in the United States for X/Open:

Prentice-Hall
200 Old Tappan Road
Tappan, NJ 07675

FIPS

You can order a copy of the POSIX.1 FIPS 151-1 from:

National Technical Information Service (NTIS)
U.S. Department of Commerce
5285 Port Royal Road
Springfield, VA 22161

Phone: (703) 487-4650

ISO

In the United States, you should order ISO standards through ANSI, at the address given above. If this is not convenient, copies of ISO standards and documents can be ordered from:

ISO
1 rue de Varembé
Case Postale 56
CH–1211
Genève 20
Switzerland

References

1. *ISO/IEC 9945-1:1990*, clause 4.7.1.2, p. 78. Institute of Electrical and Electronics Engineers, Inc., New York, 1990.

2. Ibid., clause 2.2.2.81, p. 19.

3. Ibid., clause 3.1.1.4, p. 52.

4. Ibid., clause 8.2.3.12, p. 161.

5. Ibid.

6. Ibid., clause B.3.2.2, p. 232.

7. *Programming Language — C*, Section 3.3.2.2, p. 42. American National Standards Institute, New York, 1990.

8. *ISO/IEC 9945-1:1990*, clause 8.2.3.11, p. 161. Institute of Electrical and Electronics Engineers, Inc., New York, 1990.

9. *P1003.1b Draft 3*, clause 2.2.2, p. 4. Institute of Electrical and Electronics Engineers, Inc., New York. Draft dated 25 June 1990.

10. Ibid., clause 6.4.1.2, p. 41.

11. Ibid., clause 6.4.2.2, p. 41.

12. *P1003.2 Draft 10*, clause 4.40.2, p. 443. Institute of Electrical and Electronics Engineers, Inc., New York. Draft dated July 1990.

13. *Programming Language — C*, Section 3.2.1.1, p. 35. American National Standards Institute, New York, 1990.

Glossary

abnormal termination: Termination of a process caused by an uncaught signal or by a call to *abort()*.

additional file access control mechanism: An access control mechanism that works in addition to the basic POSIX.1 file access control rules. Such a mechanism can only further restrict file access.

AEP (application environment profile): A description of the facilities that a system must provide to support a particular class of application.

alternate file access control mechanism: An access control mechanism that replaces the basic POSIX.1 file access control rules. Such a mechanism must be explicitly enabled on a per-file basis by the file owner or by a user with appropriate privileges.

appropriate privileges: An implementation-defined mechanism of associating with a process privileges with respect to certain function calls.

ASCII: The American Standard Code for Information Interchange; the most widely used character representation on computers in the United States.

asynchronous: Not synchronized.

atomic: Behaving as if it were a single, indivisible operation. Thus, an *atomic write* to a file cannot write data interleaved with data from another write to the same file.

baud rate: The rate of transmission of data, roughly in bits per second including parity, start, and stop bits as well as data bits. As a rule, the baud rate is about ten times the rate in bytes transferred per second. Thus, 2400 baud corresponds to about 240 bytes per second.

block special file: A file that refers to a device. Traditionally, such devices have been mass storage (disk or tape) devices, but the POSIX.1 standard does not specify anything about the use of block special files.

blocked signal: A signal that is currently in the process's signal mask and that, if generated, will be blocked from delivery to the process. Some signals (e.g., SIGKILL and SIGSTOP) cannot be blocked.

break condition: A continuous stream of zero bits transmitted over an asynchronous serial line.

BSD: Acronym for Berkeley Software Distribution. Many UNIX and POSIX features originated in one or another version of BSD.

canonical input mode: A terminal input mode in which data is not made available for reading until an entire line (delimited by a newline, EOF, or EOL character) has been entered.

caught signal: A signal that is delivered to a process and for which a signal-handling function has been installed by the process. When the signal is caught, the process is interrupted and the signal-handling function is entered.

character special file: A file that refers to a device. A *terminal* is one example of a character special file. Other character special files may have characteristics that are not specified by the POSIX.1 standard.

child process: A process created by another process, which becomes the *parent process* of the new process.

conformance document: A document that must accompany a system claiming conformance to the POSIX.1 standard. It specifies the system's behavior in all aspects that the standard describes as implementation-defined.

conforming implementation: An implementation of an operating system that supports all required interfaces defined within POSIX.1, with the functional behavior described therein.

conforming POSIX.1 application: Any application that is either an *ISO/IEC conforming POSIX.1 application* or a *<national body> conforming POSIX.1 application*.

conforming POSIX.1 application using extensions: An application that uses facilities that are outside the POSIX.1 standard, but that are consistent with the standard, and that documents the use of such facilities.

controlling terminal: A terminal that may be associated with a session. If a session has a controlling terminal, then certain characters input from that terminal may be treated specially, and members of background process groups of the session are restricted from certain kinds of access to the controlling terminal.

current working directory: The directory from which relative pathnames are resolved. Every process has a current working directory at any given moment.

directory special file: A file that is a directory, i.e., that contains entries that name links to other files.

directory stream: An opaque data type from which a process can sequentially read directory entries.

dot: A special pathname, " . ". When dot occurs as a pathname component, it refers to its predecessor.

dot-dot: A special pathname, " . . ". When dot-dot occurs as a pathname component, it refers to the parent directory of its predecessor.

duplicate file descriptor: A file descriptor that refers to the same *open file description* as another file descriptor.

effective group ID: The group ID of a process that is used to determine its group access privileges. The effective group ID of a process may (but need not) be used to set the group ID of files created by the process.

effective user ID: A user ID associated with a process that is used to determine its owner access privileges. The effective user ID of a process may (but need not) be associated with certain appropriate privileges.

environment strings: A vector of strings of the form "name=value" that are accessible to the process and are inherited by its child processes.

Epoch: The time January 1, 1970, 0:00 UCT (formerly GMT).

feature test macro: A symbol that, if defined, makes certain symbols visible in headers that are included by an application.

FIFO special file: A type of special file in which data is always read and written in a first-in-first-out discipline.

file descriptor: An integer that is associated with an open file. Each file descriptor is also associated with an *open file description* that contains data about the open file.

file group class: The class of all processes that are not members of a file's *file owner class* but that have an *effective group ID* or *supplementary group ID* equal to the file's group ID.

file handle: A file descriptor or FILE pointer associated with an open file or stream.

file link count: The system-wide total number of directory entries for a file.

file mode: A field in the file's stat structure that describes the file's type and access permission bits.

file mode creation mask: A mask associated with a process. When a process creates a file, bits set in the process's file mode creation mask are cleared in the file's access permission bits.

file other class: The class of all processes that are not in a file's *file owner class* or *file group class*.

file owner class: The class of all processes whose effective user ID is equal to the owner ID of the file.

file serial number: A number that uniquely identifies a file within a POSIX.1 file system (but not necessarily within the whole file hierarchy).

FIPS: A federal information processing standard.

FIPS 151-1: A *FIPS* that specifies conformance with IEEE Std. 1003.1-1988, the original POSIX.1 standard, and that specifies some additional requirements as well.

format-creating utility: A utility that is present on a POSIX.1 conforming system and that creates archives in the POSIX.1 `tar` or `cpio` format.

format-reading utility: A utility that is present on a POSIX.1 conforming system and that reads archives created in the POSIX.1 `tar` or `cpio` format.

group database: A system database that contains the group name, group ID, and user names for each group.

hard link: See *link*.

header: An object that, when specified for inclusion in a C program, causes the program to behave as if certain text were present in place of the statement that includes the header.

implementation-defined: Describing a value or behavior that the standard does not specify, but that the implementation is required to document, for correct programs and data.

internationalization: The process of making programs, and particularly user interfaces, independent of a particular natural language or locale-dependent convention.

ISO 646: An international standard character representation for roman alphabets. Closely related to but not identical to *ASCII*.

ISO/IEC conforming POSIX.1 application: An application that uses only the facilities described in POSIX.1 and approved conforming language bindings for any ISO or IEC standard and that documents such dependencies.

job control: A set of operating system features that allow processes to be stopped, continued, and moved from the foreground to the background or vice versa.

link: A directory entry for a file. Sometimes referred to as a *hard link*, to distinguish it from a *symbolic link*.

login name: A user name that is associated (in an unspecified way) with a session.

<National Body> Conforming POSIX.1 Application: An application that uses only the facilities described in POSIX.1 and approved conforming language bindings for any standard of a member body of ISO or IEC and that documents such dependencies.

noncanonical input mode: A terminal input mode in which data is not collected into lines but is made available for reading based on timing and the number of characters that have been entered.

nonlocal goto: A transfer of control from a function to a point outside that function.

normal termination: Process termination by a call to *exit()* or *_exit()* or by returning from *main()*.

open file description: A system data structure associated with an open file, in which the file pointer and several file flags are maintained. Associated with one or more *file descriptors*.

orphaned process group: A process group in which the parent of every member is either also a member of the process group or is a member of a different session.

parent process: The process that created a given process, or—if that process has exited—a process that has inherited a given process.

pathname resolution: The process of associating a file with a pathname.

pathname-variable limits: System limits that may vary from one place to another within the file hierarchy.

pending signal: A signal that has been generated for a process but has not yet been delivered, typically because it is blocked from delivery.

pipe: An unnamed FIFO, created by the *pipe()* call and only accessible to descendants of the process that created it.

portable filename character set: The set of characters: A–Z, a–z, 0–9, ., _, - (all upper- and lower-case roman letters, all digits, period, underscore, and hyphen).

process: A program in a state of execution.

process group: A collection of processes.

process group leader: A process whose process ID is the same as the process group ID of its process group.

real group ID: An ID associated with a process. At process creation, it identifies the group of the user who created the process, but it may change during the process's lifetime.

real user ID: An ID associated with a process. At process creation, it identifies the user who created the process, but it may change during the process's lifetime.

reentrant with respect to signals: Having well-defined behavior when invoked from a *signal handler*.

regular file: A file that is a randomly accessible sequence of bytes.

reserved symbol: An identifier that is reserved for use by system implementors. If an application uses a reserved symbol, the results are *undefined*.

saved set-user-ID: A process attribute that saves a user ID for possible later setting as the process's effective user ID.

session: A collection of process groups. A session may possibly be associated with a *controlling terminal*.

session leader: The process that created a *session*.

set-user-ID program: A program that has the S_ISUID bit of its *file mode* set. Such a program, when executed, becomes a process whose effective user ID is the owner of the program file.

signal: A mechanism by which a process is notified of an event occurring in the system.

signal delivery: The time when the appropriate action for a signal with respect to a process is taken.

signal generation: The time when an event occurs that causes a signal for a process.

signal handler: A function that is executed when a signal is delivered to a process.

signal mask: A set of signals that are currently blocked from delivery to a process.

special character: A character that, when entered from a terminal, has some effect other than simply becoming part of the input stream for that terminal.

strictly conforming POSIX.1 application: An application that requires only the facilities described in the POSIX.1 standard and the applicable language standards. Such an application must accept any behavior described by POSIX.1 as *unspecified* or *implementation-defined* and, for symbolic constants, must accept any value in the range permitted by POSIX.1.

supplementary group ID: An attribute of a process that is used along with the process's *effective group ID* to determine the process's file access permissions.

SVID: The *System V Interface Definition* published by AT&T.

symbolic link: A type of special file that refers to another file. Symbolic links are not supported by the adopted POSIX.1 standard but have been proposed for inclusion in a revision of the standard.

System V: A version of the UNIX operating system developed and marketed by AT&T. At this writing, the latest version of System V is System V Release 4.

terminal: A type of *character special file* that obeys the interface description in Clause 7 of the POSIX.1 standard (see Chapter 7 of this book).

trigraph: A sequence of three ISO 646 characters that can be used in a C program to represent one of the nine characters that are part of the C source language character set but are not part of ISO 646. All trigraphs begin with the characters "??".

undefined: Describing a value or behavior for which the standard imposes no requirements for erroneous programs or data.

unspecified: Describing a value or behavior for which the standard imposes no requirements for correct programs and data.

user database: A system database that contains the user name, user ID, group ID, initial working directory, and initial user program for each user in the system.

XPG/3: The third issue of the *X/Open Portability Guide*.

Index